W9-ACZ-990

a guide to
PHILOSOPHICAL BIBLIOGRAPHY
and RESEARCH

THE CENTURY PHILOSOPHY SERIES
Justus Buchler, editor

a guide to
PHILOSOPHICAL BIBLIOGRAPHY
and RESEARCH

RICHARD T. DE GEORGE
the university of kansas

APPLETON-CENTURY-CROFTS
Educational Division
New York   MEREDITH   CORPORATION

PRINTED IN THE UNITED STATES OF AMERICA
390-26005-3

PREFACE

NOT EVERY OUTSTANDING philosopher has been a scholar. Scholarship is no substitute for genius. Genius or not, however, technical competence in research is a prerequisite for successful scholarship; and scholarship is a sound basis on which to build if one is interested in contributing to human knowledge in any field, including philosophy.

Productive research usually consists of a detailed, systematic, purposeful search. It initially involves selecting, defining (or redefining), and evaluating a problem. If, once the problem has been clarified, it seems worthy of investigation, the researcher usually forms a tentative hypothesis about the way he hopes to solve it. He then proceeds to collect, organize, and evaluate the evidence for and against his hypothesis. Often this requires compiling a preliminary bibliography, reading the important pertinent work already written on the problem, evaluating this data, correcting what has been incorrectly claimed in the past, and presenting the new material, data, or arguments that the researcher has discovered.

Research in philosophy to some extent depends on what one conceives philosophy to be. Whether it be considered the analysis of concepts, the systematic building of conceptual schemes, the search for ultimate causes, or a combination of these or other tasks, it is never *ex nihilo*. Knowledge of the literature on the topic is necessary to know what has not already been said or what can be said better. Thus any topic, historical or systematic, requires some background research. Mastery of research tools and techniques helps to remove much of the drudgery and frustration from the initial stages of research and also helps guarantee complete coverage of the literature in question.

This book serves as a guide to the sources, bibliographies, and other tools of philosophical research—their existence, usefulness, and use. As a guide it makes no claim to being exhaustive. It does, however, contain a great deal of information that will be valuable not only to the student while in college or graduate school, but also to those who have embarked on a career in philosophy. Starting with dictionaries as sources of definition, it proceeds through encyclopedias, histories of philosophy, philosophical classics, bibliographical tools and specialized bibliographies, library and trade catalogs, philosophical journals, guides to writing and publishing, and biographical sources. It ends with information and works concerning philosophical professional life. It can serve as an introduction for the beginner who wishes to get an overview of the sources and tools of philosophical research, a guide for students writing papers and theses, and a handy reference manual for the teacher and professional.

Each chapter begins with a brief general introduction. Annotations have been added to those entries that are not self-explanatory and for which more information seemed desirable to help the reader evaluate the usefulness of the item listed. Value judgments have been entered in a number of cases, but only when I have felt there was a consensus among scholars on the item in question. For the most part rare items, dated and superseded works, and bibliographies compiled before 1900 have been omitted, unless they have been reprinted recently or are still of general use. By utilizing the specialized guides and bibliographies contained herein, the reader should be able to locate such unlisted specialized and older material with relative ease. "See also" references will lead the reader to additional items on a topic, and this device has been used to avoid reprinting items that could correctly be listed under more than one heading. The Index is an author, subject, and title index and can be used as a means of unifying material on a topic or author which may be spread through various sections and chapters.

Since this guide was prepared primarily for English-speaking students and scholars, items in English are given fullest and most prominent treatment. Entries in other languages have—with a certain few obvious exceptions—been restricted to those written in French, German, Italian, Latin, Russian, and Spanish. There are, however, abundant sources listed for locating works in other languages. Where the number of items in a section is considerable, and where appropriate, entries have been grouped by language.

In addition to the general guidelines of selection enumerated here, I have attempted to indicate in the various introductions the additional criteria of selection that I have employed in choosing the items for that section. As is inevitable, my choice of criteria and my employment of those criteria will not meet with universal approval. There is ample room for individual scholars to lament the omission of some particular work or class of works. I can only hope that my selection has included a large majority of the basic sources, and sufficiently specific references to where other tools and sources can be found, so that this guide may be of general usefulness to readers with a variety of philosophic interests and inclinations.

The style I have employed for listing entries is basically that of the Library of Congress, with slight modifications where these seemed called for, and items have been checked against the Library of Congress Catalogue for accuracy and uniformity whenever this was appropriate.

I wish to express my thanks to the many colleagues and friends who have made suggestions on the work as a whole and on particular entries, and to the students who helped me achieve the present form and content by their critical use of earlier drafts of this guide. Suggestions for modification, correction, deletion, or addition of items and sections will be welcome from any interested reader.

R. D. G.

CONTENTS

a guide to
PHILOSOPHICAL BIBLIOGRAPHY
and RESEARCH

An asterisk (*) preceding an entry or title indicates that it was listed in the October 1969 issue of *Paperbound Books in Print* (Vol. 14, No. 10). Where details concerning publisher, imprint date, number of pages, etc., vary for the paperbound and the hardbound editions of a book, the information listed refers to the hardbound edition.

1. DICTIONARIES

DEFINITION OF TERMS is a frequent first step in philosophical discussions. Unabridged English dictionaries (1.1) are useful as a source for determining ordinary and specialized usage, currently accepted meanings, derivations, and in some cases the history of individual words. Though technical philosophical meanings are frequently listed, they are usually not very detailed. Philosophical dictionaries (1.2) provide definitions and explanations of philosophical terms, often with references to their use by prominent philosophers and to their development in the history of philosophy, and frequently with brief bibliographies. The discussions are usually much more detailed than those found in unabridged general dictionaries.

Specialized philosophical dictionaries are of three main types: those limited to the terms of one of the branches of philosophy (1.3), those concerned with ideas or terms as found or used in a particular period or by a particular school or movement (1.4), and those devoted exclusively to the meanings given terms by an individual philosopher. The latter can sometimes also serve as indexes to the works of a particular author and will be found in the appropriate sections of chapter 4. Dictionaries in related disciplines (1.5) are useful in ascertaining the meanings of specialized terms in those disciplines. The polyglot dictionaries listed in section 1.6 give various foreign language equivalents for philosophical terms. For a recommended list of general bilingual dictionaries, see section 8.2.

1.1 UNABRIDGED ENGLISH LANGUAGE DICTIONARIES

For an annotated list of English language dictionaries of all types, see Winchell (5.1.3), pp. 92–102.

1.1.1 **Century dictionary and cyclopedia** with a new atlas of the world. Rev. and enl. ed. New York, Century, 1911. 12v.

1st ed. 1889–91.
Though based on common usage and so somewhat out of date, it is still useful for its etymologies, quotations, and references.

C. S. Peirce was the editorial contributor of many of the items in philosophy.

1.1.2 **Funk & Wagnalls new standard dictionary** of the English language. Prepared by more than 380 specialists and other scholars under the supervision of I. K. Funk, Calvin Thomas, F. H. Vizetelly. New York, Funk & Wagnalls, 1964. 2816 pp.

1.1.3 **The Oxford English dictionary,** being a corrected reissue, with an introduction, supplement, and bibliography, of A New English dictionary of historical principles; founded mainly on the materials collected by the Philological Society and ed. by James A. H. Murray, Henry Bradley, W. A. Craigie, and C. T. Onions. Oxford, Clarendon Press, 1933. 12v. and supplement.

Gives the history of each word included, with many quotations exemplifying usage in various historical periods.

1.1.4 **The Random House dictionary** of the English language. Jess Stein, ed. in chief; Laurence Urdang, managing ed. New York, Random House, 1967. 2059 pp.

Also contains concise French, Spanish, Italian, and German bilingual (with English) dictionaries, and a basic manual of style.

1.1.5 **Webster's new international dictionary** of the English language. A Merriam-Webster. William Allan Neilson, ed. in chief; Thomas A. Knott, general ed.; Paul W. Carhart, managing ed. 2d ed., unabridged. Springfield, Mass., Merriam, 1961. 3194 pp.

1.1.6. **Webster's third new international dictionary** of the English language, unabridged. A Merriam-Webster. Philip Babcock Gove, ed. in chief, and the Merriam-Webster editorial staff. Springfield, Mass., Merriam, 1961. 2662 pp.

New, and different from the 2d edition, with emphasis on English as it is currently used.

1.2 PHILOSOPHICAL DICTIONARIES: GENERAL

This list is restricted to the more important, the widely used, and the relatively recent philosophical dictionaries in the major Western languages. For a history of philosophical dictionaries, together with descriptive listings of such dictionaries in all languages, see William Gerber's article "Philosophical Dictionaries and Encyclopedias" in the *Encyclopedia of Philosophy* (2.2.1), vol. VI, pp. 170–199.

1.2.1 **Baldwin, James M.,** *ed.* Dictionary of philosophy and psychology, including many of the principal conceptions of ethics, logic,

aesthetics, philosophy of religion, mental pathology, anthropology, biology, neurology, physiology, economics, political and social philosophy, philology, physical science, and education, and giving a terminology in English, French, German, and Italian. New York, Macmillan, 1901–05. 3v. in 4.

A 2d ed., 1910, simply contains minor corrections.

Reprinted: Gloucester, Mass., Peter Smith, 1960. 2v.

Entries cover both terms and persons. An index of Greek, Latin, French, German, and Italian terms gives the equivalent in these languages of English terms. Vol. III (in 2 parts) is devoted to bibliographies (see 5.3.1).

Though long a standard reference work, the first two volumes, except for historical purposes, have been superseded by the *Encyclopedia of Philosophy* (2.2.1).

Contributors included J. Dewey, W. James, G. E. Moore, C. Peirce, and J. Royce.

1.2.2 **Bruckmann, William D.** Keystones and theories of philosophy; a handbook to aid in the study of philosophy containing definitions of terms, and a brief historical conspectus, with a chart "General diagrammatic survey of philosophy." New York, Benzinger Brothers, 1946. 230 pp.

Primarily scholastic in outlook.

1.2.3 **The great ideas; a syntopicon of Great books** of the Western world. Mortimer Adler, ed. in chief. Chicago, Encyclopaedia Britannica, 1952. 2v.

Vols. II and III of *Great Books of the Western World*.

The *Syntopicon* covers 102 ideas, with exposition, references to the Great Books series, and lists of additional readings.

1.2.4 ★ **Gutmann, James,** *ed.* Philosophy A to Z. Based on the work of Alwin Diemer, Ivo Frenzel, and others. [Translation by Salvatore Altanasio.] New York, Grosset & Dunlap, 1963. 343 pp.

Based on 1.2.19. Contains long articles on broad topics; includes bibliographies.

1.2.5 **★ Runes, Dagobert D.,** *ed.* Dictionary of philosophy. 16th rev. ed. New York, Philosophical Library, 1960. 342 pp.

1st ed. 1942.
Useful, despite the fact that a number of its distinguished contributors objected to the final form of the published volume.

1.2.6 **Urmson, James Opie,** *ed.* The concise encyclopedia of Western philosophy and philosophers. London, Hutchinson; New York, Hawthorn, 1960. 431 pp.

Reliable, informative articles by a number of different scholars on concepts, terms, and philosophers.
Contributors include A. J. Ayer, I. Berlin, A. C. Ewing, E. Nagel, G. Ryle, and P. F. Strawson; but individual articles are not signed.

1.2.7 **★ Voltaire, François Marie Arouet de.** Philosophical dictionary. Translated, with an introduction and glossary by Peter Gay. New York, Basic Books, 1962. 2v.

See 1.2.13. The latest of the English editions. More popular than technical, the work is now only of historical interest.

See also: 1.2.33, 1.2.34.

French

1.2.8 **Cuvillier, Armand.** Nouveau vocabulaire philosophique. 3. éd. Paris, A. Colin, 1958. 204 pp.

1st ed. 1956.
Supersedes his *Petit vocabulaire de la langue philosophique,* 1st ed., 1925.

1.2.9 **Foulquié, Paul,** et **R. Saint-Jean.** Dictionnaire de la langue philosophique. Paris, Presses Universitaires de France, 1962. 776 pp.

A useful dictionary which gives etymologies, definitions, synonyms, and quotations from individual philosophers.

1.2.10 **Jolivet, Regis.** Vocabulaire de la philosophie, suivi d'un tableau historique des écoles de philosophie. 4. éd. Lyon-Paris, Emmanuel Vitte, 1957. 227 pp.

1st ed. 1942.
Also in Spanish translation: Buenos Aires, 1953.

1.2.11 **★ Julia, Didier.** Dictionnaire de la philosophie. Paris, Librairie Larousse, 1964. 319 pp.

Covers both terms and philosophers, but more popular than scholarly.

1.2.12 **Lalande, André.** Vocabulaire technique et critique de la philosophie. 10. éd. Paris, Presses Universitaires de France, 1967. 1324 pp.

1st ed., in parts, 1902–22.
French terminology with Greek, Latin, German, English, and Italian definitions.
Excellent, but no bibliography. The best of the French philosophical dictionaries.

1.2.13 **Voltaire, François Marie Arouet de.** Dictionnaire philosophique, comprenant les 118 articles parus sous ce titre du vivant de Voltaire, avec leurs suppléments parus dans les Questions sur l'Encyclopédie. Avec introduction, variants et notes par Julien Benda. Paris, Garnier frères, 1936. 2v.

The best of the many varying editions. *See* 1.2.7.

German

1.2.14 **Apel, Max.** Philosophisches Wörterbuch. Berlin, Walter de Gruyter, 1958. 5 völlig neubearbeitete von Peter Ludz. 315 pp.

1st ed. 1930.
Includes some short bibliographies.

1.2.15 **Austeda, Franz.** Wörterbuch der Philosophie. 2. Aufl. Berlin und München, Verlag Lebendiges Wissen, 1962. 270 pp.

1st ed., *Kleines Wörterbuch der Philosophie,* 1954.
Contains short articles and biographical sketches.

1.2.16 **Brugger, Walter.** Philosophisches Wörterbuch. 13., überarb. u. erw. Aufl. Freiburg, Herder, 1967. 578 pp.

1st ed. 1948.

Spanish translation: Barcelona, 1953; Italian translation: Turin, 1961.

Explanations of terms, bibliographies, and a historical survey of philosophy.

1.2.17 Eisler, Rudolf. Wörterbuch der philosophischen Begriffe. 4. Aufl. Berlin, Mittler & Sohn, 1927–30. 3v.

1st ed. of Vol. I, 1889.

Vols. II and III completed by K. Roetz.

Comprehensive, with good bibliographies. Still one of the better philosophical dictionaries.

1.2.18 Eisler, Rudolf. Handwörterbuch der Philosophie. 2. Aufl. neuhrsg. von R. Müller-Freienfels. Berlin, Mittler & Sohn, 1922. 785 pp.

1st ed. 1913.

Neudr. Mikro-Aufg.: Düsseldorf, Microbuch und Film Gessels., 1949.

A condensation of 1.2.17. Gives bibliographical references.

1.2.19 Das Fischer Lexikon, Enzyklopädie des Wissens. Bd. II, Philosophie. Hrsg. von Alwin Diemer und Ivo Frenzel. Frankfurt und Hamburg, Fischer Bücherei, 1958. 376 pp.

A collection of 26 articles on broad topics. See 1.2.4.

1.2.20 Herders kleines philosophisches Wörterbuch. Hrsg. von Max Müller und A. Halder. 7. Aufl. Freiburg in Br., Herder Verlag, 1965. 206 pp.

1st ed. 1958.

Contains a bibliographical appendix and some biographical articles.

1.2.21 Hoffmeister, Johannes. Wörterbuch der philosophischen Begriffe. 2. Aufl. Hamburg, F. Meiner, 1955. 687 pp.

1st ed. 1944.

A revised edition of a work edited by Friedrich Kirchner and Carl Michaelis, 1st ed. 1866; 6th ed., by C. Michaelis, 1911.

Includes terms, concepts, and some bibliography; no biography.

1.2.22 Klaus, Georg, und **Manfred Buhr.** Philosophsiches Wörterbuch. 3. Aufl. Leipzig,

VEB Bibliographisches Institut, 1965. 634 pp.

1st ed. 1964.

Includes terms, categories, concepts. Marxist-Leninist in orientation.

1.2.23 Neuhäusler, Anton Otto. Grundbegriffe der philosophischen Sprache. München, Ehrenwirth, 1963. 275 pp.

Brief bibliographies after each article.

1.2.24 Rothacker, Erich. Archiv für Begriffsgeschichte; Bausteine zu einem historischen Wörterbuch der Philosophie. Bonn, H. Bouvier, 1955– .

In progress.

Vols. II, Part II (1958), III (1958), IV (1959), V (1960), VII (1962), VIII (1963) have already appeared.

Encyclopedic in scope and execution.

1.2.25 Schmidt, Heinrich. Philosophisches Wörterbuch. 18. Aufl., neubearb. von Georgi Schischkoff. Stuttgart, A. Kröner, 1969. 690 pp.

1st ed. 1912.

Treats concepts and philosophers (biographies and bibliographies) in alphabetical order.

A widely used German work.

See also: 2.2.3.

Italian

1.2.26 Abbagnano, N. Dizionario di filosofia. Torino, Unione Tipografico-Editrice Torinese, 1961. 905 pp.

An English translation is in preparation by University of Chicago Press.

The best of the Italian philosophic dictionaries.

1.2.27 Biraghi, A. Dizionario di filosofia. Milano, Communità, 1956. 787 pp.

Includes a dictionary of Greek and German terms.

1.2.28 Lamanna, Eustachio Paolo, e **Francesco Adorno.** Dizionario di termini filosofici. 9. ed. Firenze, F. Le Monnier, 1960. 104 pp.

1st ed. 1951.
Entries are very brief.

1.2.29 **Miano, V.** (in collaborazione con alcuni professori). Dizionario filosofico. Torino, Società editrice internazionale, 1952. 693 pp.

Thomistic in orientation.

1.2.30 **Ranzoli, Cesare.** Dizionario di scienze filosofiche. 5. ed. augmentata e rev. da Maria Pigatti Ranzoli. Milano, Hoepli, 1952. 1313 pp.

1st ed. 1905.
Updated periodically.

1.2.31 **Semprini, Giovanni.** Nuovo dizionario di coltura filosofica e scientifica. Torino, Società Editrice Internazionale, 1951. 470 pp.

Primary emphasis is on philosophy.

See also: 1.2.16.

Russian

1.2.32 **Blauberg, I. V., P. V. Kopnin, i I. K. Pantin.** Kratkii slovar' po filosofii. Moskva, Izd. politicheskoi literatury, 1966. 359 pp.

Marxist-Leninist in orientation.

1.2.33 **Rozental', M. M., i P. F. Iudin.** Kratkii filosofskii slovar'. 5. izd. Moskva, Gos. Izd. politicheskoi literatury, 1955. 567 pp.

1st ed. 1939.
English adaptation by Howard Selsam, New York, International Publishers, 1949, 128 pp. Also translated into many other languages.
Marxist-Leninist orientation of the Stalinist era.
Superseded by 1.2.34.

1.2.34 **Rozental', M. M., i P. F. Iudin.** Filosofskii slovar'. Moskva, Izd. politicheskoi literatury, 1963. 544 pp.

English translation and adaptation by R. R. Dixon and M. Saifulin, Moscow, Progress Publishers, 1967, 494 pp.

Spanish

1.2.35 **Ferrater Mora, José.** Diccionario de filosofía. 5. ed. Buenos Aires, Editorial Sudamericana, 1965. 2v.

1st ed. 1941.
Covers concepts, movements, schools, and persons. Bibliographies.
Reliable and useful, one of the better philosophical dictionaries.

1.2.36 **Pallares, Eduardo.** Diccionario de filosofía. México, Editorial Porrúa, 1964. 652 pp.

Bibliography: pp. 641–652.

1.2.37 **Zaragüeta Bengoechea, Juan.** Vocabulario filosófico. Madrid, Espasa-Calpe, 1955. 571 pp.

Usually indicates German, French, English, and Italian equivalents.
Generally scholastic in orientation.

See also: 1.2.10, 1.2.16.

1.3 PHILOSOPHICAL DICTIONARIES: SPECIALIZED BY BRANCH

Aesthetics

1.3.1 **Caillois, Roger.** Vocabulaire esthétique. Paris, Editions de la Revue Fontaine, 1946. 141 pp.

Essays on a variety of topics connected with art and aesthetics.

1.3.2 **Mantegazza, Paolo.** Dizionario delle cose belle. Milano, Fratelli Treves, 1891. 346 pp.

Contains articles on terms and on "beautiful things."

1.3.3 **Ovsiannikov, M. F., i V. A. Razumnii.** Kratkii slovar' po estetike. Moskva, Izd. politicheskoi literatury, 1936. 542 pp.

Covers about 250 terms and concepts of Marxist-Leninist aesthetics.

Ethics

1.3.4 **Ferm, Vergilius,** *ed.* Encyclopedia of morals. New York, Philosophical Library, 1956. 682 pp.

Articles were contributed by a number of contemporary philosophers, including L. W. Beck, W. Frankena, and W. Kaufmann.
Contains bibliographies.

1.3.5 **Kratkii slovar' po etike.** Pod. red. O. G. Drobnitskogo, I. S. Kona. Moskva, Izd. politicheskoi literatury, 1965. 543 pp.

Contains more than 270 terms and concepts of Marxist-Leninist ethics and communist morality.

1.3.6 **Macquarrie, John.** Dictionary of Christian ethics. Philadelphia, Westminster, 1967. 366 pp.

Articles by many different contributors including Harvey Cox, Joseph Fletcher, and D. M. MacKinnon.

1.3.7 **Mathews, Shailer,** and **Gerald Birney Smith,** *eds.* A dictionary of religion and ethics. New York, Macmillan, 1921. 513 pp.

Contributors include F. Boas, G. H. Mead, and J. H. Tufts.
Bibliographies.

See also: 1.5.14, 2.2.2.

Logic

1.3.8 **Dictionary of symbols of mathematical logic.** Ed. by R. Feys and F. B. Fitch. Amsterdam, North-Holland Publishing Company, 1969. 171 pp.

"The purpose of the present 'Dictionary' is to enable the reader to find with some ease the meaning and interpretation of symbols currently used in mathematical logic (symbolic logic)."

1.3.9 **Diez y Lozano, Baldomero.** Vocabulario de lógica. 2. ed. Murcia, Spain, Imp. Lourdes, 1928. 198 pp.

1st ed. 1925.

1.4 PHILOSOPHICAL DICTIONARIES: SPECIALIZED BY PERIOD, MOVEMENT, OR TYPE

Ancient Greek Philosophy

1.4.1 **Goclenius, Rudolf.** Lexicon philosophicum quo tamquam clave philosophiae fores aperiuntur. Marburg, Rudolf Hutwelcker, 1615. 2v.

Reprinted: Hildesheim, G. Olms, 1964.
Latin definitions and explanations of Greek terms. Still useful.

1.4.2 **Peters, F. E.** Greek philosophical terms: a historical lexicon. New York, New York University Press, 1967. 234 pp.

Includes translations, definitions, and references to use by specific philosophers; it has an English-Greek index with cross-references, making knowledge of Greek unnecessary for its use.

1.4.3 **Schwartz, George T.** Index zu philosophischen Problemen in der klassischen griechischen Literatur. Bern, Francke Verlag, 1956. 109 pp.

Gives references to pre-Aristotelian Greek literature and philosophy.

Existentialism

1.4.4 ★ **Winn, Ralph B.** A concise dictionary of existentialism. New York, Philosophical Library, 1960. 122 pp.

Quotations from Kierkegaard, Heidegger, Jaspers, Marcel, Sartre, and de Beauvoir.

Scholastic Philosophy

1.4.5 **Signoriello, Nuntius.** Lexicon peripateticum philosophico-theologicum in quo Scholasticorum distinctiones et effata praecipua explicantur. 5. ed. Roma, Pustet, 1931. 470 pp.

1st ed. 1854.
A dictionary of scholastic distinctions and principles.

1.4.6 **Wuellner, Bernard, S. J.** Dictionary of scholastic philosophy. Milwaukee, Bruce Publishing Co., 1956. 138 pp.

Includes more than 37,000 words and phrases.

A reference work primarily for the undergraduate student.

1.5 DICTIONARIES: RELATED FIELDS

For annotated lists of dictionaries of most areas of the humanities, the sciences, and the social sciences, see Winchell (5.1.3).

Classics (Greek and Roman)

1.5.1 **Daremberg, Charles,** and **Edmond Saglio.** Dictionnaire des antiquités grecques et romaines d'après les textes et les monuments. Paris, Hachette, 1873–1919. 5v. and index.

Contains long, informative articles with bibliographies. Broad in scope.

1.5.2 **Oxford classical dictionary.** Ed. by M. Cary, A. D. Nock, and others. Oxford, Clarendon Press, 1949. 971 pp.

A standard reference work.

Literature

1.5.3 * **Beckson, Karl,** and **Arthur Ganz.** A reader's guide to literary terms: a dictionary. New York, Noonday, 1960. 230 pp.

1.5.4 **Columbia dictionary of modern European literature.** Horatio Smith, gen. ed. New York, Columbia University Press, 1947. 899 pp.

1.5.5 **Lexikon der Weltliteratur im 20. Jahrundert.** 2. Aufl. Freiburg, Herder, 1960–61. 2v.

1.5.6 **Thrall, William Flint,** and **Addison Hibbard.** A handbook to literature. Rev. and enl. by C. Hugh Holman. New York, Odyssey, 1960. 598 pp.

Mythology

1.5.7 **Dowson, John.** A classical dictionary of Hindu mythology and religion, geography, history and literature. 8th ed. London, Routledge and Paul, 1953. 411 pp.

1st ed. 1879.

1.5.8 **Funk & Wagnalls standard dictionary of folklore,** mythology and legend. Maria Leach, editor; Jerome Fried, assoc. editor. New York, Funk & Wagnalls, 1949–50. 2v.

Psychology

1.5.9 * **Drever, James.** A dictionary of psychology. Rev. by Harvey Wallerstein. Baltimore, Penguin, 1964. 320 pp.

1.5.10 **English, Horace B.,** and **Ava C. English.** A comprehensive dictionary of psychological and psychoanalytic terms: a guide to usage. New York, Longmans, Green & Co., 1958. 594 pp.

1.5.11 **Warren, H. C.** Dictionary of psychology. Boston, Houghton Mifflin, 1934. 372 pp.

Definitions of English and foreign terms; also bibliography of other dictionaries.

Religion and Theology

1.5.12 **Dictionnaire de spiritualité,** ascétique et mystique, doctrine et histoire. Publié sous la direction de J. de Guibert. Paris, Beauchesne, 1932– .

In progress.

1.5.13 **Dictionnaire de théologie catholique.** Publié sous la direction de A. Vacant, E. Mangenot et E. Amann. Paris, Letouzey, 1909–50. 15v.

Good not only for theology but also for medieval philosophy.

1.5.14 **Dizionario di teologia morale.** Diretto da F. Roberti. Roma, Editrice Studium, 1954, 1503 pp.

1.5.15 **Humphreys, Christmas.** A popular

dictionary of Buddhism. London, Arco, 1962. 233 pp.

1.5.16 **Jüdisches Lexikon;** ein enzyklopädisches Handbuch des jüdischen Wissens . . , hrsg. von Georg Herlitz und Bruno Kirschner. Berlin, Jüdischer Verlag, 1927–30. 4v. in 5.

1.5.17 **Lexikon für Theologie und Kirche.** 2 völlig. neubearb. Aufl. Hrsg. von Josef Höfer und Karl Rahner. Freiburg, Herder, 1957–65. 10v.

    1st ed. 1930–38.
    Roman Catholic.

1.5.18 **Oxford dictionary of the Christian Church.** Ed. by F. L. Cross. London, Oxford University Press, 1957. 1492 pp.

    Biographies, definitions of terms, development of doctrine.

1.5.19 **Parente, Pietro, Antonio Piolanti, e Salvatore Garofalo.** Dictionary of dogmatic theology. Trans. by E. Doronzo. Milwaukee, Bruce, 1951. 310 pp.

    Translation of *Dizionario di teologia dogmatica*, 2. ed., Roma, Studium, 1945.

1.5.20 **Die Religion in Geschichte und Gegenwart.** Handwörterbuch für Theologie und Religionswissenschaft. 3 völlig neubearb. Aufl. hrsg. von Kurt Galling. Tübingen, J. C. B. Mohr, 1956–62. 6v.

    1st ed. 1909–13.

1.5.21 **Soothill, William Edward,** and **Lewis Hodous.** A dictionary of Chinese Buddhist terms, with Sanskrit and English equivalents and a Sanskrit-Pali index. London, Kegan Paul, 1937. 510 pp.

See also: 1.3.7.

Science and Technology

1.5.22 **Beadnell, Charles Marsh.** Dictionary of scientific terms as used in the various sciences. London, Watts, 1942. 232 pp. (with a supplement of 13 pp.).

1.5.23 **Chambers's technical dictionary.** Ed. by C. F. Tweney and L. E. C. Hughes. 3d ed. rev. with suppl. New York, Macmillan, 1958. 1028 pp.

    1st ed. 1940.

Social Sciences

1.5.24 ★ **Fairchild, H. P.** Dictionary of sociology. New York, Philosophical Library, 1944. 342 pp.

1.5.25 **Kolb, William L.,** and **Julius Gould.** Dictionary of the social sciences. New York, Free Press, 1964. 762 pp.

    Covers terms in current usage in political science, anthropology, sociology, economics, and social psychology.

1.5.26 **Zadrozny, John Thomas.** Dictionary of social science. Washington, D. C., Public Affairs Press, 1959. 367 pp.

1.6 DICTIONARIES: SPECIALIZED POLYGLOT

1.6.1 **Ballestrem, Karl G.** Russian philosophical terminology. Dordrecht, Holland, D. Reidel Publishing Company, 1964. 117 pp.

    Gives English, French, and German equivalents of Russian terms. Includes English, French, and German indexes.

1.6.2 **Inoue, Tetsujiro.** Dictionary of English, German, and French philosophical terms with Japanese equivalents by Tetsujiro Inouye, Yujiro Motora, Rikizo Nakashima. Tokyo, Maruzen Kabushiki-Kaisha, 1912. 209 pp.

1.6.3 **Von Ostermann, Georg F.** Manual of foreign languages for the use of librarians, bibliographers, research workers, editors, translators and printers. 4th ed. New York, Central Books, 1952. 414 pp.

    Covers about 130 languages and dialects.

See also: 1.2.1, 1.2.12, 1.2.37, 1.5.21.

2. ENCYCLOPEDIAS

ENCYCLOPEDIAS OFFER a quick and summary presentation of a large number of philosophical topics and the biography and thought of major philosophers. Their articles are usually more comprehensive and their treatment broader and deeper than can be found even in specialized dictionaries. Encyclopedias also provide an excellent source for compiling a preliminary bibliography and for ascertaining the standard works on a topic. The general encyclopedias listed in 2.1 include the most important and the largest in the world. Their pholosophical entries have for the most part been written by experts in the field and their treatment of major philosophical topics is often extensive and thorough. Many of the articles on philosophy and the bibliographies supplied in the better of these works are as good as, and sometimes superior to, those in the more specialized encyclopedias.

Of the philosophical encyclopedias listed in 2.2, the *Encyclopedia of Philosophy* (2.2.1) deserves special mention, since it is the most recent, comprehensive, and reliable of the encyclopedias, and can be recommended as a general reference for almost any philosophical topic. The better philosophical encyclopedias are able to cover many more philosophical topics than is possible in even the best of the general encyclopedias.

Specialized encyclopedias in other fields (2.3) serve as excellent introductions to particular aspects of these fields. Many of them also include articles on philosophically pertinent topics. The encyclopedias of religion are especially useful for philosophical topics which are historically related to theology and religion. Questions dealing with methodology, ethics, and social philosophy are usually well covered in the encyclopedias of the natural and social sciences.

The index should always be consulted first in any encyclopedia having one.

2.1 ENCYCLOPEDIAS: GENERAL

For a discussion and an annotated list of general encyclopedias see Winchell (5.1.3), pp. 81–91.

2.1.1 **Chambers's encyclopedia.** London, George Newnes Ltd., 1959. 15v.

> Based on the 1950 ed.

Articles tend to be short. Major articles include bibliographies of standard works.

2.1.2 **Collier's encyclopedia.** 2d ed. New York, The Crowell-Collier Publishing Co., 1962. 24v.

> 1st ed. 1949–51. 20v.
> Continuous revisions. Articles on philosophy are of generally high quality.

See pp. 3–10 of v. 24 for general bibliographical material in philosophy.

2.1.3 Columbia encyclopedia. 3d ed. New
York, Columbia University Press, 1963.
2388 pp.

1st ed. 1935.
Articles are brief; those in biography are
generally better than the other articles.

2.1.4 Encyclopedia Americana. New York,
Americana Corp. 30v.

1st ed. 1903–04. New ed. 1918–20; since
then continuously revised. Bibliographies.
Articles on philosophy are somewhat un-
even, but many are by well-known American
philosophers.

2.1.5 Encyclopaedia Britannica. Chicago,
Encyclopaedia Britannica. 24v.

1st ed. 1768–61. 14th ed. 1929; since then
continuously revised. 24v. (incl. Index).
Bibliographies. Britannica of the Year, 1933- .
The most famous edition is the 11th (29v.,
London and New York, 1910-11).
The present edition is largely rewritten; the
philosophical articles are of generally high
quality. A. J. Ayer, Max Black, Brand Blanshard, and Gilbert Ryle are among the
contributors.

French

2.1.6 Encyclopédie française. Paris, Comité
de l'Encyclopédie Française, 1935–64. 20v.

Vol. XIX: Philosophie, Religion (1957),
424 pp.

2.1.7 La grande encyclopédie. Paris, H.
Lamirault et Cie., 1886–1902. 31v.

Very good bibliographies, especially of
works in French.

2.1.8 Grande Larousse encyclopédique.
Paris, Larousse, 1960–64. 10v.

The articles on philosophy are generally
short; bibliographies are at back of each
volume.
Supersedes Larousse du XXᵉ siècle.

German

2.1.9 Der grosse Brockhaus. 16. Aufl.
Wiesbaden, F. A. Brockhaus, 1952–60. 12v.;
Ergänzungsbd., 2v.

Good bibliographies in German, English,
and other languages.

2.1.10 Der grosse Herder. 5. Aufl. Freiburg,
Herder, 1953–56. 10v.

Supplemented by 2v., 1962.

Italian

2.1.11 Dizionario enciclopedico italiano.
Roma, Istituto della Enciclopedia Italiana,
1955–61. 12v.

No bibliographies.

2.1.12 Enciclopedia italiana di scienze,
lettere ed arti. Roma, Istituto della Enciclopedia Italiana, 1929–39. 36v.

5v. of supplements, 1938–61.
Articles on philosophy are often long and
detailed.
Bibliographies in Italian, English, and other
languages.

Russian

2.1.13 Bol'shaia sovetskaia entsiklopediia.
2. izd. Moskva, "Sovetskaia Entisiklopediia,"
1949–58. 51v.

Bibliographies in philosophy are usually
only in Russian.
The articles are from the Marxist-Leninist
point of view of the Stalinist era.
The third edition of 30 volumes, to be
completed in 1974, was begun in 1969.

Spanish

**2.1.14 Enciclopedia universal illustrada
europeo-americana.** Barcelona, Hijos de
J. Espasa, 1905–33. 80v. in 81. v. 1–70 in 71,
and 10v. supplement. Seven additional supplements, 1934–58.

Bibliographies in Spanish, English, other
languages.

Especially good on Spanish and Latin American topics of the 19th century or earlier.

2.2 ENCYCLOPEDIAS: PHILOSOPHICAL

For an historical and detailed review of philosophical encyclopedias see William Gerber's article "Philosophical Dictionaries and Encyclopedias" in the *Encyclopedia of Philosophy* (2.2.1), vol. VI, pp. 170–199.

2.2.1 Encyclopedia of philosophy. Ed. in chief, Paul Edwards. New York, Macmillan and Free Press, 1967. 8v.

Contains 1450 articles, written by 500 scholars from 24 nations. An excellent source for almost any topic in philosophy. Detailed and annotated bibliographies follow each article.

The best single reference book in philosophy.

2.2.2 Encyclopedia of religion and ethics. Ed. by James Hastings. Edinburgh, Clark, 1908–26. 12v. and Index.

Reprinted: N. Y., Scribner, 1955.
Aims "at containing articles on every religious belief or custom, and on every ethical movement, every philosophical idea, every moral practice" (p. v). Bibliographies.

An excellent reference work, despite its age.

See also: 1.2.6, 1.2.24, 1.3.4.

Italian

2.2.3 Enciclopedia filosofica. Venezia-Roma, Istituto Per la Collaborazione Culturale, 1957–58. 4v.

An excellent reference work on philosophers and philosophy. International bibliographies.

A 2d ed., Firenze, G. C. Sansoni, 1968– , projected for 6v., is in progress.

A German revised edition, *Lexikon der Philosophie*, ed. by W. Brugger, H. G. Gadamer, R. Guardini, H. Kuhn, and L. Landgrebe, Freiburg, Herder, 1969– , is also in progress.

Russian

2.2.4 Filosofskaia entsiklopediia. Moskva, "Sovetskaia Entsiklopediia," 1960– .

In progress.
6v. projected. Bibliographies.
Marxist-Leninist in orientation.

2.3 ENCYCLOPEDIAS: RELATED FIELDS

Education

2.3.1 Cyclopedia of education. Ed. by Paul Monroe with the assistance of departmental editors and more than 1000 individual contributors. New York, Macmillan, 1911–13. 5v.

Contributors included John Dewey, Paul Carus, Morris Cohen, and A. O. Lovejoy.
Now dated.

Religion

2.3.2 Encyclopaedia of Islam. New ed., ed. by H. A. R. Gibb, J. H. Kramers, E. Lévi-Provençal, J. Schacht. Leiden, Brill; London, Luzac & Co., 1954– .

In progress.
1st ed. 1911–38, 4v. in 8. Supplement, 1934–38.
A basic reference work on Islam.

2.3.3 Jewish encyclopedia; a descriptive record of the history, religion, literature, and customs of the Jewish people from the earliest times to the present day. Prepared under the direction of Cyrus Adler. New York, Funk & Wagnalls, 1901–06. 12v.

Long the standard encyclopedia in English in its field.

2.3.4 The Mennonite encyclopedia; a comprehensive reference work on the Anabaptist-Mennonite movement. Scottdale, Pa., Mennonite Publishing House, 1955–59. 4v.

2.3.5 New Catholic encyclopedia. Ed. in chief, Most Rev. William J. McDonald, D. D. New York, McGraw-Hill, 1967. 15v.

"An international work of reference on the teachings, history, organization and activities of the Catholic Church, and on all institutions, religions, philosophies, and scientific and cultural developments affecting the Catholic Church from its beginnings to the present." Includes articles on philosophy.

2.3.6 **New Schaff-Herzog encyclopedia of religious knowledge.** New York, Funk & Wagnalls, 1908–12. 12v. and Index.

Reprinted: Grand Rapids, Mich., Baker Book House, 1949–50. 13v.
Based on *Realencyklopädie*, founded by J. J. Herzog. Supplemented and to some extent revised by: *Twentieth Century Encyclopedia of Religious Knowledge*. Grand Rapids, Mich., Baker Book House, 1955. 2v.
Good bibliographies; especially useful for Protestant theology.

2.3.7 **Sacramentum mundi:** an encyclopedia of theology. Ed. by Karl Rahner with Cornelius Ernst and Kevin Smyth. New York, Herder and Herder, 1968–70. 6v.

A compendium of postconciliar Catholic theology.
Also German, French, Italian, Spanish, and Dutch editions.

2.3.8 **Universal Jewish encyclopedia.** Ed. by Isaac Landman. New York, Universal Jewish Encyclopedia, Inc., 1939–43. 10v.

Science

2.3.9 **Harper encyclopedia of science.** Ed. by James R. Newman. New York, Harper & Row, 1963. 4v.

Includes articles on logic and the history and philosophy of science.

Also covers astronomy, biochemistry and biophysics, biology, chemistry, geology, mathematics, meteorology, physics, and technology.

2.3.10 **International encyclopedia of unified science.** Foundations of the unity of science. Chicago, University of Chicago Press, 1938– .

In progress.
Includes articles by Bohr, Carnap, and Dewey, among others.
More a collection of monographs than an encyclopedia in the ordinary sense.

2.3.11 **McGraw-Hill encyclopedia of science and technology;** an international reference work. New York, McGraw-Hill, 1960. 15v.

Covers most of the sciences in a relatively nontechnical manner.

Social Sciences

2.3.12 **Encyclopedia of the social sciences.** Ed. in chief, E. R. A. Seligman. New York, Macmillan, 1930–35. 15v.

Covers the broad area of the social sciences, and includes a number of articles on philosophy.
Supplemented by 2.3.13.

2.3.13 **International encyclopedia of the social sciences.** David L. Sills, editor. New York, Macmillan and Free Press, 1968. 17v.

Good bibliographies in English, French, and German.
"Designed to complement, not to supplant, its predecessor the *Encyclopedia of the Social Sciences*." (p. xix).

3. HISTORIES OF PHILOSOPHY

HISTORIES OF PHILOSOPHY can provide a summary introduction to a philosopher's thought, interpretations of particular authors and works, background material on individuals, works and movements, and bibliographies.

The following lists include the more important, scholarly histories of philosophy published in English or in major European languages. Many of them are standard reference works and most of them contain bibliographies and bibliographical references to more specialized studies on particular philosophers and periods. Section 3.1 includes a number of multivolumed histories which cover two or more periods of the history of philosophy. The appropriate volumes are not relisted in the later sections, but the work as a whole is referred to by its number.

There are a great many undergraduate texts and popular presentations of the history of philosophy. No attempt has been made to list them here and such English language works which are still in print can be found by consulting *Subject Guide to Books in Print* (6.2.7).

Additional works on the history of philsophy in particular countries and on particular branches of philosophy can be found by using the bibliographies in the works listed in 3.6 and 3.7, by consulting the appropriate articles in the encyclopedias listed in chapter 2, by referring to the bibliographies listed in sections 5.4 to 5.6, and by utilizing the general bibliographies listed in section 5.3. For a survey of material which has appeared in philosophical journals since 1966 on the history of philosophy, see 7.3.42.

3.1 HISTORIES OF PHILOSOPHY: GENERAL

3.1.1 **Bréhier, Emile.** The history of philosophy. Chicago, Chicago University Press, 1963–69. 7v.

A translation of 3.1.12.
* Vol. I, The Hellenic age, trans. by Joseph Thomas, 1963;
* vol. II, The Hellenistic and Roman age, trans. by Wade Baskin, 1965;
* vol. III, The Middle Ages and the Renaissance, trans. by Wade Baskin, 1965;

* vol. IV, The Seventeenth Century, trans. by Wade Baskin, 1966;
vol. V, The Eighteenth Century, trans. by Wade Baskin, 1967;
vol. VI, The Nineteenth Century; period of systems, 1800–1850, trans. by Wade Baskin, 1968;
vol. VII, Contemporary philosophy—since 1850, trans. by Wade Baskin, 1969.
Excellent bibliographies.

3.1.2 **Caponigri, A. Robert,** and **Ralph McInerny.** A history of Western philosophy. Chicago, Regnery, 1964– .

V. 1, From the beginnings of philosophy to Plotinus, 1964;

v. 2, From St. Augustine to Ockham, 1970;

v. 3, From the Renaissance to the romantic age, 1964;

5v. projected. Taken over by Notre Dame University Press.

Bibliographical references conclude each chapter.

3.1.3 * **Copleston, F. C.** A history of philosophy. Westminster, Md., The Newman Press, 1946–66. 8v.

Vol. I, Greece and Rome;

vol. II, Mediaeval philosophy: Augustine to Scotus;

vol. III, Ockham to Suarez;

vol. IV, Descartes to Leibniz;

vol. V, Hobbes to Hume;

vol. VI, Wolff to Kant;

vol. VII, Fichte to Nietzsche;

vol. VIII, Bentham to Russell.

Reliable and objective. This is one of the best general histories of philosophy available in English. There is some criticism from a Thomistic point of view. The bibliographies are good for both sources and secondary works.

3.1.4 * **Ferm, Vergilius,** *ed.* History of philosophical systems; contributions by forty-one professors of America, Canada, Europe, and Asia. New York, Philosophical Library, 1950. 642 pp.

Essays on 47 schools, systems, and branches of philosophy.

Includes bibliographies.

3.1.5 **Gilson, Etienne,** *general ed.* A history of philosophy. New York, Random House, 1962– .

In progress.

4v. projected.

See 3.3.6, 3.4.3, 3.5.2.

3.1.6 **Jaspers, Karl.** The great philosophers. Ed. by Hannah Arendt, trans. by Ralph Manheim. New York, Harcourt, Brace & World, 1962–66. 2v.

V. 1, * Part I: Socrates, Buddha, Confucius, Jesus; Part II: Plato, Augustine, Kant.

v. 2, Anaximander, Heraclitus, Parmenides, Plotinus, Anselm, Nicholas of Cusa, Spinoza, Lao-Tzu, Nagarjuna.

Includes bibliographies.

3.1.7 **O'Connor, Daniel J.,** *ed.* A critical history of Western philosophy. New York, Free Press, 1964. 604 pp.

Twenty-nine scholarly studies by various philosophers of figures and periods in the history of philosophy from the early Greeks to the present.

Good bibliographies, pp. 576–594.

3.1.8 **Radhakrishnan, Sir Sarvepalli,** *ed.* History of philosophy, Eastern and Western. London, Allen and Unwin, 1952–53. 2v.

Essays on the history of Eastern and Western philosophy by various scholars.

Bibliographies throughout.

3.1.9 **Randall, John Herman.** The making of the modern mind; a survey of the intellectual background of the present age. Rev. ed. Cambridge, Mass., Houghton Mifflin, 1954. 696 pp.

A history of cultural development.

Bibliographies at the end of each chapter.

3.1.10 **Randall, John Herman.** The career of philosophy. New York, Columbia University Press, 1962– .

In progress.

3v. projected.

V. 1, From the Middle Ages to the Enlightenment, 1962;

v. 2, From the German Enlightenment to the age of Darwin, 1965.

Bibliographical footnotes.

3.1.11 * **Windelband, Wilhelm.** A history of philosophy. Trans. by James Tufts. Rev. ed. Macmillan, 1901. 2v.

1st ed. 1893.

Reprinted: N. Y., Harper, 1958

A translation of *Geschichte der Philosophie,* 1889.

Idealist in outlook. The ample bibliographical sections throughout the text have not been updated.

French

3.1.12 **Bréhier, Emile.** Histoire de la philosophie. Paris, Presses Universitaires de France, 1926–32. 2v. in 7.

See 3.1.1. Also later editions of each of the parts.

The French edition includes two supplementary volumes: Paul Masson-Oursel, *La philosophie en Orient*, 3. éd., 1948, and Basile Tatakis, *Philosophie Byzantine*, 1949.

A standard work. Excellent bibliographies.

3.1.13 **Chevalier, J.** Histoire de la pensée. Paris, Flammarion, 1955–66. 4v.

V. 1, La pensée antique, 1955;

v. 2, La pensée chrétienne, des origines à la fin du XVIe siècle, 1956;

v. 3, De Descartes à Kant, 1961;

v. 4, De Hegel à Bergson, 1966.

Full bibliographies throughout.

3.1.14 **Rivaud, Albert.** Histoire de la philosophie. Paris, Presses Universitaires de France, 1948–67. 5v. in 6.

V. 1, Des origines à la Scholastique, 1948;

v. 2, De la Scholastique à l'époque classique, 1950;

v. 3, L'époque classique, 1950;

v. 4, Philosophie française et philosophie anglaise de 1700 à 1830, 1962;

v. 5, Philosophie allemande, de 1700 à 1850: Ptie. 1, De l'Aufklarung à Schelling, 1968; Ptie. 2., De Hegel à Schopenhauer, 1968.

General bibliography in v. 1 and bibliographies at end of most chapters.

German

3.1.15 **Schilling, Kurt.** Geschichte der Philosophie. München, Reinhardt, 1951–53. 2v.

V. 1, Die alter Welt; das christlich-germanische Mittelalter, 1951;

v. 2, Die Neuzeit, 1953.

Useful biliographies.

3.1.16 **Ueberweg, Friedrich.** Grundriss der Geschichte der Philosophie. 11. and 12. Aufl.

Berlin, E. S. Mittler und Sohn, 1923–28. 5v.

1st ed. 1862–66, 3v. The 11th and 12th editions are famous for their extremely full bibliographies.

Reprinted: v. 1–3, Bâle, B. Schwabe, 1951–60.

V. 1, Die Philosophie des Altertums, 12. Aufl., herausgegeben von Karl Praechter, 1926;

v. 2, Die patristische und scholastische Philosophie, 11. Aufl., herausgegeben von Bernhard Geyer, 1928;

v. 3, Die Philosophie der Neuzeit bis zum Ende des 18. Jahrhunderts, 12. Aufl., herausgegeben von Max Frischeisen-Köhler und Willy Moog, 1924;

v. 4, Die deutsche Philosophie des neunzehnten Jahrhunderts und der Gegenwart, 12. Aufl., herausgegeben von Traugott Konstantin Osterreich, 1923;

v. 5, Die Philosophie des Auslandes vom Beginn des 19. Jahrhunderts bis auf die Gegenwart, 12. Aufl. herausgegeben von Traugott Konstantin Osterreich, 1928.

Though a standard reference for historical research, there is no systematic index. Bibliographies are massive, but not exhaustive. They cover the period of roughly up to 1920.

The two-volume English translation, *History of Philosophy, from Thales to the Present Time*, 1887, is from the 4th German edition, and does not have the bibliographical data which makes the history so useful.

A new German edition, in 8v., under the direction of Paul Wilpert, has been announced by Schwabe and Co. (Basel).

Italian

3.1.17 **Abbagnano, Nicola.** Storia della filosofia. Torino, Unione Tipografico-Editrice Torinese, 1949–50. 2v. in 3.

V. 1, Filosofia antica; filosofia patristica; filosofia scholastica;

v. 2, pt. 1, Filosofia moderna sino all fine del secolo XVII; pt. 2, Filosofia del romanticismo; filosofia contemporanea.

Includes bibliographies.

3.1.18 **De Ruggiero, Guido.** Storia della filosofia. Bari, Laterza, 1920–34. 14v.

Written from a neo-Hegelian point of view. Bibliographies.

See also: 5.1.15.

Russian

3.1.19 **Akademiia nauk SSSR.** Institut filosofii. Istoriia filosofii. V shesti tomakh. Moskva, 1957–65. 6v. in 7.

Bibliography, vol. VI, pp. 474–544.

3.2 HISTORIES OF ANCIENT PHILOSOPHY

3.2.1 **Armstrong, A. H.,** ed. The Cambridge history of later Greek and early medieval philosophy. Cambridge, The University Press, 1967. 711 pp.

A scholarly work by eight contributors covering a period from the 4th century B.C. to the beginning of the 12th century A.D.
Bibliography, pp. 670–691.

3.2.2 **Burnet John.** Early Greek philosophy. See 4.1.8.

3.2.3 **Diogenes Laërtius.** Lives of eminent philosophers, with an English translation by R. D. Hicks. Loeb classical library. Cambridge, Mass., Harvard University Press, 1958–59. 2v.

Greek and English on facing pages. First printed 1925.
For a critical edition of the Greek text see, Diogenes Laërtius, *Vitae philosophorum*; recognovit brevisque adnotatione critica instruxit H. S. Long, Oxonii, E. Typographeo Clarendoniano, 1964, 2v.
An account, by a Third Century writer, of the lives and doctrines of the chief Greek philosophers, containing biographical data and fragments of their work, culled primarily from secondary sources.

3.2.4 ★ **Gomperz, Theodor.** Greek thinkers; history of ancient philosophy. New York, Charles Scribner's Sons, 1901–12. 4v.

Reprinted: Humanities Press, 1955.

A translation of *Griechische Denker; eine Geschichte der antiken Philosophie*, Leipzig, Veit, 1893–1909, 3v.

3.2.5 **Guthrie, W. K. C.** A history of Greek philosophy. Cambridge, The University Press, 1962– .

In progress.
5v. projected.
V. 1, The earlier presocratics and the Pythagoreans, 1962;
v. 2, The presocratic tradition from Parmenides to Democritus, 1965;
v. 3, The fifth-century enlightenment, 1969.
Bibliographies at the end of each volume.

3.2.6 **Kirk, G. S.,** and **J. E. Raven.** The presocratic philosophers. See 4.1.11.

3.2.7 **Owens, Joseph.** A history of ancient Western philosophy. New York, Appleton-Century-Crofts, 1959. 434 pp.

Includes bibliography.

3.2.8 ★ **Robinson, John Mansley.** An introduction to early Greek philosophy; the chief fragments and ancient testimony with connecting commentary. Boston, Houghton Mifflin, 1968. 339 pp.

Includes a bibliographical essay and notes on sources.

3.2.9 **Zeller, E.** A history of Greek philosophy from the earliest period to the time of Socrates. Trans. by S. F. Alleyne. London, Longmans, Green & Co., 1881. 2v.

Translation of the first part of *Die Philosophie der Griechen* (3.2.13).

3.2.10 ★ **Zeller, E.** Outlines of the history of Greek philosophy. 13th rev. ed. Trans. by L. R. Palmer. New York, Meridian, 1955. 349 pp.

1st American ed. 1931; 1st German ed. 1883; 13th ed. 1928.

A translation of *Grundriss der Geschichte der griechischen Philosophie*.

See also: 3.1.1, 3.1.2, 3.1.3, 3.1.6.

French

3.2.11 **Rivaud, Albert.** Les grands courants de la pensée antique. 4. éd. Paris, A. Colin, 1941. 220 pp.

1st ed. 1929.

See also: 3.1.12, 3.1.13, 3.1.14.

German

3.2.12 **Kranz, W.** Die griechische Philosophie. 4. Aufl. Brême, Schünemann, 1958. 353 pp.

1st ed. 1950.

3.2.13 **Zeller, E.** Die Philosophie der Griechen in ihrer geschichtlichen Entwicklung. 7. Aufl. Leipzig, Reisland, 1920–23. 3v. in 6.

Reprinted: Olms, Hildesheim, 1963. 1st ed. 1844–52.
English translation: *Philosophy of the Greeks*, trans. by S. F. Alleyne and others, 1881–88, 9v. *See also* 3.2.8.
Ample bibliographical notes.

See also: 3.1.15, 3.1.16.

Italian

3.2.14 **Zeller, E.,** and **R. Mondolfo.** La filosofia dei greci nel suo sviluppo storico. 5. ed. Firenze, La Nuova Italia, 1961. 4v.

Monumental, with many references.

See also: 3.1.17.

3.3 HISTORIES OF MEDIEVAL AND RENAISSANCE PHILOSOPHY

3.3.1 **De Wulf, Maurice.** History of mediaeval philosophy. 3d ed. London, Longmans, Green & Co., 1935–37. 2v.

English translation by E. E. Messenger of first 2v. of 3.3.8.
Reprinted: New York, Dover, 1952– .
A standard work. Excellent bibliographies.

3.3.2 **Gilson, Etienne.** History of Christian philosophy in the Middle Ages. New York, Random House, 1955. 829 pp.

Translation of 3.3.9.
A basic reference work. Bibliography, pp. 552–804.

3.3.3 ★ **Gilson, Etienne.** The spirit of mediaeval philosophy. Trans. by A. H. C. Downes. London, Sheed and Ward, 1936. 490 pp.

Gifford Lectures, 1931–32.
A translation of *L'esprit de la philosophie médiévale*, Paris, Vrin, 1932.

3.3.4 ★ **Husik, I.** A history of mediaeval Jewish philosophy. New York, Meridian, 1958. 466 pp.

1st ed. 1916.
Bibliography: pp. 433–37.

3.3.5 **Kristeller, Paul Oskar.** Studies in Renaissance thought and letters. Roma, Edizioni di Storia e Letteratura, 1956. 680 pp.

Bibliography: pp. 591–628.
A collection of essays, rather than a systematic history.

3.3.6 **Maurer, Armand.** Medieval philosophy. New York, Random House, 1962. 435 pp.

Bibliography and notes: pp. 380–426.

3.3.7 **Wolfson, Harry A.** The philosophy of the Church Fathers. 2d rev. ed. Cambridge, Mass., Harvard University Press. 635 pp.

1st ed. 1956.
Includes bibliographies.

See also: 3.1.1, 3.1.2, 3.1.3, 3.1.6, 3.1.10.

French

3.3.8 **De Wulf, Maurice.** Histoire de la philosophie médiévale. 6. éd. Louvain, Institut Supérieur de Philosophie, 1934–47. 3v.

Its annotated bibliographies supplement those in Ueberweg (3.1.16).

3.3.9 **Gilson, Eteinne.** La philosophie au moyen âge des origines patristiques à la fin du XIVe siècle. 3 éd. Paris, Payot, 1952. 782 pp.

1st ed. 1922.
Its bibliographies supplement those of De Wulf (3.3.8).

See also: 3.1.13, 3.1.14.

German

3.3.10 **Grabmann, Martin.** Mittelalterliches Geistesleben; Abhandlungen zur Geschichte der Scholastik und Mystik. München, Max Hueber, 1926–56. 3v.

A standard reference work. Bibliography: v. 3, pp. 10–35.

3.3.11 **Grabmann, Martin.** Die Geschichte der scholastischen Methode. Freiburg, Herder, 1909–11. 2v.

Reprinted: Basel/Stuttgart, 1961.

See also: 3.1.15, 3.1.16.

3.4 HISTORIES OF MODERN PHILOSOPHY

3.4.1 ★ **Cassirer, Ernst.** The philosophy of the enlightenment. Trans. by Fritz C. A. Koelln and James P. Pettegrove. Princeton, Princeton University Press, 1951. 366 pp.

A translation of *Die Philosophie der Aufklärung*, 1932.
An excellent study of 18th century thought, with bibliographical footnotes.

3.4.2 **Collins, James.** A history of modern European philosophy. Milwaukee, Bruce, 1954. 854 pp.

Annotated bibliographies of sources and secondary works.
Objective and reliable. Criticism from Thomistic point of view.
Parts of this work have been published separately in paperbound editions.

3.4.3 **Gilson, E.,** and **Thomas Langan.** Modern philosophy; Descartes to Kant. New York, Random House, 1963. 570 pp.

Notes and bibliography: pp. 457–560.

3.4.4 ★ **Hazard, Paul.** European thought in the 18th century from Montesquieu to Lessing. Trans. by J. Lewis May. Cleveland, World Publishing Co., 1963. 477 pp.

Translation of *La pensée européene au XVIII ème siècle: De Montesquieu à Lessing*, 1963.

Bibliographical footnotes.

3.4.5 ★ **Höffding, Harald.** A history of modern philosophy. Trans. by B. E. Meyer. New York, Humanities Press, 1950. 2v.

Reissue: New York, Dover, 1955. 2v.
A translation of *Geschichte der neueren Philosophie*, Leipzig, Reisland, 1895–96, 2v.

3.4.6 **Lévy-Bruhl, Lucien.** A history of modern philosophy in France. Trans. by G. Coblence. Chicago, The Open Court Co., 1899. 500 pp.

Bibliography: pp. 483–494.

3.4.7 ★ **Löwith, Karl.** From Hegel to Nietzsche; the revolution in nineteenth-century thought. Trans. by David E. Green from 3d German ed. New York, Holt, Rinehart, and Winston, 1964. 464 pp.

A translation of *Von Hegel zu Nietzsche: Der revolutionäre Bruch im Denken des neunzehnten Jahrhunderts*. Zürich, Europa Verlag, 1941.
Bibliography: pp. 389–395; and extensive bibliographical information in the notes.

3.4.8 ★ **Merz, John Theodore.** A history of European thought in the nineteenth century. New York, Dover, 1965. 4v.

1st ed., Edinburgh, W. Blackwood, 1904–12, 4v.
Treats topics, not individuals.
Bibliography in the footnotes.

3.4.9 ★ **Stephen, Sir Leslie.** History of English thought in the eighteenth century. 3d ed. New York, P. Smith, 1949. 2v.

1st ed. 1876.
A standard work. Includes bibliographies.

See also: 3.1.1, 3.1.2, 3.1.3, 3.1.6, 3.1.10, 3.4.4, 3.7.22.

French

3.4.10 **Maréchal, J., S. J.** Précis d'histoire de la philosophie moderne, de la Renaissance à Kant. 2. éd. Paris, Desclée de Brouwer, 1951. 355 pp.

1st ed. 1933.
The second editon contains a bibliographical supplement from 1933–1949.

3.4.11 **Sortais, Gaston.** La philosophie moderne depuis Bacon jusqu'à Leibniz. Paris, P. Lethielleux, 1920–22. 2v.

Includes bibliographies.

See also: 3.1.13, 2.1.14, 3.7.21, 3.7.23.

German

3.4.12 **Kroner, R.** Von Kant bis Hegel. Tübigen, Mohr, 1921–24. 2v.

Reprinted: 1961, 2v. in 1.

See also: 3.1.15, 3.1.16, 3.4.1, 3.4.5, 3.4.7, 3.6.23, 3.6.24, 3.7.20, 3.7.22.

3.5 HISTORIES OF CONTEMPORARY PHILOSOPHY

3.5.1 * **Bochenski, I. M.** Contemporary European philosophy. Trans. by D. Nicholl and K. Aschenbrenner. Berkeley, University of California Press, 1956. 326 pp.

Translation of *Europäische Philosophie der Gegenwart*, 2. Aufl., Bern, Francke, 1951.
Bibliography: pp. 267–321.

3.5.2 **Gilson, Etienne, Thomas Langan,** and **Armand Maurer.** Recent philosophy; Hegel to the present. New York, Random House, 1966. 876 pp.

The notes, pp. 671–864, contain a wealth of bibliographical material.

3.5.3 **Klibansky, Raymond,** *ed.* Philosophy in mid-century; a survey. Firenze, La Nuova Italia, 1958. 4v.

Surveys the period from 1949 to the end of 1955. Includes bibliographies.
Continued by 3.5.4.

3.5.4 **Klibansky, Raymond,** *ed.* Contemporary philosophy; a survey. Firenze, La Nuova Italia, 1968–69. 4v.

Follows and complements 3.5.3.
Includes bibliographies.

3.5.5 * **Passmore, John A.** A hundred years of philosophy. New York, Macmillan, 1957. 523 pp.

Bibliography: pp. 479–502.
Rev. ed. 1966, 574 pp., contains only an abbreviated bibliography, pp. 547–549.

3.5.6 **Sciacca, Michele Federico.** Philosophical trends in the contemporary world. Trans. by Attilio Salerno. Notre Dame, University of Notre Dame Press, 1964. 656 pp.

Bibliographical footnotes.
A translation of *La filosofla, oggi, dalle origini romantiche della filosofia contemporaneo ai problemi attuali*, Milano, Mondadori, 1945.

3.5.7 **Sciacca, Michele Federico.** Les grands courants de la pensée mondiale contemporaine. Publié sous la direction de M. F. Sciacca. Milan, Marzorati, 1958–61. 4v.

Pt. I, a survey by countries; Pt. II, a survey by movements.
By various authors. Includes bibliographies.

3.5.8 **Spiegelberg, Herbert.** The phenomenological movement; a historical introduction. 2d ed. The Hague, Nijhoff, 1965. 2v.

Contains good bibliographies on individual philosophers in the movement.

3.5.9 * **Urmson, James O.** Philosophical analysis; its development between the two World Wars. Oxford, Clarendon Press, 1956. 202 pp.

3.6 HISTORIES OF PHILOSOPHY: BY COUNTRY

American Philosophy

3.6.1 **American philosophic addresses 1700–1900.** Ed. by Joseph L. Blau. New York, Columbia University Press, 1946. 762 pp.

Contains a biobibliography at the beginning of each address.

3.6.2 **Blau, Joseph L.** Men and movements in American philosophy. Englewood Cliffs, N. J., Prentice-Hall, 1958. 403 pp.

> 1st published 1952.
> Covers American philosophy from its Puritan background through John Dewey.
> Bibliographical references are included in "Footnotes and suggested reading": pp. 357–383.

3.6.3 **Contemporary American philosophy.** 34 personal statements. Edited by G. P. Adams and W. P. Montague. New York, Macmillan, 1930. 2v.

> Biobibliographical information on the authors is included.

3.6.4 **Reck, Andrew.** Recent American philosophy; studies of ten representative thinkers. New York, Pantheon Books, 1964. 343 pp.

> Contains studies of the philosophy of R. B. Perry, W. E. Hocking, G. H. Mead, J. E. Boodin, W. M. Urban, D. H. Parker, R. W. Sellars, A. O. Lovejoy, E. Jordan, and E. S. Brightman.
> Includes bibliographical references.

3.6.5 **Reck, Andrew.** The new American philosophers; an exploration of thought since World War II. Baton Rouge, Louisiana State University Press, 1968. 362 pp.

> A sequel to 3.6.4. Contains studies of the philosophy of C. I. Lewis, S. C. Pepper, B. Blanshard, E. Nagel, J. H. Randall, J. Buchler, S. Hook, F. S. C. Northrop, J. K. Feibleman, J. Wild, C. Hartshorne, and P. Weiss.
> Biobibliographical material throughout.

3.6.6 ★ **Schneider, Herbert.** A history of American philosophy. 2d rev. ed. New York, Columbia University Press, 1963. 523 pp.

> 1st ed. 1946.
> A standard work with excellent bibliographies.

3.6.7 ★ **Smith, John E.** The spirit of American philosophy. New York, Oxford University Press, 1963. 219 pp.

3.6.8 **Werkmeister, W. H.** A history of philosophical ideas in America. New York, Ronald Press, 1949. 599 pp.

See also: 3.6.22.

British Philosophy

3.6.9 **Contemporary British philosophy.** New York, Macmillan, 1924–56. 3v.

> First Series, 1924; second series, 1925. Ed. by J. H. Muirhead. Reprinted: 1953. Third series, 1956, ed. by H. D. Lewis.
> Statements of their philosophy by British philosophers. The first two volumes included such figures as Broad, Bosanquet, and Russell. All volumes include bibliographies.

3.6.10 **Metz, Rudolf.** A hundred years of British philosophy. Trans. by J. W. Harvey et al. Ed. by J. H. Muirhead. London, Allen and Unwin, 1938. 828 pp.

> 2d impression: New York, Macmillan, 1951.
> A translation of *Die philosophischen Strömungen der Gegenwart in Grossbritannien*, Leipzig, Meiner, 1935, 2v.
> Includes bibliographies.

3.6.11 **Paul, Leslie.** The English philosophers. London, Faber & Faber, 1953. 380 pp.

> Bibliography: pp. 353–366.

3.6.12 **Pucelle, J.** L'idéalisme en Angleterre de Coleridge à Bradley. Neuchâtel, La Baconnière, 1955. 295 pp.

> Includes bibliographical references.

3.6.13 ★ **Sorley, W. R.** A history of British philosophy to 1900. Cambridge, The University Press, 1956. 386 pp.

> Bibliography: pp. 323–379.
> First published as *A History of English Philosophy*, 1920.
> Covers the period from John Scotus Erigena to the end of the Victorian era. Includes biographical material and treats "early and now almost forgotten philosophers" as well as the great writers, e.g., it treats the critics and contemporaries of Locke as well as Locke himself.

Very full bibliography. Comparative chronological table of the chief works in English philosophy along with the dates of some other writings, English and foreign, and of some leading events, pp. 303–321.

3.6.14 * **Warnock, G. J.** English philosophy since 1900. Oxford, Oxford University Press, 1958. 180 pp.

Includes bibliography.

See also: 3.4.9, 3.5.5, 3.5.9.

Chinese Philosophy

3.6.15 * **Creel, H. G.** Chinese thought, from Confucius to Mao Tsê-tung. Chicago, University of Chicago Press, 1953. 292 pp.

Bibliography: pp. 266–271.

3.6.16 **Forke, Alfred.** Geschichte der alten chinesischen Philosophie. 2., unveränderte Aufl., Hamburg, Cram, W. de Gruyter, 1964. 594 pp.

1st ed. 1927.

3.6.17 **Forke, Alfred.** Geschichte der mittelalterlichen chinesischen Philosophie. 2., unveränderte Aufl., Hamburg, Cram, W. de Gruyter, 1964. 410 pp.

1st ed. 1934.

3.6.18 **Forke, Alfred.** Geschichte der neueren chinesischen Philosophie. 2., unveränderte Aufl. Hamburg, Cram, W. de Gruyter, 1964. 693 pp.

1st ed. 1938.

3.6.19 **Fung-Yu-lan.** A history of Chinese philosophy. Trans. by Derk Bodde. 2d ed. Princeton, Princeton University Press, 1952–53. 2v.

V. 1, 1st ed., London, Allen and Unwin, 1937.
A basic work. Bibliographies: v. 1, pp. 410–422; v. 2, pp. 726–754.
Abridged version: * *A Short History of Chinese Philosophy,* New York, Macmillan, 1948, 368 pp.

French Philosophy

3.6.20 **Belin, J. P.** Le mouvement philosophique en France de 1748 à 1789. Paris, Belin, 1913. 381 pp.

Bibliography: pp. 5–10.
Reprinted: N. Y., Burt Franklin.

3.6.21 **Benrubi, J.** Les sources et les courants de la philosophie contemporaine en France. Paris, F. Alcan, 1933. 2v.

3.6.22 **Farber, Marvin,** *ed.* Philosophic thought in France and the United States; essays representing major trends in contemporary French and American philosophy. Buffalo, University of Buffalo Press, 1950. 775 pp.

Bibliographies throughout.

German Philosophy

3.6.23 **Hartmann, Nicolai.** Die Philosophie des deutschen Idealismus. Berlin und Leipzig, W. de Gruyter, 1923–29. 2v.

3.6.24 **Wundt, Max.** Die deutsche Schulphilosophie im Zeitalter der Aufklärung. Tübingen, J. C. B. Mohr, 1945. 346 pp.

Reprinted: Hildsheim. Olms, 1964.

See also: 3.4.12.

Indian Philosophy

3.6.25 **Dasgupta, Surendra Nath.** A history of Indian philosophy. Cambridge, The University Press, 1922–55. 5v.

A basic work.

3.6.26 **Radhakrishnan, Sir Sarvepalli.** Indian philosophy. 2d ed. New York, Macmillan, 1951. 2v.

Islamic Philosophy

3.6.27 **Corbin, Henry.** Histoire de la philosophie islamique. Paris, Gallimard, 1964– .

In progress.
V. 1, Des origines jusqu'à la mort d'Averroës.

3.6.28 * **De Boer, T. J.** The history of philosophy in Islam. Trans. by E. Jones. 2d. ed. New York, Dover, 1933. 229 pp.

Reissue, 1961.
Translated from *Geschichte der Philosophie im Islam*, Stuttgart, Frommann, 1901.

Italian Philosophy

3.6.29 **Sciacca, M. F.,** *ed.* Storia della filosofia italiana. Milano, Bocca, 1941– .

In progress.
Multivolume, each with bibliographies.
Alliney, G. *I pensatori della seconda metà del s. XIX*, 1942. Bibliography: pp. 341–423.
Sciacca, M. F. *Il secolo XX.* 2. ed., 1947. 2v.
At end of 2d vol., bibliography of Italian philosophy since 1894, pp. 705–900.

Jewish Philosophy

3.6.30 **Cahn, Zvi.** The philosophy of Judaism; the development of Jewish thought throughout the ages, the Bible, the Talmud, the Jewish philosophers, and the Cabala, until the present time. New York. Macmillan, 1962. 524 pp.

Bibliography: pp. 507–511.

3.6.31 * **Guttmann, Julius.** Philosophies of Judaism; the history of Jewish philosophy from Biblical times to Franz Rosenzweig. Trans. by D. Silverman. New York, Holt, Rinehart and Winston, 1964. 464 pp.

Bibliography: pp. 399–411.

Russian Philosophy

3.6.32 **Masaryk, Thomas Garrigue.** The spirit of Russia; studies in history, literature and philosophy. Trans. from the German original by Eden and Cedar Paul with additional chapter and bibliographies by Jan Slavik, the former translated and the latter condensed and translated by W. R. and Z. Lee. New York, Macmillan, 1919. 2v.

3d impression, 1961.
Bibliography: pp. 627–653.

3.6.33 **Zenkovsky, V. V.** A history of Russian philosphy. Trans. by George L. Kline. London, Routledge and Kegan Paul, 1953. 2v.

A basic work.

Spanish Philosophy

3.6.34 **Carreras y Artau, Tomás.** Historia de la filosofía española; filosofía cristiana de los siglos XIII al XV. Madrid, Real academia de ciencias exactas, físicas y naturales, 1939–43. 2v.

Includes bibliographies.

3.7 HISTORIES OF PHILOSOPHY: BY BRANCH

Aesthetics

3.7.1 * **Beardsley, Monroe C.** Aesthetics from ancient Greece to the present. New York, Macmillan, 1966. 414 pp.

3.7.2 **Bosanquet, B.,** *ed.* A history of aesthetics. 2d ed. London, Allen and Unwin, 1904.

Reprinted: New York, Meridian, 1957.
Includes bibliography.

3.7.3 **Gilbert, Katharine E.,** and **Helmut Kuhn.** A history of esthetics. Rev. ed. Bloomington, Ind., Indiana University Press, 1953. 613 pp.

Includes bibliographies.

Ethics

3.7.4 **Bourke, Vernon J.** History of ethics; a comprehensive survey of the history of ethics from the early Greeks to the present time. Garden City, N. Y., Doubleday, 1968. 432 pp.

Bibliography: pp. 353–417.

3.7.5 **Brinton, C. C.** A history of Western morals. New York, Harcourt Brace, 1959. 502 pp.

3.7.6 **Dittrich, Ottmar.** Geschichte der Ethik. Die Systeme der Moral vom Altertum bis zum Gegenwart. Leipzig, Meiner, 1926–32. 4v.

Good and quite complete up to its time. Bibliographies.

3.7.7 ★ Mac Intyre, Alasdair. A short history of ethics. New York, Macmillan, 1966. 280 pp.

Treats about 30 major figures from the Sophists to Sartre.

3.7.8 ★ Sidgwick, Henry. Outlines of the history of ethics. With an additional chapter by A. G. Widgery. 6th ed. London, Macmillan, 1931. 342 pp.

Reprinted: Boston, Beacon, 1964.
1st ed. 1886.

Logic

3.7.9 Bochenski, I. M. A history of formal logic. Trans. and ed. by Ivo Thomas. Notre Dame, Notre Dame University Press, 1961. 567 pp.

A translation of *Formale Logik*, Freiburg and Munich, 1956.

Good bibliographies.

3.7.10 Kneale, William, and **Martha Kneale.** The development of logic. Oxford, Oxford University Press, 1962. 761 pp.

3.7.11 Rescher, Nicholas. The development of Arabic logic. Pittsburgh, University of Pittsburgh Press, 1964. 262 pp.

Complete bibliography.

Metaphysics

3.7.12 ★ Lovejoy, A. O. The great chain of being; a study in the history of an idea. Cambridge, Mass., Harvard University Press, 1936. 382 pp.

Reprinted: Harper, 1960.

See also: 3.7.23.

Political and Legal Philosophy

3.7.13 ★ Cairns, H. Legal philosophy from Plato to Hegel. Baltimore, Johns Hopkins Press, 1949. 583 pp.

3.7.14 Cook, T. I. A history of political philosophy from Plato to Burke. New York, Prentice-Hall, 1936. 725 pp.

Includes bibliographies.

3.7.15 ★ Friedrich, Carl Joachim. The philosophy of law in historical perspective. 2d ed. Chicago, University of Chicago Press, 1963. 296 pp.

1st ed. 1958.
Bibliography: pp. 277–284.
An English version of *Die Philosophie des Rechts in historischer Perspektive*, Berlin, Springer, 1955, 153 pp.

3.7.16 Plamenatz, J. P. Man and society; political and social theory. New York, McGraw-Hill, 1963. 2v.

V. 1, Political and Social Theory: Machiavelli through Rousseau;
v. 2, Political and Social Theory: Bentham through Marx.

3.7.17 ★ Popper, K. R. The open society and its enemies. 5th ed. rev. London, Routledge and Kegan Paul, 1966. 2v.

1st ed. 1945.
Bibliography in "Notes" at the end of each volume.

3.7.18 Sabine, G. H. A history of political theory. 3d ed. rev. and enl. New York, Holt, Rinehart and Winston, 1961. 948 pp.

Bibliographies at the end of each chapter.

3.7.19 Vecchio, G. del. Philosophy of law. Trans. by Thomas Owen Martin from the 8th ed., 1952. Washington, Catholic University of America Press, 1953. 474 pp.

"History of Philosophy of Law," pp. 23–243, contains abundant bibliographical references. This section, which is part of del Vecchio's *Lezioni di filosofia del diritto*, was published separately as *Storia della filosofia del diritto*, 2. ed., Milano, Guiffre, 1958, 200 pp.

Theory of Knowledge

3.7.20 Aster, Ernst von. Geschichte der neueren Erkenntnistheorie (von Descartes bis

Hegel). Berlin und Leipzig, W. de Gruyter, 1921. 638 pp.

3.7.21 **Bayer, R.** Epistémologie et logique depuis Kant jusqu'à nos jours. Paris, Presses Universitaires de France, 1954. 369 pp.

  Bibliographical footnotes.

3.7.22 **Cassirer, E.** Das Erkenntnisproblem in der Philosophie u. Wissenschaft der neueren Zeit. 3. Aufl. Berlin, Bruno Cassirer, 1922–57. 4v.

1st ed. 1907–21. 3v.
  V. 4 appeared first in English translation: ★ *The Problem of Knowledge*; *Philosophy, Science and History Since Hegel*, New Haven, Yale University Press, 1950, 334 pp.

3.7.23 **Maréchal, Joseph.** Le point de départ de la métaphysique; leçons sur le développement historique et théorique du problème de la connaissance. Paris, Desclée De Brouwer, 1926–49. 5v.

  Editions of individual volumes vary.

4. SOURCES: BIBLIOGRAPHIES, STANDARD EDITIONS, AND COLLECTED WORKS OF INDIVIDUAL PHILOSOPHERS

HISTORIES OF PHILOSOPHY can never replace a study of the original works of philosophers themselves. Definitive texts of the works of many major philosophers are available. Often these are collected into a series containing the complete works of the author in question. For some major philosophers there are several different collections of their complete works and care should be taken to use the most accurate, which is usually the most recent. Critical editions note variant readings, anomalies in the text, and so on. "Complete works" should be distinguished from "collected works" (which make no claim to completeness), and both of these should be distinguished from "selected works." Any of these, as well as individual works, may be "critical editions." A "standard" text or edition is the one generally cited in secondary sources.

Because of difficulties of translation, no translation is wholly adequate for serious research. However, many translations are more or less useful approximations of the original. Whenever a translation is used, it should, if possible, be used in conjunction with the original text. Where several translations of a work are available, one should ascertain the most accurate translation of those available. This can be done by checking them against the original (if one knows the language of the original) or by relying on the appraisal of qualified scholars. Factors making for a good translation include: intelligibility and fluency of the translation; consistency in the translation of key words in the original; accuracy in the translation of these key words.

The following lists are intended as initial guides to bibliographies of individual philosophers and to the best collections of the complete works, critical editions, or standard editions of major philosophers. Individual works of philosophers are not listed, unless there are several editions and one of them is the standard edition. Not unreasonably, the works of most contemporary philosophers have not yet been collected. A list of the individual works of most important contemporary philosophers can be found by consulting the *Encyclopedia of Philosophy* (2.2.1), other recent encyclopedias or recent dictionaries, histories of contemporary philosophy, or the appropriate trade bibliographies (6.2). Translations of individual works of ancient, medieval, and modern philosophers can usually be found by consulting the various histories of philosophy listed in the appropriate sections of chapter 3.

Bibliographies of individual authors are sometimes difficult to find, especially if they have not been separately published. Arnim (5.2.1), Besterman (5.2.2), and the

Bibliographic Index (5.2.3) can be consulted, as well as the other sources listed in chapter 5. The present chapter includes only the most recent and inclusive bibliography on any given philosopher, if this has superseded earlier and briefer ones. In some instances no bibliography of sufficient comprehensiveness or usefulness is available, and so none has been listed.

In the case of some philosophers indexes to their works have been compiled. When these form part of a specific edition, they have been so noted following the edition. If separately published, they are separately listed, as are dictionaries and lexicons of individual philosophers.

The number of philosophers listed in the following sections is obviously limited. I have tried to include the generally recognized major figures through the modern period, and at least some of the important philosophers of the twentieth century. A number of important authors have not been listed simply because no significant bibliography of their works is available and their works have yet to appear in a collected edition. These are clearly bibliographical and not philosophical criteria for exclusion, and the omission of any particular name does not necessarily indicate a value judgment about his philosophical contribution or about his importance in the history of philosophy.

Items in the following sections are listed alphabetically within each of the periods of the history of philosophy.

4.1 ANCIENT PHILOSOPHY

General Bibliographies

4.1.1 **Bibliography on the survival of the classics.** Ed. by the Warburg Institute. London, Warburg Institute, 1934–38. 2v.

4.1.2 **Engelmann, W. V.** Bibliotheca scriptorum classicorum . . . 1700–1878. 8. Aufl. Leipzig, Engelmann, 1880–82. 2v.

Bibliography of editions, translations, and commentaries.
Continued by 4.1.3.

4.1.3 **Klussmann, Rudolf.** Bibliotheca scriptorum classicorum et graecorum et latinorum. Die Literatur von 1878–1896. Leipzig, Reisland, 1909–13. 2v. in 4.

Continued by 4.1.4.

4.1.4 **Lambrino, Scarlat.** Bibliographie de l'antiquité classique de 1896 à 1914. Paris, Soc. d'Edit. "Les Belles Lettres," 1951– .

In progress.
V. 1, "Auteurs et textes"; v. 2, "Matières et disciplines," has not appeared.
Continued by 4.1.5.

4.1.5 **Marouzeau, J.** Dix années de bibliographie classique, bibliographie critique et analytique de l'antiquité gréco-latine pour la période 1914-1924. Paris, Soc. d'Edit. "Les Belles Lettres," 1927–28. 2v.

V. 1, "Auteurs et textes"; v. 2, "Matières et disciplines."

4.1.6 **Mondolfo, Rodolfo.** Guia bibliográfica de la filosofía antigua. Buenos Aires, Editorial Losada, 1959. 102 pp.

See also: 1.4.1–1.4.3, 1.5.1, 1.5.2, and 5.1.14 (No. 5), as well as the histories of ancient philosophy listed in 3.1 and 3.2.

Presocratics

4.1.7 Diels, Hermann. Die Fragmente der Vorsokratiker. 12. Aufl. hrsg. von Walther Kranz. Zürich, Weidmann, 1966–67. 3v.

Greek texts with German translations.
This is the standard collection and best edition of the fragments of the Presocratics. V. 3 is a *Wort-index*, by W. Kranz.

Translations and Commentaries

4.1.8 * Burnet, John. Early Greek philosophy. 4th ed. London, Macmillan, 1930. 375 pp.

Reprinted: New York, Meridian, 1957. 1st ed. 1892.
Translations and commentaries. A basic and standard reference work.

4.1.9 Freeman, Kathleen. Ancilla to the Pre-Socratic philosophers; a complete translation of the fragments in Diels' *Fragmente der Vorsokratiker* (4.1.7). Cambridge, Mass., Harvard University Press, 1948. 162 pp.

4.1.10 Freeman, Kathleen. The Pre-Socratic philosophers; a companion to Diels, *Fragmente der Vorsokratiker*. Cambridge, Mass., Harvard University Press, 1947. 486 pp.

Gives first a summary of what is known of the life, then of the teaching of each thinker, with references for every statement made.

4.1.11 * Kirk, G. S., and **J. E. Raven.** The Presocratic philosophers; a critical history with a selection of texts. Cambridge, The University Press, 1962. 486 pp.

Selected quotations in Greek and English with scholarly interpretations and discussions. It contains the most important texts.
Bibliography: pp. 446–449.

See also: 3.2.8.

Aristotle
(384–322 B.C.)

Bibliography

4.1.12 Mioni, Elpidio. Aristotelis codices graeci qui in bibliothecis venetis adservantur.

Miscellanea erudita, vol. VI. Patavii, In Aedibus Antenoreis, 1958. 162 pp.

4.1.13 Moraux, Paul. Les listes anciennes des ouvrages d'Aristote. Louvain, Editions universitaires de Louvain, 1951. 391 pp.

4.1.14 Schwab, Moïse. Bibliographie d'Aristote. Paris, Welter, 1896. 380 pp.

Reprinted: W. C. Brown.

See also: 5.3.3 (pp. 214–264); 5.1.14 (No. 5).

Dictionary and Index

4.1.15 Kiernan, Thomas P. Aristotle dictionary. New York, Philosophical Library, 1962. 524 pp.

Lists each subject word in English, with references to the Greek text.
Based on 4.1.17.

4.1.16 Organ, Troy W. An index to Aristotle in English translation. Princeton, Princeton University Press, 1949. 181 pp.

Based on 4.1.18.

See also: 4.1.17.

Works

4.1.17 Aristotelis opera. I. Bekker [ed.]. Berlin, Prussian Academy, 1831–70.

This is the edition usually cited in scholarly works. V. 5 includes the *Index Aristotelicus*, ed. by Hermanus Bonitz (reprinted separately, Berlin, de Gruyter, 1961, 878 pp.), which is a complete concordance of the Greek texts.
A new edition of vols. I, II, IV, and V, ed. by Olof Gigon, was printed: Berlin, de Gruyter, 1960–61.

See also: 4.1.15.

4.1.18 The works of Aristotle; translated into English. Ed. by J. A. Smith and W. D. Ross. Oxford, The University Press, 1908–52. 12v.

See also: 4.1.17 and 4.1.19.

4.1.19 **The Basic works of Aristotle.** Ed. by Richard McKeon. New York, Random House, 1941. 1487 pp.

Includes the Oxford translation (4.1.18) of the major works in their entirety, and selections from minor works.
Bibliography: pp. xxxv–xxxix.

4.1.20 **Aristotle.** Works. Loeb classical library. Cambridge, Mass., Harvard University Press, 1933– .

In progress.
Greek and English on facing pages.

Epictetus
(c. 50–c. 130)

Bibliography

4.1.21 **Oldfather, W. A.** Contributions toward a bibliography of Epictetus. Urbana, University of Illinois Press, 1927. 201 pp.

See also: *A Supplement*, ed. by Marian Harman, with a preliminary list of Epictetus manuscripts by W. H. Friedrich and C. U. Faye, Urbana, University of Illinois Press, 1952, 177 pp.

Works

4.1.22 **Epictetus.** Trans. by W. A. Oldfather. Loeb classical library. Cambridge, Mass., Harvard University Press. 2v.

1st published, 1926–28.
Text with English translations. For the works of Epictetus see also the edition by H. Schenkl, Leipzig, Teubner, 1916, 740 pp.

Epicurus
(341 B.C.–270 B.C.)

Works

4.1.23 **Epicurea.** Edidit H. Usener. Leipzig, Teubner, 1887. 445 pp.

Text and commentary. Standard edition.

4.1.24 **Epicurus,** the extant remains with short critical apparatus, translation and notes. Ed. by C. Bailey. Oxford, 1926. 432 pp.

Greek texts with English translations. The Bailey translation is also available in W. J. Oates, *The Stoic and Epicurean Philosophers*, New York, Random House, 1957.

Lucretius
(c. 99–55 B.C.)

Bibliography and Index

4.1.25 **Gordon, Cosmo Alexander.** A bibliography of Lucretius. London, Hart-Davis, 1962. 318 pp.

4.1.26 **Paulson, J.** Index Lucretianus. Goto-burgi, W. Zachrisson, 1911. 177 pp.

Works

4.1.27 **De rerum natura.** Ed. and trans. by C. Bailey. Oxford, Clarendon Press, 1947. 3v.

A critical edition with full English commentary and translation.

Marcus Aurelius Antoninus
(121–180)

Works

4.1.28 **Farquharson, A. S. L.,** *ed.* The meditations of the Emperor Marcus Antoninus. Oxford, Clarendon Press, 1944. 2v.

A critical edition with English translation and commentary.

Plato
(c. 428–347 B.C.)

Bibliography

4.1.29 **Cherniss, H. F.** "Plato Studies, 1950–57," Lustrum, IV (1959), 5–308; V (1960), 323–648.

4.1.30 **Plato manuscripts:** a catalogue of microfilms in the Plato microfilm project, Yale University Library. Edited by Robert S. Brumbaugh and Rulon Wells, with the assistance of Donna Scott and Harry V. Botsis. New Haven, Yale University Library, 1962. 2v.

Part I: Mss. in Belgium, Denmark, England, Germany, and Italy.

Part II: Mss. in Austria, Czechoslovakia, France, Holland, and Spain; post-1600 mss. in Belgium, Denmark, England, Germany, and Italy; addenda to Part I.

4.1.31 The Plato manuscripts; a new index, prepared by the Plato microfilm project of the Yale University Library under the direction of Robert S. Brumbaugh and Rulon Wells. New Haven, Yale University Press, 1968. 163 pp.

Based on the Yale microfilm collection (4.1.30), it lists all the pre-1500 manuscript material held by libraries throughout the world. It includes an Index by Library, an Index by Dialogue, Collations, and a List of Papyri.

4.1.32 Rosenmeyer, T. G. "Platonic Scholarship, 1945–1955," Classical Weekly, L (1957), 172–182, 197–201, 209–211.

4.1.33 Sciacca, M. F. Platone. (Guide bibliografiche.) Milano, Vita e Pensiero, 1945. 58 pp.

See also: 5.1.14 (No. 12); 5.3.3 (pp. 146–212).

Dictionaries

4.1.34 Ast, Fred (Astius, D. Fredericus). Lexikon Platonicum sive vocum Platonicarum index. Bonn, Habelt, 1956. 3v. in 2. Leipzig, Weidmann, 1835–38. 3v.

Reprinted: Bonn, Habelt, 1956, 3v. in 2.

4.1.35 ★ Stockhammer, Morris. Plato dictionary. New York, Philosophical Library, 1963. 287 pp.

Based on the Jowett translation (4.1.36).

Works

4.1.36 Platonis opera. Ed. by J. Burnet. Oxford, 1899–1906. 5v.

Complete Greek text of Plato's works. The standard, critical edition.

Modern editions refer to the pagination of Plato's works edited by J. Serranus and H. Stephanus, 3v., with Latin translation, Paris, 1578.

4.1.37 Platon. Oeuvres complètes. Collection des Universités de France publiée sous le patronage de l'Association Guillaume Budé. Paris, Société d'édition "Les belles lettres," 1920–64. 14v. in 27.

Also published in 12v. in 19, 1951–66.

Greek text and French translation. Editors for individual volumes vary.

The critical apparatus is fuller than that found in 4.1.36.

4.1.38 Plato. The collected dialogues of Plato, including the letters. Ed. by Edith Hamilton and Huntington Cairns, with an introduction and prefatory notes. New York, Pantheon Books, 1961. 1743 pp.

Translations are by L. Cooper, B. Jowett, A. E. Taylor, and others.

4.1.39 The dialogues of Plato. Trans. by Benjamin Jowett. 4th ed., revised by D. J. Allan and H. E. Dale. Oxford, The University Press, 1952.

1st ed. 1871.

Also published by New York, Random House.

A complete and somewhat poetic translation of the dialogues.

4.1.40 Plato. [Selected works.] Trans. by F. M. Cornford, with running commentaries.

Accurate translations of individual works, including the ★ Timaeus, Parmenides, ★ Republic, ★ Theaetetus, and the ★ Sophist, in separate volumes.

Publishers vary.

4.1.41 Plato. Works. Loeb classical library. Cambridge, Mass., Harvard University Press. 12v.

First published 1921–53.

Greek and English on facing pages.

Plotinus
(205–70)

Bibliography

4.1.42 Marien, B. Bibliografia critica degli studi Plotiniani con rassegna delle loro recensioni, rev. e curata da V. Cilento. Bari, Laterza, 1949. 668 pp.

Pt. 2 of vol. III of the Italian translation of and commentary on the *Enneads* by V. Cilento. Reprinted separately: Wm. C. Brown, 1949.

Works

4.1.43 **Plotini opera.** Ediderunt P. Henry et Hans R. Schwyzer. Oxonii, e Typ. Clarendoniano, 1964– .

In progress.
A critical edition which, when completed, will supersede all other editions.

4.1.44 **Plotinus.** With an English translation by A. H. Armstrong. Loeb classical library. Cambridge, Mass., Harvard University Press, 1966– .

In progress.
6v. projected.
Greek and English on facing pages. The Greek text is essentially that of P. Henry and H. R. Schwyzer (4.1.43).

4.1.45 **Enneads.** Translated by Stephen MacKenna. 3d ed., rev. by B. S. Page. New York, Pantheon Books, 1962. 636 pp.

1st ed. 1927–30. 5v.
English translation without Greek texts.

4.1.46 **Enneades.** . . . texte établi et trad. par Emile Bréhier. Paris, Soc. d'édit. "Les Belles Lettres," 1924–38. 6v.

Good for its notes, but not for its Greek text. Pp. 200–297 of vol. VI contain an index of Greek words and an analytic index of subject matter.

Sextus Empiricus

Works

4.1.47 **Sexti Empirici opera.** Recensuit H. Mutschmann et J. Mau. Leipzig, Teubner, 1958–62. 4v.

4.1.48 **Sextus Empiricus.** Trans. by R. G. Bury. Loeb classical library. Cambridge, Mass., Harvard University Press. 4v.

First published 1933–49.
Greek text with English translation.

4.2 MEDIEVAL AND RENAISSANCE PHILOSOPHY

General Bibliographies

Medieval

4.2.1 **Bibliographia patristica;** internationale patristiche Bibliographie. Berlin, Walter de Gruyter, 1959– . Annual.

4.2.2 **Chevalier, C. U. J.** Répertoire des sources historiques du Moyen Age. Nouv. éd. Paris, Picard, 1894–1907. 2v. in 4.

V. 1, Bio-bibliographie; v. 2, Topobibliographie.
An important general reference work on the Middle Ages.

4.2.3 **Farrar, C. P.,** and **A. P. Evans.** Bibliography of English translations from medieval sources. New York, Columbia University Press, 1946. 534 pp.

An annotated list of translations up to 1943 of works produced during the period from Constantine the Great to 1500.

See also: 1.4.5, 1.4.6, 5.1.14 (Nos. 17 and 18), and 7.2.82, as well as the histories of philosophy listed in 3.1 and 3.3.

Renaissance

4.2.4 **Kristeller, Paul Oskar.** Catalogus translationum et commentariorum; medieval and Renaissance Latin translations and commentaries. Annotated lists and guides. Washington, D. C., Catholic University of America Press, 1960– .

Lists Latin translations and commentaries of Greek and Latin authors up to 1600.

4.2.5 **Kristeller, Paul Oskar.** Iter Italicum. A finding list of uncatalogued or incompletely catalogued humanistic manuscripts of the Renaissance in Italian and other libraries. London, Warburg Institute, 1965– .

Four or 5v. projected.

Lists philosophical and literary manuscripts of scholars active between 1300 and 1600.

4.2.6 Kristeller, Paul Oskar. Latin manuscript books before 1600; a list of printed catalogues and unpublished inventories of extant collections. Rev. ed. New York, Fordham University Press, 1960. 234 pp.

4.2.7 Riedl, J. O. [et al.]. A catalogue of Renaissance philosophers (1350–1650). Milwaukee, Marquette University Press, 1940. 179 pp.

General Collections

The writings of medieval philosophers have been collected into basic editions. References to some of these collections will be made from the list of individual philosophers in this section.

4.2.8 Beiträge zur Geschichte der Philosophie und Theologie des Mittelalters, Texte und Untersuchungen. Münster, Aschendorff, 1891– .

In progress.

An important and extensive collection on the philosophy of the Middle Ages. 40v. to date.

4.2.9 Corpus scriptorum ecclesiasticorum latinorum. Vienna, Hoelder-Pichler-Tempsky; Leipzig, Akademische Verlagsgesellschaft, 1866– .

In progress.

Contains critical editions of selected works of the Latin Fathers. 77v. to 1969.

Johnson Reprint Corp. has reprinted a large part of the series.

4.2.10 Gilson, Etienne, *ed.* Etudes de philosophie médiévale. Paris, 1922–47. 35v.

Monographs on patristic and medieval philosophers, with some critical texts.

4.2.11 Migne, J.-P., *ed.* Patrologiae cursus completus. Series ecclesiae graecae. Paris, J.-P. Migne, 1857–1866. 162v.

Works of Greek ecclesiastical writers from 1st to 15th centuries, with Latin translations.

4.2.12 Migne, J.-P., *ed.* Patrologiae cursus completus. Series ecclesiae latinae. Paris, J.-P. Migne, 1844–64. 221v. [of which the last four are indices].

Contains uncritical editions of works of Latin ecclesiastical writers from 2d through 12th centuries. It is the basic source for this period of medieval philosophy.

Supplementum. A. Hamman, ed. Paris, Garnier, 1958.

Translated Collections

4.2.13 Ancient Christian writers; the works of the Fathers in translation. Westminster, Md., Newman Press, 1946– .

36v. had appeared by 1968.

4.2.14 The Fathers of the church. Ed. dir., Roy J. Defarrari. Washington, D. C., Catholic University of America Press. 1947– .

English translations.

100v. projected of which 60 had appeared by 1969.

The collection was founded by Ludwig Schopp.

Publisher varies.

4.2.15 Select library of Nicene and post-Nicene Fathers. New York, The Christian Literature Co., 1886–1900. 28v.

2 series of 14v. each. English translations with notes.

See also: 7.4.12.

Abelard, Peter
(1079–1142)

Works

4.2.16 Opera omnia. Accurante J.-P. Migne. Paris, 1855.

Vol. CLXXVIII of 4.2.12.

The most complete collection available, but should be used with later, critical editions when possible.

4.2.17 Ouvrages inédits d'Abélard. Publiés par V. Cousin. Paris, Imprimerie royale, 1836. 677 pp.

4.2.18 **Peter Abelards philosophische schriften.** Hrsg. von Bernhard Geyer. Münster, Aschendorff, 1919–33. 4v.

Vol. XXXI, 1–4 of 4.2.8.
Critical edition of Abelard's logical works.

4.2.19 **Petri Abaelardi opera.** [Accurante] V. Cousin, C. Jourdain et E. Despois. Parisiis, A. Durand, 1949–59. 2v.

Albert the Great
(1200–1280)

Bibliography

4.2.20 **Catania, Francis J.** "A bibliography of St. Albert the Great," The modern schoolman, XXXVII (1959), 11–28.

4.2.21 **Schooyans, Michel.** "Bibliographie philosophique de saint Albert le grand (1931–1960)," Revista da Universidade Cathólica de São Paulo, XXI (1961), 36–88.

4.2.22 **Weiss, Melchior.** Primordia novae bibliographiae b. Alberti Magni. . . . Editio secunda. Parisiis, Ludovicum Vivès, 1905. 120 pp.

Works

4.2.23 **Alberti Magni . . . Opera omnia.** Münster, Aschendorf, 1951– .

In progress.
40v. projected.
New critical edition of the complete works by the Albertus-Magnus-Institute of Cologne.
Earlier edition of the works edited by P. Jammy, 21 folio volumes, 1651. Reprinted: A. Borgnet. Paris, Vives, 1890–99. 38v.

St. Anselm of Canterbury
(1033–1109)

Works

4.2.24 **Sancti Anselmi . . . opera omnia.** Ad fidem codicum recensuit F. S. Schmitt. Sekau-Rome-Edinburgh, 1938–61. 6v.

Reprinted: Stuttgart, Fromman-Holzboog, 1968–69. 7v. in 2.

The standard, critical edition of Anselm's works. Supersedes the complete works ed. by G. Gerberon (1675) and reproduced in vols. CLVIII–CLIX of 4.2.12.

4.2.25 ★ **Saint Anselm's basic writings.** Trans. by Sidney Deane. 2d ed. La Salle, Ill., Open Court Publishing Company, 1962. 288 pp.

1st ed. 1903.
Contains English translations of the *Proslogium, Monologium, Liber pro Insipiente* of Gaulino, and *Cur deus homo.*

Augustine, St.
(354–430)

Bibliography

4.2.26 **Andresen, Carl.** Bibliographia Augustiniana. Darmstadt, Wisseschaftliche Buchgesellschaft, 1962. 127 pp.

Includes works by and about Augustine. The best of the bibliographies.
For later works see the bibliographical supplements of the *Revue des études augustiniennes* (7.3.14).

4.2.27 **Bavel, Tarsicius van.** Répertoire bibliographique de Saint Augustin 1950–1960. Instrumenta Patristica, vol. III. The Hague, Nijhoff, 1963. 992 pp.

4.2.28 **Nebreda, E.** Bibliographia Augustina seu Operum collectio quae divi Augustine vitam et doctrinam quadantenus exponunt. Romae, Typ. Pol. "Cuore di Maria," 1928. 272 pp.

Reprinted: W. C. Brown Co.
A critical bibliography of St. Augustine's works, collected editions, and books about him; indexes.

See also: 5.1.14 (No. 10).

Concordance

4.2.29 **Lenfant, D.** Concordantiae augustinianae. Parisiis, 1656–65. 2v.

Works

4.2.30 Sancti Aurelii Augustini . . . opera omnia. Paris, 1679–1700. 11v.

Benedictine edition of the Maurists.
Reprinted in 4.2.12, vols. XXXII–XLVII. Paris, 1845–49.
This is the basis of a critical edition being published with a French translation in *Bibliothéque augustinienne* (Paris, Desclée de Brouwer).

4.2.31 Writings of Saint Augustine. 14v. in 4.2.14.

Includes bibliographies.

4.2.32 Basic writings of Saint Augustine. Ed. by W. J. Oates. New York, Random House, 1948. 2v.

A convenient collection of texts primarily from 4.2.15.

See also: 4.2.15.

Averroes
(c. 1126–c. 1198)

Works

4.2.33 Aristotelis opera cum Averrois commentariis. Venice, 1562–74. 12v.

Reprinted: Frankfurt am Main, 1962.
A Latin translation of Aristotle with commentaries by Averroes.
A new edition is in preparation by the Mediaeval Academy of America.

4.2.34 Müller, M. J. Philosophie und Theologie von Averroes. München, Franz, 1859–75. 2v.

Arabic text and German translation.

Avicenna
(980–1037)

Bibliography

4.2.35 Anawati, G. C. Essai de bibliographie avicennienne. Cairo, Dar-al-Maaref, 1950. 20 pp. [French text], 31–435 pp. [Arabic text].

Section 4 lists works about Avicenna in languages other than Arabic.

4.2.36 Ergin, Osman. Ibni Sina bibliográfyasi. Bibliographie d'Avicenne. Istanbul, O. Yalçin Matbassi, 1956. 168 pp.

4.2.37 Naficy, Said. Bibliografie des principaux travaux européens sur Avicenne. Téhéran, Université de Téhéran, 1953. 30 pp.

295 entries.

Lexicon

4.2.38 Goichon, A. M. Lexique de la langue philosophique d'Ibn Sina (Avicenne). Paris, Desclée de Brouwer, 1938. 496 pp.

Works

4.2.39 Opera philosophica. Venetiis, 1508. 320 pp.

Reprinted: New York, Johnson Reprint Co 1961.
There is no collected edition in the original.

Bacon, Francis
(1561–1626)

Bibliography

4.2.40 Gibson, Reginald W. Francis Bacon: a bibliography of his works and of Baconiana to the year 1750. Oxford, Scrivener Press, 1950. 369 pp.

4.2.41 ★ Patrick, J. Max. Francis Bacon. British Council; British book news; bibliographical series of supplements (no. 131). 1961. 43 pp.

4.2.42 Woodward, Parker. Francis Bacon's works (acknowledged, vizared, or suspected). London, Sweeting & Co., 1912. 105 pp.

Works

4.2.43 The works of Francis Bacon. Collected and ed. by James Spedding, R. L. Ellis and D. D. Heath. London, Longmans, 1857–74. 14v.

Reprinted: Stuttgart, Frommann, 1962.

The last 7v. are *The Letters and Life of Francis Bacon* including all his occasional works.

This is the standard edition of his works.

Bacon, Roger
(c. 1220–1292)

Bibliography

4.2.44 **Alessio, F.** "Un seculo di studi su Ruggero Bacone (1848–1957)," Revista critica di storia della filosofia, XIV (1959), 81–108.

Works

4.2.45 **The "Opus Majus" of Roger Bacon.** Ed. with an introduction and analytical table, by J. H. Bridges. Oxford, Clarendon Press, 1897–1900. 3v.

Reprinted: Johnson Reprint Co., 1964.

4.2.46 **Opera hactenus inedita Fratris Rogeri Baconis.** Edidit Robert Steele. Oxford, Clarendon Press, 1905–40. 16v.

4.2.47 **The Opus Majus of Roger Bacon.** Trans. by R. B. Burke. Philadelphia, University of Pennsylvania Press, 1928. 2v.

Reprinted: New York, 1962.
English translation of 4.2.45.

Bernard of Clairvaux, St.
(1090–1153)

Works

4.2.48 **S. Bernardi . . . Opera omnia.** Paris, 1844–64.

Vol. CLXXXII–CLXXXV of 4.2.12.
A nine-volume critical edition by Dom J. Leclerq is in preparation.

Boethius, Anicius Manlius Severinus
(c. 480–524)

Concordance

4.2.49 **Cooper, Lane.** A concordance of Boethius; the five theological tractates and the Consolation of philosophy. Cambridge, Mass.,

The Mediaeval Academy of America, 1928. 467 pp.

Works

4.2.50 **Opera omnia.** Paris, 1847.
Vol. LXIII–LXIV of 4.2.12.

4.2.51 **Boethius.** De consolatione philosophiae. Edidit L. Bieler. Turnholti, Brepols, 1957. 124 pp.

Vol. XCIV of *Corpus Christianorum Series Latina*.
Another edition, edited by G. Weinberger, Vienna, Tempsky, 1934, 229 pp., is vol. LXVII of 4.2.9.

4.2.52 **Boethius.** The theological tractates, with an English translation by H. F. Stewart . . . and E. K. Rand . . . The consolation of philosophy, with the English translation of "I. T." (1609) rev. by H. F. Stewart. Loeb classical library. Cambridge, Mass., Harvard University Press, 1962. 420 pp.

First published 1918.
Latin and English on facing pages.

4.2.53 **Boethius.** In Isagogen Porphyrii commenta. Copiis a G. Scheps comparatis suisque usus recensuit S. Brandt. Lipsiae, G. Freytag, 1906. 423 pp.

Vol. XLVIII of 4.2.9.

Bonaventure, St.
(c. 1217–1274)

Bibliography and Lexicon

4.2.54 **Bibliographia Franciscana.** Rome, 1962– .

Published as part of *Collectanea Franciscana*, 1931– ; published separately since 1942; contains current bibliographies.

See also pp. 929–944 of E. Gilson, *Der heilige Bonaventura*, Leipzig, J. Hegner, 1929; and vol. I of L. Amoros (and others) *Obras de S. Buenaventura*, Madrid, Biblioteca de Autores Cristianos, 1945–59, 6v.

4.2.55 **Vicetia, Antonius Maria a, O. F. M., et Joannes a Rubino, O. F. M.** Lexikon

Bonaventurianum philosophico-theologicum in quo termini theologici distinctiones et effata praecipua scholasticorum a Seraphico Doctore declarantur. Venice, 1880. 338 pp.

Works

4.2.56 **S. Bonaventurae . . . Opera omnia.** [Ed. by] I. Jeiler, O. F. M., et al. Quaracchi, Ex Typographia Collegii S. Bonaventurae, 1882–1902. 10v.

A critical edition.

4.2.57 **The works of St. Bonaventure.** Trans. by José de Vinck. Paterson, N. J., St. Anthony Guild Press, 1960– .

In progress.
An English translation.

Bruno, Giordano
(1548–1600)

Bibliography

4.2.58 **Salvestrini, Virgilio, e Luigi Firpo.** Bibliografia di Giordano Bruno 1582–1950. Firenze, Sansoni, 1958. 407 pp.

Works

4.2.59 **Jordani Bruni Nolani opera latine conscripta.** Recensebat Francisco Fiorentino, Vittorio Imbriani, C. M. Tallarigo, Felice Tocco et Girolamo Vitelli. Neapoli, D. Morano, 1879–91. 3v.

Reissue: 1962.

4.2.60 **Le Opere italiane di Giordano Bruno,** con noti di Giovanni Gentile. Bari, 1907–08. 2v.

Cajetan, Cardinal (Thomas de Vio)
(1468–1534)

Bibliography

4.2.61 **Congar, M.-J.** Bio-bibliographie de Cajétan. Saint-Maximin (Var), Edit. de la Revue thomiste, 1935. 47 pp.

Originally appeared in the *Revue thomiste*, XVII, 1934–35, 3–39.

Duns Scotus, John
(c. 1266–1308)

Bibliography and Lexicon

4.2.62 **Schäfer, Odulfus.** Bibliographia de vita, operibus et doctrina Iohannis Duns Scoti, doctoris subtilis ac Mariani, saec. XIX–XX. Romae, Orbis Catholicus-Herder, 1955. 223 pp.

For recent works see the continuing bibliography in *Bibliographia Francisciana.*

See also: 5.1.14 (No. 22).

4.2.63 **Fernandez Garcia, Marianus, O. F. M.** Lexicon scholasticum philosophico-theologicum in quo termini, definitiones, distinctiones et effata seu axiomaticae propositiones philosophiam ac theologiam spectantes a B. Joanne Duns Scoto exponuntur, declarantur. Ad Claras Aquas (Quarracchi), Collegium S. Bonaventurae, 1910. 1056 pp.

Works

4.2.64 **Opera omnia.** Studio et cura Commissionis Scotisticae ad fidem codicum edita, praeside Carlo Balić. Civitas Vaticana, Typis polyglottis Vaticanis, 1950– .

In progress.
Complete and critical edition. Includes bibliographies.
Will supersede the *Opera omnia,* ed. by L. Wadding, Lyons, 1639, 12v. (reprinted: Vives, 1891–95, 26v.), which contains some spurious works.

Erasmus, Desiderius
(1466–1536)

Bibliography

4.2.65 **Haeghen, Ferdinand van der.** Bibliotheca Erasmiana: répertoire des oeuvres d'Erasme. Nieuwkoop, B. de Graff, 1961. 3 pts. in IV.

Reprint of the Gand, 1893 ed.
See also other volumes published by Ghent University, 1897– .

4.2.66 **Margolin, Jean Claude.** Douze années de bibliographie érasmienne, 1950–1961. Paris, Vrin, 1963. 204 pp.

Works

4.2.67 **Opera omnia.** [Ed.] Beatus Rhenanus. Basilea, H. Frobenium et N. Episcopium, 1540–42. 9v.

4.2.68 **Opera omnia emendatiora.** [Ed.] Joannes Cleriucus. Leyden, P. Vander Aa, 1703–06. 11v.

Reprinted: Hildesheim, Olms, 1961.
A new edition is in progress, edited by Dr. C. Reedijk.

4.2.69 **A supplement to the Opera omnia.** Ed. with intr. and notes by Wallace K. Ferguson. The Hague, Nijhoff, 1933. 373 pp.

4.2.70 **Opus epistolarum.** [Ed. by] P. S. Allen, H. M. Allen, and H. W. Garrod. Oxford, Clarendon Press, 1906–58. 12v.

This contains the complete correspondence.
For an English translation of the letters up to 1517 see *The Epistles of Erasmus*, ed. and trans. by F. M. Nichols, New York, Longmans, Green, & Co., 1901–08, 3v. Reprinted: New York, 1962.

Erigena, John Scotus
(c. 810–c. 877)

Works

4.2.71 **Joannis Scoti Opera quae supersunt omnia.** Edidit H. J. Floss, 1853.

Vol. CXXII (1853) of 4.2.12.

Farabi, Al–
(c. 870–950)

Bibliography

4.2.72 **Rescher, Nicholas.** Al-Farabi; an annotated bibliography. Pittsburgh, University of Pittsburgh Press, 1962.

For corrections and additions see the review by W. I. Quinn in *The New Scholasticism*, XXXVII (1963), 528–533.

Ficino, Marsilio
(1433–1499)

Works

4.2.73 **Marsilii Ficini opera.** Basilea, Per Henricum Petri, 1576. 2v.

Reproduced Torino, Bottega d'Erasmo, 1959. See also, *Supplementum Ficinianum*, ed. by P. O. Kristeller, Florence, Olschki, 1937, 2v., which lists manuscripts and editions and gives a chronology of Ficino's works.

Kindi, Yakub ibn Ishak al–
(Ninth Century)

Bibliography

4.2.74 **Rescher, Nicholas.** Al-Kindi; an annotated bibliography. Pittsburgh, University of Pittsburgh Press, 1964. 55 pp.

Machiavelli, Niccolo
(1469–1527)

Works

4.2.75 **Opere.** A cura di Sergio Bertelli e Franco Gaeta, ed. Feltrinelli, 1960– .

In progress.
A critical edition which supersedes all earlier editions, none of which was complete.

4.2.76 **Machiavelli; the chief works and others.** Ed. by Allan Gilbert. Durham, N. C., Duke University Press, 1965. 3v.

The best English translation.
Supersedes the earlier edition in 4v. ed. by E. Farneworth, 2d ed., 1775.

Maimonides
(1135–1204)

Bibliography

4.2.77 **Gorfinkle, Joseph I.** "A bibliography of Maimonides," *in* I. Epstein, ed., Moses Maimonides (1135–1204), London, Sancino, 1935, pp. 229–248.

See also: 5.1.14 (No. 19).

Works

4.2.78 **The guide of the perplexed.** Trans., introduction and notes by S. Pines. Chicago, University of Chicago Press, 1963. 658 pp.

4.2.79 **Le guide des égarés.** Ed. par Salomon Munk. 2. éd. Paris, A. Franck, 1960. 3v.

1st ed. 1856–66. Arabic text and French translation.

Nicholas of Cusa
(1401–1464)

Bibliography

4.2.80 **Kleinen, H., und R. Danzer.** "Cusanus-Bibliographie, 1920–1961," Mitteilungen und Forschugensbeiträge der Cusanus-Gesellschaft, I (1961), 95–126.

Concordance

4.2.81 **Zellinger, Eduard.** Cusanus-Konkordanz. München, Hüber, 1960. 331 pp.

Works

4.2.82 **Nicolai Cusae cardinalis opera.** Parisiis, 1514. 3v.

Reprinted: Frankfurt, Minerva, 1962.

4.2.83 **Opera omnia.** [Ed.] E. Hoffmann and P. Wilpert. Lipsiae, Meiner, 1932–59. 14v.

4.2.84 **Philosophisch-theologische Schriften** [von] Nikolaus von Kues. Hrsg. und eingeführt von Leo Gabriel. Wein, Herder, 1964– .

In progress.
A jubilee edition with Latin and German texts.

Lombard, Peter
(c. 1095–1160)

Works

4.2.85 **[Works.]** Contained in 4.2.12, vols. CXCI and vol. CXCII.

Pico della Mirandola, Count Giovanni
(1463–1494)

Bibliography

4.2.86 **Ludovici, Sergio Samek.** Catalogo della mostra delle opere di Giovanni Pico della Mirandola. Modena, Biblioteca communale, 1963. 71 pp.

Works

4.2.87 **Opera omnia.** Basileae, Henricpetrina, 1572–73. 2v.

4.2.88 **Commentationes Joannis Pici Mirandulae.** E. Garin, ed. Firenze, Vallecchi, 1942– .

In progress.
A critical edition.

Suárez, Francisco
(1548–1617)

Bibliography

4.2.89 **Múgica, Plácido.** Bibliografía suareciana, con una introd. sobre el estado actual de los estudios por Eleuterio Elorduy. Granada, Universidad de Granada, Cátedra Suárez, 1948. 103 pp.

4.2.90 **Scorraille, R. de.** François Suarez de la compagnie de Jésus, d'apès ses lettres, ses autres écrits inédits et un grand nombre de documents nouveaux. Paris, P. Lethielleux, 1912–13. 2v.

The most complete bibliography up to its time.

4.2.91 **Smith, Gerard.** "A Suarez bibliography," *in* Jesuit thinkers of the Renaissance, ed. by Gerard Smith, Milwaukee, Marquette University Press, 1939, pp. 227–238.

Works

4.2.92 **Opera omnia.** Paris, Vives, 1856–78. 28v. in 30.

An incomplete edition. A complete, critical edition is in progress.

Thomas Aquinas, St.
(c. 1225–1274)

Bibliography

4.2.93 **Eschmann, I. T.** "A Catalogue of St. Thomas's Works: Bibliographical Notes," *in* E. Gilson, The Christian philosophy of St. Thomas Aquinas, New York, 1956, pp. 381–439.

A complete list of Aquinas' works with editions, chronology, and translations.

See also: 5.1.14 (Nos. 13/14 and 15/16); and 5.5.18–5.5.20.

Index, Lexicons, and Dictionaries

4.2.94 **Defarrari, Roy Joseph.** A Latin-English dictionary of St. Thomas Aquinas, based on the Summa Theologica and selected passages of his other works. Boston, St. Paul, 1960. 1115 pp.

An abridged edition of 4.2.96.

4.2.95 **Defarrari, Roy Joseph,** and **Sister M. I. Barry.** A complete index of the Summa Theologica of St. Thomas Aquinas. Washington, D. C., The Catholic University of America Press, 1956. 386 pp.

A list of terms and where they appear.

4.2.96 **Defarrari, Roy Joseph, Sister M. Involata,** and **Ignatius McGuiness.** A lexicon of St. Thomas Aquinas based on the Summa Theologica and selected passages of his other works. Washington, D. C., Catholic University of America Press, 1948–53. 5v.

Arranged by Latin words, with English meanings, Latin quotations, and indication of source.

4.2.97 **Schütz, Ludwig.** Thomas-lexikon. 2. Aufl. Paderborn, Schöningh, 1895. 889 pp.

Reprinted: New York, F. Ungar, 1957. 1st ed. 1881.
A useful concordance.

4.2.98 **Stockhammer, Morris.** Thomas Aquinas dictionary. New York, Philosophical Library, 1965. 219 pp.

Works

4.2.99 **Opera omnia.**

There are many different editions. The Leonine edition (Rome, 1882–) is a critical edition. Prior to 1950, 16v. were published. A new critical edition began with vol. XVII and is in progress at Rome, Le Saulchoir (France), Ottawa, Torrente (Spain), and Yale University.

The Parma edition (1852–73, 25v., reprinted N. Y., 1948–50) is not a critical edition but is almost complete.

Other famous editions are the Piana edition of 1570 (Pius V), and the Vives edition of Paris, 1871–80, 34v.

4.2.100 **Summa theologiae.** New York, McGraw-Hill, 1964– .

In progress.
60v. projected.
A critical edition with Latin and English on facing pages.

4.2.101 **Thomas Aquinas, Saint.** Basic writings. Edited and annotated, with an introduction, by Anton C. Pegis. New York, Random House, 1945. 2v.

The text is a revision of the English Dominican Translation of St. Thomas (by Father Laurence Shapcote, O. P.) begun in 1911.

William of Ockham
(c. 1285–1349)

Bibliography and Lexicon

4.2.102 **Baudry, L.** Guillaume d'Occam, sa vie, ses oeuvres, ses idées sociales et politiques. vol. I: L'Homme et les oeuvres. Paris, Vrin, 1949. 317 pp.

4.2.103 **Heynck, V.** "Ockham-Literatur 1919-1949," Fraziskanische Studien, XXXII (1950), 164–183.

Continued by 4.2.104.

4.2.104 **Reilly, James P.** "Ockham bibliography: 1950–1967," Franciscan Studies, XXVIII (1968), 197–214.

Continues 4.2.103.

4.2.105 **Baudry, Léon.** Lexique philosophique de Guillaume d'Ockham. Etude des notions fondamentales. Paris, Lethielleux, 1958. 298 pp.

Works

4.2.106 **Opera plurima.** Lyon, Johannes Trechsel, 1494–96. 4v.

Reprinted: London, Gregg Press, 1962. Contains the major political and theological works.

4.2.107 **Opera omnia philosophica et theologica.** St. Bonaventure, New York, Franciscan Institute, 1967– .

In progress.
25v. projected.
Under the general editorship of E. M. Buytaert. A critical edition of the nonpolitical works.

4.2.108 **Guillelmi de Ockham opera politica.** Accuravit G. Sikes [et al.]. Manchester, University Press, 1940– .

In progress.
Complete, critical Latin edition of the political works.

4.2.109 ★ **Ockham.** Philosophical writings; a selection edited and translated by Ph. Boehner. London, Nelson, 1957. 147, 154 pp.

A selection of Latin texts with facing English translations.

4.3 MODERN PHILOSOPHY

For general bibliographies see the histories of modern philosophy listed in 3.1 and 3.4

Bentham, Jeremy
(1748–1832)

Bibliography

4.3.1 **Halévy, Elie.** The growth of philosophic radicalism. Trans. by Mary Morris. London, Faber & Gwyer, 1928. 554 pp.

Contains a Bentham bibliography by Charles W. Everett: pp. 522–546.

4.3.2 **Milne, Alexander Taylor.** Catalogue of the manuscripts of Jeremy Bentham in the library of University College, London. 2d ed. London, University of London, Athlone Press, 1962. 104 pp.

Works

Many of Bentham's writings are preserved at University College, London.

4.3.3 **The collected works of Jeremy Bentham.** General ed., J. H. Burns. London, Athlone Press, 1968– .

In progress.
38v. projected.
This will be a comprehensive, definitive edition. When completed it will replace *The Works of Jeremy Bentham*, ed. by J. Bowring, Edinburgh, William Tait, 1838–43, 11v. (reprinted: N. Y., Russell and Russell, 1962), which is an incomplete collection.

Berkeley, George
(1685–1753)

Bibliography

4.3.4 **Jessop, T. E.** A bibliography of George Berkeley. . . . With an inventory of Berkeley's manuscript remains by A. Luce. London, Oxford University Press, 1934. 100 pp.

Continued by 4.3.5.

4.3.5 **Turbayne, C. M.,** and **Robert X. Ware.** "A bibliography of George Berkeley, 1933–1962," Journal of philosophy, LX (1963), 93–112.

A continuation of 4.3.4.

Works

4.3.6 **The works of George Berkeley,** Bishop of Cloyne. Ed. by A. A. Luce and T. E. Jessop. London, T. Nelson, 1948–57. 9v.

Reprinted: Nelson, 1964.
A critical edition. Also has a useful introduction and notes.

Brentano, Franz
(1838–1917)

Bibliography

4.3.7 **Gilson, Lucie.** Méthode et métaphysique selon F. Brentano. Paris, Vrin, 1955.

Bibliography, pp. 16–23.

4.3.8 **Mayer-Hillebrand, Franziska.** "Rückblick auf die bisherigen Bestrebungen zur Erhaltung und Verbreitung von Fr. Brentanos philosophischen Lehren und kurze Darstellung dieser Lehren," Zeitschrift für Philosophische Forschung, XVII (1963), 146–169.

Covers works on and reviews of Brentano's writings.

Works

4.3.9 **Gesammelte philosophische Schriften.** Hrsg. von O. Kraus und A. Kastil. Leipzig, Meiner, 1922–30. 10v.

Butler, Joseph
(1692–1752)

Works

4.3.10 **The works of Joseph Butler.** Ed. by The Rt. Hon. W. E. Gladstone. 2d ed. Oxford, Clarendon Press, 1910. 2v.

1st ed. 1897.

Comte, Auguste
(1798–1857)

Bibliography

4.3.11 **Ducassé, Pierre.** La méthode positive et l'intuition comtienne; bibliographie. Paris, Alcan, 1939. 172 pp.

Works

4.3.12 **Oeuvres.** Paris, Editions Anthropos, 1968– .

In progress.
12v. projected.
A reprinted collection of Comte's works as published in various editions from 1844–95.

An English condensation, *The Positive Philosophy of Auguste Comte*, trans. by H. Martineau, London, Bohn, 1853, 2v., was repudiated by some positivists.

Descartes, René
(1596–1650)

Bibliography and Index

4.3.13 **Sebba, Gregor.** Bibliographia Cartesiana; a critical guide to the Descartes literature, 1800–1960. The Hague, Nijhoff, 1964. 510 pp.

4.3.14 **Gilson, Etienne.** Index scholastico-cartésien. Paris, Alcan, 1913. 354 pp.

Indicates how Descartes uses scholastic terms.

Works

4.3.15 **Oeuvres de Descartes.** Publiées par C. Adam et P. Tannery. Paris, Cerf, 1896–1913. 12v. and supplement.

The collected, critical, standard edition.
The supplement is a general index.
The edition has been re-edited and published in a 7v. edition by the Centre national de la recherche scientifique, Paris, Vrin, 1964.

4.3.16 ★ **The philosophical works of Descartes.** Trans. by E. S. Haldane and G. T. R. Ross. Cambridge, The University Press, 1968. 2v.

A reprint of the corrected 1934 edition. 1st ed. 1911–12.
The most complete of the English editions.

Diderot, Denis
(1713–1784)

Bibliography

4.3.17 **Cabeen, D. C.,** *ed.* A critical bibliography of French literature. Syracuse, N. Y., Syracuse University Press, 1957–61. 4v.

See vol. IV, pp. 165–194, for a Diderot bibliography.

Works

4.3.18 **Oeuvres complètes.** Notices, notes . . . par J. Assézat et M. Tourneux. Paris, Garnier, 1875–77. 20v.

Dilthey, Wilhelm
(1833–1911)

Bibliography

4.3.19 **Zeeck, Hans.** "Im Druck erschienene Schriften von Wilhelm Dilthey," Archiv für Geschichte der Philosophie, XXV (1912), 154–160.

Works

4.3.20 **Gesammelte Schriften.** 2. Aufl. Stuttgart, Teubner, 1962–67. 14v.

1st ed. 1914–36, 12v., was not complete.

Feuerbach, Ludwig Andreas
(1804–1872)

Works

4.3.21 **Gesammelte Werke.** Hrsg. von W. Schuffenhauer. Berlin, Akademie Verlag, 1967– .
In progress.
16v. projected.

4.3.22 **Sämmtliche Werke.** Neu. hrsg. von Wilhelm Bolin und Friedrich Jodl. 2. Aufl. Stuttgart, Fromman, 1959. 13v.

Includes critical apparatus and bibliographies of works by and about him.

4.3.23 **Ausgewählte Briefe von und an Ludwig Feuerbach.** Hrsg. von W. Bolin. Leipzig, O. Wigand, 1904. 2v.

Fichte, Johann Gottlieb
(1762–1814)

Bibliography

4.3.24 **J. G. Fichte-Bibliographie.** Hrsg. von Hans Michael Baumgartner und Willi Jacobs. Stuttgart, Frommann.

To be published in conjunction with 4.3.25.

Works

4.3.25 **Gesamtausgabe der Bayerischen Akademie der Wissenschaften.** Hrsg. von Reinhard Lauth und Hans Jacob. Stuttgart, F. Frommann, 1964– .

In progress.
26v. projected.
The complete works, which will supersede all other editions.

4.3.26 **Johann Gottlieb Fichtes Nachgelassene Werke.** Hrsg. von I. H. Fichte. Bonn, A. Marcus, 1834–35. 3v.

Reprinted: Berlin, de Gruyter, 1962.

4.3.27 **Johann Gottlieb Fichtes Sämmtliche Werke.** Hrsg. von J. H. Fichte. Berlin, Veit, 1845–46. 8v.

Reprinted: Berlin, de Gruyter, 1964–65.

4.3.28 **Werke.** Hrsg. von F. Medicus. Leipzig, Meiner, 1908–12. 6v.

Reprinted: 1954– .
Not complete, but better than the J. H. Fichte edition (4.3.27).

4.3.29 **Fichtes Briefweschel,** kritische gesamtausgabe gesammelt und hrsg. von Hans Schultz. 2. Aufl. Leipzig, H. Haessel, 1930. 2v.

Frege, Gottlob
(1848–1925)

Bibliography

4.3.30 **Stroll, Avrum.** "On the first flowering of Frege's reputation," Journal of the history of philosophy, IV (1966), 72–81.

Lists articles on Frege, 1950–65, pp. 79–81.
For a list of works by and on Frege, see *Encyclopedia of Philosophy* (2.2.1), p. 237.

Green, Thomas Hill
(1836–1882)

Works

4.3.31 **The works of Thomas Hill Green.** Ed. by R. L. Nettleship. 2d ed. London, Longmans, Green & Co., 1889–90.

Reprinted: N. Y., Kraus Reprint Co. 1st ed. 1885–88.

Contains all his works except his introduction to Hume's *Works* and his ★ *Prolegomena to Ethics*, ed. by A. C. Bradley, 5th ed., Oxford, Clarendon Press, 1929.

Hegel, Georg Wilhelm Friedrich
(1770–1831)

Bibliography

4.3.32 **Janeff-Sofia, Janko.** "Bibliographie der deutschen Hegel-Literatur für hundert Jahre (1828–1928)," Literarische Berichte aus dem Gebiete der Philosophie [5.4.15], 1931 (Heft 24), pp. 35–49; "Bibliographie der ausländischen Hegel-Literatur," ibid., 1930 (Heft 23), pp. 40–48.

4.3.33 **Kern, W.** "Hegel-bücher 1961–1966; ein auswahlbericht," Theologie und Philosophie, XLII (1967), 79–88 and 402–418.

Annotated.

4.3.34 **Nadler, K.** "Wandlung des Hegelbildes in Deutschland seit der Jahrhundertwende; zur deutschen Hegelbibliographie von 1900–1933," Idealismus, Jahrbuch für die idealistische Philosophie, I (1934), 227–256.

See also: *Hegel-Studien* (7.3.27), 1961– , for continuing bibliography.

Works

4.3.35 **Gesammelte Werke.** Herausgegeben in auftrag der deutschen Forschungsgemeinschaft. Hamburg, Meiner, 1968– .

1st complete critical edition.
In progress.

4.3.36 **Sämmtliche Werke.** Jubiläumsausgabe. Neu. hrsg. von Hermann Glockner. Stuttgart, Frommann, 1927–40. 26v.

Based on the 1832–45 ed. 19v. in 22.
V. 23–26 are a *Hegel-Lexikon*; also separately reprinted in a 2d ed. in 2v., 1957.

4.3.37 **Sämmtliche Werke:** neue kritische Ausgabe. Hrsg. von Johannes Hoffmeister. Hamburg, F. Meiner, 1952–60. 30v.

A critical edition, originally planned by G. Lasson in 1907, and replanned by Hoffmeister.

Hobbes, Thomas
(1588–1679)

Bibliography

4.3.38 **Macdonald, Hugh,** and **Mary Hargreaves.** Thomas Hobbes; a bibliography. London, The Bibliographical Society, 1952. 83 pp.

4.3.39 **Pacchi, A.** "Bibliografia Hobbesiana dal 1840 a oggi," Rivista Critica di Storia della Fillosofia, XVII (1962), 528–47.

Includes editions of and works on Hobbes, 1840–1962.

Works

4.3.40 **The English works of Thomas Hobbes.** Ed. by Sir William Molesworth. London, J. Bohn, 1839. 11v.

Reprinted: Oxford, 1962.
The standard edition, together with 4.3.41; contains an index.

4.3.41 **Thomae Hobbes Malmesburiensis opera philosophica quae Latine scripsit omnia . . .** collecta studio et labore Gu. Molesworth. London, J. Bohn, 1839–45. 5v.

Reprinted: Oxford, 1961.
The standard edition, together with 4.3.40.

Hume, David
(1711–1776)

Bibliography

4.3.42 **Jessop, T. E.** A bibliography of David Hume and of Scottish philosophy from Francis Hutcheson to Lord Balfour. London, A. Brown, Hull, 1938. 201 pp.

4.3.43 **Ronchetti, E.** "Bibliografia humiana dal 1937 al 1966," Revista critica di storia della filosofia," XXII (1967), 495–520.

Works

4.3.44 Philosophical works. Ed. by T. H. Green and T. H. Grose. London, 1874–75. 4v.

Reprint of 1886 ed., Aalen, Scientia Verlag, 1964.
Superseded by 4.3.45 and 4.3.46 for those works; the standard edition for other works.

4.3.45 ⋆ Enquiries concerning the human understanding and concerning the principles of morals. Ed. by L. A. Selby-Bigge. 2d ed. Oxford, Clarendon, 1902.

1st ed. 1894.
Standard edition; includes index.

4.3.46 ⋆ A treatise of human nature. Ed. by L. A. Selby-Bigge. Oxford, Clarendon Press, 1888.

Reprinted: 1955.
The standard edition; includes index.

Husserl, Edmund
(1859–1938)

Bibliography

4.3.47 Patocka, Jan. "Husserl-Bibliographie," *Revue internationale de philosophie*, I (1939), 374–397.

Continued by: Raes, Jean, "Supplément à la bibliographie de Husserl," ibid., IV (1950), 469–475; G. Maschke and I. Kern, ibid., XIX (1965), 153–202; and H. L. van Breda, "Bibliographie der bis zum 30. Juni 1959 veröffentlichten Schriften Edmund Husserls," *Edmund Husserl 1859–1959*, The Hague, Nijhoff, 1959, pp. 289–306.

Works

4.3.48 Husserliana: Edmund Husserl, Gesammelte Werke. Hrsg. von H. L. van Breda. The Hague, Nijhoff, 1950– .

In progress.
Based on the collection of the Husserl-Archiv in Louvain, Belgium. The New School for Social Research (N. Y.) contains a complete set of Husserl's inedita, photocopied from the original transcriptions held at the Louvain archives.

James, William
(1842–1910)

Bibliography

4.3.49 McDermott, John J. The writings of William James; a comprehensive edition. New York, Modern Library, 1967.

Annotated bibliography of the writings of William James, pp. 811–858.

4.3.50 Perry, Ralph Barton. Annotated bibliography of the writings of William James. New York, Longmans, Green & Co., 1920. 69 pp.

Reprinted: Wm. C. Brown.
Annotated.

Kant, Immanuel
(1724–1804)

Bibliography

4.3.51 Bibliography of writings by and on Kant which have appeared in Germany up to the end of 1887.

First published as supplements to *The Philosophical Review*, v. 2–4 (1893–95), 380 pp. Also published separately, Boston, 1896.

4.3.52 Baer, Joseph and Co. Kant-bibliothek; Schriften von und über Immanuel Kant. Frankfurt am Main, Joseph Baer and Co., 1903. 48 pp.

Works

4.3.53 Kants gesammelte Schriften. Herausgegeben von der Preussischen Akademie der Wissenschaften zu Berlin. Berlin, Walter de Gruyter, 1902–56. 23v.

The standard critical edition.
Supplemented by: Vorlesungen, v. 24–28, 1966– ; and *Allegmeiner Kantindex zu Kants gesammelten Schriften*, 1967– .
When completed, this index will supersede Rudolf Eisler, *Kant-lexikon*, Berlin, Mittler, 1930, 642 pp.; and Heindrich Ratke, *Systematisches Handlexikon zu Kants Kritik der reinen Vernunft*, Leipzig, Meiner, 1929, 330 pp. V. 1–15

will be an index of the text location of every word in the above 23 volumes; v. 16–19 will be an index of word frequencies; v. 20 will be an index of persons and sources.

Kierkegaard, Soren Aabye
(1813–1855)

Bibliography

4.3.54 **Himmelstrup, Jens.** Søren Kierkegaard; international bibliografi. København, Nyt Nordisk Forlag, Arnold Busck, 1962. 216 pp.

Includes works by and about Kierkegaard, 1835–1955. Continued for 1956–1962 by M. Allessandro Cortese, "Una nuova bibliografia Kierkegaardiana," *Revista di filosofia neoscholastica*, LV (1963), 98–108.

4.3.55 **Nielsen, Edith Ortmann.** Søren Kierkegaard; bidrag til en bibliografi. Contributions towards a bibliography. København, Munksgaard, 1951. 96 pp.

See also: 5.1.14 (No. 4).

Works

4.3.56 **Søren Kierkegaards samlede vaerker:** udgivne af A. B. Drachmann, J. L. Heiberg og H. O. Lange. 3. udgeve. Københaven, Gyldendal, 1962–64. 20v.

1st ed. 1901–06. 14v.

4.3.57 **Søren Kierkegaards Papirer.** Udgivne of P. A. Heiberg, V. Kuhr, og S. Torsting. Københagen, Gyldendal, 1909–48. 11v. in 20.

A 2d ed. is in progress, 1968– .

4.3.58 **Gesammelte Werke.** Hrsg. von H. Gottsched und C. Schrempf. Jena, Diederichs, 1903–25. 12v.

A German translation.

4.3.59 **Soren Kierkegaard's Journals and Papers.** Ed. and trans. by Howard V. and Edna H. Hong. Bloomington, Ind., Indiana University Press, 1967– .

In progress.
5v. projected.
Contains translations of portions of 4.3.56.

La Mettrie, Julien Offray de
(1709–1751)

Works

4.3.60 **Oeuvres philosophiques de La Mettrie.** Paris, C. Tutot, 1796. 3v.

Leibniz, Gottfried Wilhelm
(1646–1716)

Bibliography

4.3.61 **Leibniz-Bibliographie.** Ein Verzeichnis der Literatur über Leibniz. Bearb. von K. Müller. Hrsg. von der Niedersächsischen Landesbibliothek, 1966. 480 pp.

4.3.62 **Ravier, Emile.** Bibliographie des oeuvres de Leibniz. Paris, Alcan, 1937. 703 pp.

Reprinted: Hildesheim, Olms, 1965.

Works

There are many unpublished Leibniz manuscripts at the Hanover Library. Microfilm copies of the unpublished papers are held by the University of Pennsylvania Library.

4.3.63 **Sämtliche Schriften und Briefe.** Hrsg. von der Preussischen Akademie der Wissenschaften. Darmstadt, O. Reichl, 1923– .

A critical edition, but still incomplete; includes bibliographies.
40v. were originally projected.

4.3.64 **Die mathematischen Schriften von G. W. Leibniz.** Hrsg. von C. I. Gerhardt. Berlin, Ascher, 1849–63. 7v.

4.3.65 **Die philosophischen Schriften von G. W. Leibniz.** Hrsg. von C. I. Gerhardt. Berlin, Weidmann, 1875–90. 7v.

Reprinted: Hidelsheim, Olms, 1960–61.

4.3.66 **Philosophical papers and letters:** a selection translated and edited, with an introduction by Leroy E. Loemker. Chicago, University of Chicago Press, 1956. 2v.

Standard English edition; bibliography, v. 1, pp. 102–113.

Lessing, Gotthold Ephraim
(1729–1781)

Works

4.3.67 **Gesammelte Werke.** Hrsg. von P. Rilla. Berlin, Aufbau-Verlag, 1954–58. 10v.

Locke, John
(1632–1704)

Bibliography

4.3.68 **Christophersen, H. O.** A bibliographical introduction to the study of John Locke. Skrifter utgitt av det Norske videnskapsakademi: Historisk-filosofisk klasse (1930, no. 8). Oslo, I Kommisjon hos J. Dybwad., 1930. 134 pp.

Continued by Roland Hall and Roger Woolhouse, "Forty years of work on John Locke (1929–1969), a bibliography," *The Philosophical Quarterly*, XX (1970), 258–268.

4.3.69 ★ **Cranston, Maurice.** Locke. London, Longmans, Green, 1961. 38 pp.

Published for the British Council; British book news bibliographical series of supplements no. 135.

4.3.70 **Long, Philip.** A summary catalogue of the Lovelace collection of papers of John Locke in the Bodleian library. Oxford bibliographical society. Publications (n.s., vol. VIII). Oxford, University Press, 1959. 64 pp.

A catalogue of the writings, many of which are still unpublished, of John Locke in the Lovelace Collection of the Bodleian Library,Oxford.

Works

4.3.71 **The works of John Locke.** 12th ed. London, C. and J. Rivington, 1824. 9v.

Reprinted in 10v., Aelen, Scientia Verlag, 1963.

1st ed. London, 1714. 3v.

One of the most complete collections; but 4.3.72 is the standard edition of the *Essay*.

4.3.72 ★ **Essay concerning human understanding.** Ed. with a critical introduction and notes by A. C. Fraser. Oxford, Clarendon Press, 1894. 2v.

The standard edition.
Reprinted: New York, Dover, 1959.

4.3.73 **An essay concerning human understanding.** Ed. with an introduction by John W. Yolton. Rev. ed. New York, Dutton (Everyman's Library), 1965. 2v.

". . . the full text of the Fifth Edition, that edition willed by Locke to Bodleian with his final approval" (p. xiv).

Lotze, Rudolf Hermann
(1817–1881)

Bibliography

4.3.74 **Santayana, George.** Lotze's system of philosophy. Ed. by Paul Kuntz. Bloomington, Ind., Indiana University Press, 1971. 274 pp.

Lists all the works of Lotze and catalogs Lotze's influence, especially on Anglo-American philosophy.

Maine de Biran
(1766–1824)

Bibliography

4.3.75 **Ghio, M. Michelangelo.** "Essai de Bibliographie Raisonée de Maine de Biran (1766–1824)," *in* Maine de Biran e la tradizione biraniana in Francia, Turin, Ed. di "Filosofia," 1962, pp. 181–199.

4.3.76 **Mayjonade, J. B.** Maine de Biran, étude biographique et bibliographique. Lille, Taffin-Lefort, 1895. 32 pp.

Works

4.3.77 Oeuvres de Maine de Biran. Publiées par Pierre Tisserand et Henri Gouhier. Paris, Alcan, 1922–49. 14v.

Definitive and standard edition.

Malebranche, Nicholas
(1638–1715)

Bibliography

4.3.78 Del Noce, A. "Bibliografia malebranchiana" *in* Malebranche nel terzo centenario della nascita, pubbl. a cura della Fac. di Filos. della Univ. Catt. del Sacro Cuore, Milano, Vita e Pensiero, 1938, pp. 361–380.

4.3.79 Rome, Beatrice K. The philosophy of Malebranche. Chicago, Regnery, 1963. 448 pp.

Bibliography, pp. 331–362.

Works

4.3.80 Oeuvres complètes de Malebranche. Direction: André Robinet. Paris, Vrin, 1958–67. 20v.

A definitive, critical edition.

V. 20, 1967, includes a biography and a bibliography.

Marx, Karl
(1818–1883)

Bibliography and Dictionary

4.3.81 Lachs, John. Marxist philosophy; a bibliographical guide.

See 5.5.14.

4.3.82 Rubel, Maximilien. Bibliographie des oeuvres de Karl Marx. Avec en appendice un répertoire des oeuvres de Friedrich Engels. Paris, Marcel Rivière, 1956. 275 pp.

——Supplement, 1960. 79 pp.

4.3.83 Stockhammer, Morris. Karl Marx dictionary. New York, Philosophical Library, 1965. 273 pp.

Works

4.3.84 Karl Marx, Friedrich Engels. Historisch-kritische Gesamtausgabe; Werke, Schriften, Briefe. Hrsg. von D. Ryazanov and V. Adoratsky. Frankfurt, Marx-Engels Institute, 1927–36.

Commonly referred to as MEGA.
A critical edition, but never completed. Of the 42v. projected only 7v. of works by Marx and Engels, a commemorative volume on Engels, and 4v. of correspondence were published.

4.3.85 Karl Marx, Friedrich Engels. Werke. Berlin, Dietz Verlag, 1956– .

In progress.
44v. projected.
Commonly referred to as MEW.

4.3.86 [Complete works.]

A complete English edition of the works in 47v., to be published simultaneously by International Publishers (N. Y.), Lawrence & Wishart (London), and Progress Publishers (Moscow), under the direction of Maurice Dobb, was announced in 1969.

Meinong, Alexius
(1853–1920)

Works

4.3.87 Gesamtausgabe. Hrsg. von R. Haller und R. Kindinger. Graz, Akademische Druck- u. Verlagsanstalt, 1968– .

In progress.
7v. projected.
The 1st 2v. are reprints of *Gesammelte Abhandlungen*, Leipzig, 1913–14.

Mill, John Stuart
(1806–1873)

Bibliography

4.3.88 ★ Cranston, Maurice. John Stuart Mill. London, Longmans, Green, 1958. 34 pp.

Published for the British Council; British book news bibliographical series of supplements no. 99.

4.3.89 MacMinn, N., J. R. Hainds, and **J. M. McCrimmon.** Bibliography of the published writings of John Stuart Mill. Edited from his manuscript with corrections and notes. (Northwestern University Studies in the Humanities, 12.) Evanston, Ill., Northwestern University Press, 1945. 101 pp.

4.3.90 The Mill newsletter. Ed. by John M. Robson. 1965– .

Published by University of Toronto Press, in association with Victoria College, University of Toronto. Carries a continuing bibliography on Mill.

Works

4.3.91 The collected works of John Stuart Mill. Toronto, University of Toronto Press, 1963– .

In progress.
20v. projected.
A critical edition.

Nietzsche, Friedrich
(1844–1900)

Bibliography

4.3.92 Mette, Hans Joachim. Der handschriftliche Nachlass Friedrich Nietzsches. Leipzig, Verlag Richard Hadl, 1932, 87 pp.

4.3.93 Reichert, Herbert W., and **Karl Schlechta.** International Nietzsche bibliography. (Chapel Hill, University of North Carolina Studies in comparative literature v. 29.) Chapel Hill, University of North Carolina Press, 1960. 133 pp.

Partially annotated; full, but not exhaustive.

Works

4.3.94 Werke. Kritische Gesamtausgabe. Hrsg. von Georgio Colli und Mazzino Montinari. Berlin, de Gruyter, 1967– .

In progress.
30v. in eight sections projected.
A critical edition which, when completed, will supersede all other editions.

4.3.95 Gesammelte Werke. Grossoktav Ausgabe. 2. Aufl. Leipzig, Kroner, 1901–13. 19v.

Not complete.
Supplemented by Richard Oehler, *Nietzsche Register,* 1926, considered vol. XX. Also separately published, Stuttgart, Kroner, 1965.

4.3.96 Gesammelte Werke. Musarionausgabe. München, Musarion, 1920–29. 23v.

The most complete edition presently available.

4.3.97 Werke in drei Bänden. Hrsg. von Karl Schlechta. 2. Aufl. München, C. Hanser, 1960. 3v.

1st. ed. 1954–56. Not complete, though it contains all of Nietzsche's books. It is supplemented by *Nietzsche-Index zu den Werken in drei Banden,* 1965. 517 pp.

4.3.98 Werke und Briefe. Historisch-kritische Gesamtausgabe. München, C. H. Beck, 1934–52. 9v.

4.3.99 The complete works of Friedrich Nietzsche. Ed. by Oscar Levy. Edinburgh and London, T. N. Foulis, 1909–13. 18v.

Reprinted: N. Y., Russell & Russell, 1964.
The most complete collection in English but defective in various ways and not entirely reliable.

Pascal, Blaise
(1623–1662)

Bibliography

4.3.100 Maire, Albert. Bibliographie générale des oeuvres de Blaise Pascal. Paris, L. Giraud-Badin, 1925–27. 5v.

Works

4.3.101 Oeuvres complètes. Ed. L. Brunschvicg, P. Boutroux, F. Gazier. Paris, Hachette, 1904–14. 14v.

Standard edition.

4.3.102 Oeuvres complètes. Texte établi et annoté par Jacques Chevalier. Paris, Gallimard, 1954. 1529 pp.

Bibliography included in "Note bibliographique," pp. xxiii–xxvi.

4.3.103 Oeuvres complètes. Texte établi, présenté et annoté par Jean Mesnard. Paris, Desclée de Brouwer, 1964–

In progress.
Includes bibliographies.

Peirce, Charles Sanders
(1839–1914)

Bibliography

4.3.104 Fisch, Max H. [and others]. "A draft of a bibliography of writings about C. S. Peirce," *in* Edward C. Moore and Richard S. Robin, Studies in the philosophy of Charles Sanders Peirce; second series, Amherst, Mass., University of Massachusetts Press, 1964, pp. 486–514.

4.3.105 Fisch, Max H. "A first supplement to 'A draft of a bibliography of writings about C. S. Peirce',' Transactions of the Charles S. Peirce Society, II (1966), 54–59.

A supplement to the bibliography in 4.3.104.

4.3.106 Robin, Richard S. Annotated catalogue of the papers of Charles S. Peirce. Amherst, University of Massachusetts Press, 1967. 268 pp.

Works

4.3.107 Collected papers of Charles Sanders Peirce. Cambridge, Mass., Harvard University Press, 1931–58. 8v.

V. 1–6, ed. by C. Hartshorne and P. Weiss, 1931–35;
v. 7–8, ed. by A. W. Burks, 1958.

Plekhanov, Georgii Valentinovich
(1856–1918)

Works

4.3.108 Sochineniia. Pod red. D. Ryazanova. Moskva, Gos. izd., 1923–27. 24v.

4.3.109 Selected philosophical works. Trans. by B. Trifonov. Moscow, Foreign Languages Publishing House, 1961– .

In progress.
5v. projected.

Rousseau, Jean-Jacques
(1712–1778)

Bibliography

4.3.110 Sénelier, Jean. Bibliographie générale des oeuvres de J.- J. Rousseau. Paris, Encyclopédie française, 1949. 282 pp.

For a continuing bibliography see *Annales de la société Jean-Jacques Rousseau* (Geneva), 1905– .

4.3.111 Dufour, Théophile. Recherches bibliographiques sur les oeuvres imprimées de J.- J. Rousseau. Paris, L. Giraud-Badin, 1925. 2v.

Works

4.3.112 Oeuvres complètes. Mises dans un nouvel ordre, avec des notes historiques et des éclaircissements, par V.-D. Musset-Pathay. Paris, P. Dupont, 1823–26. 25v.

4.3.113 Oeuvres complètes de Jean-Jacques Rousseau. Ed. publiée sous la direction de Bernard Gagnebin et Marcel Raymond. Paris, Bibliothèque de la Pléiade, 1959– .

In progress.
5v. projected.

4.3.114 Correspondance complète de Jean-Jacques Rousseau. Ed. critique établie et annotée par R. A. Leigh. Genève, Institut et musée Voltaire, 1965– .

In progress.
Until completed, see *Correspondance générale,*

éd. par P.-P. Plan et Th. Dufour, Paris, Colin, 1924–34, 20v.

Royce, Josiah
(1855–1916)

Bibliography

4.3.115 **Cotton, J. H.** Royce on the human self. Cambridge, Mass., Harvard University Press, 1954. 347 pp.

Bibliography: pp. 305–311.

4.3.116 **Loewenberg, Jacob.** "A bibliography of the unpublished writings of Josiah Royce," The philosophical review, XXVI (1917), 578–582.

4.3.117 **Oppenheim, F. M.** "Bibliography of the published works of J. Royce," *and* A. A. Devaux, "Bibliographie des traductions d'ouvrages de Royce et des études sur l'oeuvre de Royce," Revue internationale de philosophie, XXI (1967), 138–158, 159–182.

4.3.118 **Rand, Benjamin.** "A bibliography of the writings of Josiah Royce," The philosophical review, XXV (1916), 515–522.

4.3.119 **Smith, John E.** Royce's social infinite. New York, Liberal Arts Press, 1950. 176 pp.

Bibliography: pp. 171–173.

See also: 4.3.120.

Works

4.3.120 **The basic writings of Josiah Royce.** Ed. with an introduction by John J. McDermott. Chicago, Chicago University Press, 1969. 2v.

Vol. II also contains "Annotated Bibliography of the Published Works of Josiah Royce," by Ignas Skrupskelis.

Schelling, Friedrich Wilhelm Joseph von
(1775–1854)

Bibliography

4.3.121 **Schneeberger, Guida.** Friedrich Wilhelm Joseph von Schelling. Eine Bibliographie. Bern, Francke, 1954. 190 pp.

Works

4.3.122 **Friedrich Wilhelm Joseph von Schellings sämmtliche Werke.** Stuttgart und Augsburg, J. G. Cotta, 1856–61. 14v. in 13.

4.3.123 **Werke.** Nach der Originalausgabe in neuer Anordnung hrsg. von Manfred Schröter. München, C. H. Beck and R. Oldenbourg, 1927–56. 10v.

Schopenhauer, Arthur
(1788–1860)

Bibliography

4.3.124 **Grisebach, Eduard.** Edita und Inedita. Schopenhaueriana: Eine Schopenhauer-Bibliographie, sowie Randschriften und Briefe Arthur Schopenhauers mit Porträt, Wappen und Facsimile der Handschrift des Meisters. Hrsg. zu seinem hundertjährigen Geburtstage. Leipzig, F. J. Brockhaus, 1888. 221 pp.

4.3.125 **Stäglich, Hans.** Johann Wolfgang von Goethe und Arthur Schopenhauer. Eine . . . Bibliographie einschlägiger Literatur. 3. Aufl. Bonn, Rhein, 1960. 64 pp.

1st ed. 1932.

Works

4.3.126 **Sämtliche Werke.** Nach der 1., von Julius Frauenstädt besorgten Gesamtaug. neu bearb. und hrsg. von Arthur Hübscher. 2. Aufl. Wiesbaden, E. Brockhaus, 1946–50. 7v.

The Frauenstädt edition first appeared in 1873–74
See also his *Schopenhauer-Register*, 2 Aufl., Stuttgart, Fromman, 1960, 530 pp., based on this edition.

4.3.127 ★ **The works of Schopenhauer,** abridged. Ed. by Will Durant. Garden City, N. Y., Garden City Pub. C., 1928. 539 pp.

An English translation of some of Schopenhauer's works.

Solovyov, Vladimir Sergeyevich
(1853–1900)

Works

4.3.128 **Sobranie sochinenii Vladmira Ser-gievicha Solov'eva.** 2. izd. St. Petersburg, Knigoizdatel'skoe tovarishchestvo "Proveschenie," 1911–14. 10v.

1st ed. 1901–07. 9v.

Spencer, Herbert
(1820–1903)

Works

4.3.129 **The works of Herbert Spencer.** Osnabrück, Zeller, 1966. 21v.

A reprint of the 1880–1907 ed.

Spinoza, Benedict (Baruch)
(1632–1677)

Bibliography

4.3.130 **Oko, Adolph S.** The Spinoza bibliography. Boston, G. K. Hall, 1964. 602 pp.

Published under the auspices of the Columbia University Libraries.
Contains reproductions of 7000 cards.
See also *Chronicon Spinozanum* (The Hague), 1921– ; and *Bibliotheca Spinozana* (Amsterdam), 1922– .

Dictionaries

4.3.131 **Richter, Gustav Theodor.** Spinozas philosophische Terminologie; historisch und immanent kritisch untersucht. Leipzig, J. A. Barth, 1913. 170 pp.

1. Abt. Grundbegriffe der Metaphysik. No more published.

4.3.132 **Spinoza dictionary.** Ed. by Dagobert D. Runes, with a foreword by Albert Einstein. New York, Philosophical Library, 1951. 309 pp.

Works

4.3.133 **Spinoza opera.** Hrsg. von C. Gebhardt. Heidelberg, C. Winter, 1925. 4v.

Standard, critical edition.

4.3.134 ★ **The chief works of Spinoza.** Trans. by R. H. M. Elwes. New York, Dover, 1955. 2v.

Reprint of the 1883–84 edition.

4.3.135 **Correspondence of Spinoza.** Ed. by A. Wolf. London, G. Allen & Unwin, 1928. 502 pp.

Includes the biographies by Colerus and Lucas.

4.3.136 ★ **Earlier philosphical writings.** Trans. by F. A. Hayes. Indianapolis, Bobbs-Merrill, 1963. 161 pp.

4.3.137 **Oeuvres complètes de Spinoza.** Texte nouvellement traduit ou revu, présenté et annoté par R. Caillois, Madeleine Frances, et P. Misrahi. Paris, Gallimard, 1954. 1604 pp.

A French translation with annotations, indices, and the biographies of Colerus and Lucas.

Vico, Giambattista
(1668–1744)

Bibliography

4.3.138 **Croce, Benedetto.** Bibliografia vichiana. Accresciuta e rielaborata da F. Nicolini. Napoli, Ricciardi, 1947–48. 2v.

Works

4.3.139 **Opere complete.** A cura di Benedetto Croce, Giovanni Gentile, e Fausto Nicolini. Bari, Laterza, 1911–14. 8v. in 11.

Standard edition.

Voltaire, François Marie Arouet de
(1694–1778)

Bibliography

4.3.140 **Cabeen, David C.,** [et al]. A critical bibliography of French literature. Syracuse, N. Y., Syracuse University Press, 1957–61. 4v.

See vol. IV, pp. 182–207 for a bibliography up to 1951.

Works

4.3.141 **Oeuvres complètes.** L. Moland, éd. Paris, Garnier, 1877–85. 52v.

The standard edition.

4.3.142 **Correspondence.** Ed. by Theodore Besterman. Genève, Institut et Musée Volatire, Les Délices, 1953– .

In progress.
French text with notes in English.

Wolff, Christian
(1679–1754)

Works

4.3.143 **Gesammelte Werke.** Hrsg. von J. Ecole [et al]. Hildesheim, G. Olms, 1962– .

In progress.
In part, photographic reproductions of earlier editions, with added new editorial material.

4.4 CONTEMPORARY PHILOSOPHY

Bergson, Henri
(1859–1941)

Bibliography

4.4.1 **A contribution to a bibliography of Henri Bergson.** New York, Columbia University Press, 1913. 56 pp.

Supplemented by: *References on Henri Bergson.* Washington, D. C., Library of Congress, 1913, 3 pp.

4.4.2 **Coviello, Alfredo.** El proceso filosófico de Bergson y su bibliografía. 2. ed. Tucumán, Argentina, Revista Sustancia, 1941. 117 pp.

Works

4.4.3 **Oeuvres.** Textes annotés par André Robinet. 2. éd. Paris, Presses Universitaires de France, 1963. 1603 pp.

Bibliographical references in "Notes," pp. 1483–1578.

Broad, Charlie Dunbar
(1887–)

Bibliography

4.4.4 **Lewy, C.** "Bibliography of the writings of C. D. Broad to the end of July 1959," *in* P. A. Schilpp, ed., The philosophy of C. D. Broad, New York, Tudor Pub. Co., 1959, pp. 831–852.

Buber, Martin
(1878–1965)

Bibliography

4.4.5 **Catanne, Moshe.** A biliography of Martin Buber's works (1897–1957). Jerusalem, Bialik Institute, 1958. 142 pp.

4.4.6 ★ **Friedman, Maurice S.** Martin Buber, the life of dialogue. New York, Harper, 1960. 312 pp.

Contains a bibliography of works by and about Buber up to 1960, pp. 283–300.

4.4:7 **Friedman, Maurice.** "Bibliography of the writings of Martin Buber," *in* P. A. Schilpp and Maurice Friedman, eds., Martin Buber, La Salle, Ill., Open Court Publishing Company, 1967, pp. 745–786.

Works

4.4.8 **Werke.** München, Kösel-Verlag, 1962– .

In progress.
Also includes bibliographies.

Camus, Albert
(1913–1960)

Bibliography

4.4.9 ★ **Cruickshank, J.** Albert Camus and the literature of revolt. London, Oxford University Press, 1959. 248 pp.

Bibliography: pp. 237–241.

4.4.10 **Fitch, Brian T.** Albert Camus; essai de bibliographie des études en langue française consacrées à Albert Camus (1937–1962). Paris, Minard, 1965. 231 pp.

Carnap, Rudolf
(1891–)

Bibliography

4.4.11 **Benson, Arthur L.** "Bibliography of the writings of Rudolf Carnap," *in* P. A. Schilpp, ed., The philosophy of Rudolf Carnap, La Salle, Ill., Open Court Publishing Company, 1963, pp. 1015–1070.

Cassirer, Ernst
(1874–1945)

Bibliography

4.4.12 **Hamburg, C. H.,** and **W. M. Solmitz.** "Bibliography of the writings of Ernst Cassirer to 1946," *in* P. A. Schilpp, ed., The philosophy of Ernst Cassirer, Evanston, Ill., Library of Living Philosophers, 1949, pp. 881–910.

For bibliography to 1964, see H. J. Paton and Raymond Klibansky, eds., *Philosophy and History: Essays Presented to Ernst Cassirer,* New York, Harper & Row, 1963, pp. 338–353.

Collingwood, Robin George
(1889–1943)

Bibliography

4.4.13 * **Collingwood, R. G.** The idea of history. Ed. by T. M. Knox. Oxford, Clarendon Press, 1946. 339 pp.

See the "preface" for a Collingwood bibliography.
See also the obituary essays by R. B. McCallum, T. M. Knox, and I. A. Richmond in *Proceedings of the British Academy,* XXIX (1943), pp. 463–480.

Croce, Benedetto
(1866–1952)

Bibliography

4.4.14 **Cione, Edmondo.** Bibliografia Crociana. Roma, Bocca, 1965. 481 pp.

Works by and about Croce.

4.4.15 **Stella, Vittorio.** "Il giudizio su Croce; consuntivo di un centenario," Giornale di metafisica, XXII (1967), 643–711.

Includes a bibliography of works published since 1962.

See also: 5.1.14, No. 7, pp. 17–18.

Works

4.4.16 **Opere complete.** Bari, Laterza, 1965– .

In progress.

Dewey, John
(1859–1952)

Bibliography

4.4.17 **Thomas, Milton Halsey.** John Dewey; a centennial bibliography. Chicago, University of Chicago Press, 1962. 370 pp.

The third edition of a bibliography of John Dewey by M. H. Thomas and H. W. Schneider, 1st published in 1929.
Supplemented by *The Dewey Newsletter,* Dewey Project, Southern Illinois University, 1967– .

Works

4.4.18 **Works of John Dewey.** Carbondale, Ill., Southern Illinois University Press, 1967– .

In progress. Three series are projected: The early works of John Dewey, 1882–1898 (15v.); The middle works of John Dewey, 1899–1924 (15v.); The later works of John Dewey, 1925–1952 (25v.); plus several volumes of miscellaneous material and an index.
This will be a definitive, critical edition of the works of Dewey.

Gentile, Giovanni
(1875–1944)

Bibliography

4.4.19 **Bellezza, Vita A.** Bibliografia degli scritti di Giovanni Gentile. Firenze, Sansoni, 1950. 141 pp.

Also issued as vol. III of 4.4.20.

Works

4.4.20 **Opere complete di Giovanni Gentile.** A cura della Fondazione G. Gentile per gli studi filosofici. Firenze, Sansoni, 1942– .

In progress.
55v. projected.

Hartmann, Nicolai
(1882–1950)

Bibliography

4.4.21 **Heimsoeth, Heinz,** und **Robert Heiss.** Nicolai Hartmann. Der Denker und sein Werk. Göttingen, Vandenhoeck & Ruprecht, 1952. 312 pp.

Contains a bibliography by Theodor Balluf, pp. 286–308.

Heidegger, Martin
(1889–)

Bibliography

4.4.22 **Lübbe, Hermann.** "Bibliographie der Heidegger Literatur 1917–1955," Zeitschrift für philosophische Forschung, XI (1957), 401–52.

Also separately printed, Meisenheim am Glan, A. Hain, 1957, 52 pp. Supplemented by G. F. Schneeberger, *Ergänzungen zu einer Heidegger-bibliographie.* Bern, 1960. 27 pp.

4.4.23 **Richardson, William J.** Heidegger; through phenomenology to thought. The Hague, Nijhoff, 1963.

Bibliography: pp. 673–688.

Jaspers, Karl
(1883–)

Bibliography

4.4.24 **Bentz, Hans Walther.** Karl Jaspers in Übersetzungen. Karl Jaspers translated. Karl Jaspers traduit. Frankfurt am Main, H. W. Bentz Verlag, 1961. 31 pp.

4.4.25 **Rossmann, Kurt.** "Bibliography of the writings of Karl Jaspers to spring, 1957," *in*

P. A. Schilpp, ed., The philosophy of Karl Jaspers, New York, Tudor Pub. Co., 1957, pp. 871–887.

4.4.26 **Werk und Wirkung.** Hrsg. von Klaus Piper. München, Piper, 1963.

Bibliography of Karl Jaspers: pp. 175–216.

Lewis, Clarence Irving
(1883–1964)

Bibliography

4.4.27 **Adams, E. M.** "The writings of C. I. Lewis," *in* P. A. Schilpp, ed., The philosophy of C. I. Lewis, La Salle, Ill., Open Court Publishing Company, 1968, pp. 677–689.

Marcel, Gabriel
(1889–)

Bibliography

4.4.28 **Troisfontaines, Roger.** De l'existence à l'être. Louvain, Nauwelaerts, 1953. 2v.

Contains a complete bibliography of Marcel's works to 1953: v. 2, pp. 381–425.

Maritain, Jacques
(1882–)

Bibliography

4.4.29 **Gallagher, Donald A.,** and **Idella Gallagher.** The achievement of Jacques and Raissa Maritain; a bibliography, 1906–1961. Garden City, N. Y., Doubleday, 1962. 256 pp.

An annotated list, including varying editions and translations.

Mead, George Herbert
(1863–1931)

Bibliography

4.4.30 **Natanson, Maurice.** The social dynamics of George Herbert Mead. Washington, Public Affairs Press, 1956. 102 pp.

Bibliography: pp. 96–102.

4.4.31 **Reck, Andrew.** "The writings of George Herbert Mead," *in* George Herbert Mead, Selected Writings, ed. by Andrew J. Reck, Indianapolis, Bobbs-Merrill, 1964, pp. lxiii–lxix.

Merleau-Ponty, Maurice
(1908–1961)

Bibliography

4.4.32 *★ Fischer, Alden L.* The essential writings of Merleau-Ponty. New York, Harcourt, Brace & World, Inc., 1969. 383 pp.

Bibliography: pp. 379–383.

Moore, George Edward
(1873–1958)

Bibliography

4.4.33 **Buchanan, Emerson,** and **G. E. Moore.** "Bibliography of the writings of G. E. Moore (to July, 1952)," *in* P. A. Schilpp, ed., The philosophy of G. E. Moore, 2d ed., La Salle, Ill., Open Court Publishing Company, 1952, pp. 689–699.

Ortega y Gasset, José
(1883–1955)

Works

4.4.34 **Obras completas.** Madrid, Revista de Occidente, 1962–65. 8v.

1st ed. 1946–47. 6v.

Russell, Bertrand Arthur William
(1872–1970)

Bibliography and Dictionary

4.4.35 **Dennon, L. E.** "Bibliography of the writings of Bertrand Russell to 1951," *in* P. A. Schilpp, ed., The philosophy of Bertrand Russell, 2d ed., New York, Tudor Pub. Co., 1952, pp. 743–804.

4.4.36 *★ Dorward, Alan.* Bertrand Russell. London, Longmans, Green & Co., 1951. 44 pp.

Published for the British Council, British book news as part of its Bibliographical series of supplements.

4.4.37 *★ Dennon, Lester E., ed.* Bertrand Russell's dictionary of mind, matter and morals. New York, Philosophical Library, 1952. 209 pp.

Santayana, George
(1863–1952)

Bibliography

4.4.38 **Escudero, C. S.** "Bibliografia general de Jorge Santayana," Miscelanea Comillas, XLIV (1965), 155–310.

Also published separately: Comillas, Pontificia Universitas Comillensis, 1965. 160 pp.

4.4.39 **Terzian, Shonig.** "Bibliography of the writings of G. Santayana to Oct. 1940," *in* P. A. Schilpp, ed., The philosophy of George Santayana, Evanston and Chicago, Northwestern University, 1940, pp. 607–668.

Works

4.4.40 **The works of George Santayana.** New York, Scribner's, 1936–40. 15v.

This collection is not complete.

Sartre, Jean-Paul
(1905–)

Bibliography

4.4.41 **Douglas, Kenneth.** "A critical bibliography of existentialism (The Paris School)," Yale French Studies special monograph, No. 1 (1950).

For a Sartre bibliography, see 301–442.

4.4.42 "**I. Sartre's works in French and English.** II. Books and pamphlets on Sartre; III. A selection of articles about Sartre," Yale French Studies, No. 30 (1963), 108–119.

Scheler, Max
(1874–1928)

Bibliography

4.4.43 **Kränzlin, Gerhard.** Max Schelers phänomenologische Systematik. Leipzig, Hirzel, 1934.

Bibliography: pp. 84–97.

4.4.44 **Hartmann, Wilfried.** Max Scheler; bibliographie. Stuttgart, Fromman, 1963. 128 pp.

Works

4.4.45 **Gesammelte Werke.** Hrsg. von Maria Scheler. Bern, Francke, 1953– .

In progress.
13v. projected.

Teilhard de Chardin, Pierre
(1881–1955)

Bibliography and Lexicon

4.4.46 **Cuénot, Claude,** et **Yves Vadé.** "Oeuvres, livres et principaux articles consacrés à Teilhard de Chardin," *in* Essais sur Teilhard de Chardin, ed. F. Russo, et al, Paris, Fayard, 1962, pp. 97–148.

See also *Archivum historicum Societas Iesu,* which annually carries a list of works about Teilhard de Chardin.

4.4.47 **Polgár, L.** Internationale Teilhard bibliographie 1955–65. Freiburg, Alber Verlag, 1965. 93 pp.

4.4.48 **Cuénot, Claude.** Nouveau lexique, Teilhard de Chardin. Paris, Ed. du Seuil, 1968. 224 pp.

Works

4.4.49 **Oeuvres.** Paris, Éditions de Seuil, 1955– .

In progress.
10v. projected.
Each volume issued separately under its own title.

Unamuno y Jugo, Miguel de
(1864–1936)

Works

4.4.50 **Obras completas.** Dirigada por Manuel García Blaco. Madrid, Aguado, 1950–1964. 15v.

Whitehead, Alfred North
(1861–1947)

Bibliography

4.4.51 **Kline, George L.** "Bibliography of writings by and about Alfred North Whitehead in languages other than English," *in* William Reese and Eugene Freeman, Process and Divinity, La Salle, Ill., Open Court Publishing Company, 1964, pp. 593–609.

4.4.52 **Lowe, Victor,** and **R. C. Baldwin.** "Bibliography of writings of Alfred North Whitehead to Nov. 1941 (with selected reviews)," *in* P. A. Schilpp, ed., The philosophy of Alfred North Whitehead, Evanston and Chicago, Northwestern University Press, 1941, pp. 701–725.

4.4.53 **Stokes, Walter E.** "A select and annotated bibliography of Alfred North Whitehead," The modern schoolman, XXXIX (1961–62), 131–151.

Wittgenstein, Ludwig Josef Johann
(1889–1951)

Bibliography

4.4.54 **Fann, K. T.** "Wittgenstein bibliography," International philospohical quarterly, VII (1967), 311–339.

Works

4.4.55 **Schriften.** Hrsg. von Friedrich Waismann. Frankfurt am Main, Suhrkamp Verlag, 1963– .

In progress.
4v. had appeared by 1969.

5. BIBLIOGRAPHIES

THE BIBLIOGRAPHIES contained in histories of philosophy, encyclopedias, and dictionaries serve as useful introductions to the pertinent literature, but they are seldom complete. Through the systematic use of the proper bibliographical tools, however, it is possible to compile a reasonably complete list of books and articles dealing with any philosophical topic or any philosopher. The compilation of a bibliography should not be a hit-or-miss endeavor and need not involve the search of an endless number of sources.

The general bibliographical guides listed in 5.1 describe bibliographical tools in related disciplines, specialized national bibliographies, and philosophical guides, some of which are especially useful for the countries in which they were written, and some of which are bibliographies in their own right.

The general bibliographies listed in 5.2 can be used to find published philosophical bibliographies and to supplement the specifically philosophical bibliographical tools listed in 5.3. Reviews of philosophical books and résumés of both books and articles can also be located using these tools.

Bibliographies have already been compiled and published on a great many philosophers and philosophical topics. Knowledge of their existence can accordingly save a great deal of time. The items of 5.4, 5.5, and 5.6 contain philosophical bibliographies specialized by language or area, movements, trends, tradition, or branch of philosophy. In some instances very full bibliographies are available. For some movements or branches of philosophy, no adequate bibliography is available. The omission of a particular movement, trend, etc., should consequently most frequently be taken as an indication of a bibliographical lacuna rather than as a negative value judgment as to its historical or philosophical importance. Bibliographies of individual philosophers are listed in chapter 4.

5.1 BIBLIOGRAPHICAL GUIDES

General

5.1.1 **Collison, Robert S.** Bibliographies, subject and national; a guide to their contents, arrangement and use. 2d ed., rev. and enl. London, Crosby Lockwood & Son Ltd., 1962. 185 pp.

A selected, annotated bibliography. See especially Part Two on universal and national bibliographies and serial publications.

5.1.2 **Walford, A. J.** Guide to reference material. London, Library Association, 1959. 543 pp.

Annotated guide to a wide variety of

reference books and bibliographies, with an emphasis on British material. A supplement of 370 pp. was issued in 1963.

A 2d ed. in 3v. is in progress: v. 1, Science and technology, 1966; v. 2, Philosophy and psychology, religion, social science, geography, biography, and history, 1968; v. 3 will cover generalia, language and literature, the arts.

5.1.3 **Winchell, Constance M.** Guide to reference books. 8th ed. Chicago, American Library Association, 1967. 741 pp.

An excellent annotated guide to general reference works in the humanities, social sciences, history and area studies, and the pure and applied sciences.

French

5.1.4 ⋆ **Malclès, L.-N.** Les sources du travail bibliographique. Genève, Droz, 1950–58. 3v. in 4.

Reprinted: 1965.
Vol. I, Bibliographies générales; vol. II, Bibliographies spécialisées: 1. Sciences humaines; vol. III: 2. Sciences exactes et techniques.
This supplements and replaces many older bibliographies. For general bibliographies and basic reference works, see vol. I. For philosophical bibliographies and basic reference works, see vol. II (2), pp. 633–683.

German

5.1.5 **Totok, Wilhelm,** und **Rolf Weitzel.** Handbuch der bibliographischen Nachschlagewerke. 2. Aufl. Frankfurt am Main, Vittorio Klostermann, 1959. 335 pp.

An annotated guide of both general reference works and those specialized by discipline.

Spanish

5.1.6 **Zammarriego, Thomas.** Enciclopedia de orientación bibliográfica. Barcelona, Flors, 1964. 4v.

An annotated guide.
See vol. II, pp. 611–793 for philosophy.

Philosophical

5.1.7 ⋆ **Borchardt, Dietrich Hans.** How to find out in philosophy and psychology. Oxford, Pergamon Press, 1968. 97 pp.

A descriptive guide to some of the basic reference works and bibliographies in philosophy.
The bibliography, pp. 75–94, contains a "List of works referred to."

5.1.8 **Gerber, William.** "Philosophical bibliographies," *Encyclopedia of Philosophy* (2.2.1), vol. VI, pp. 166–169.

An historico-descriptive account of philosophical bibliographies.

5.1.9 **Higgins, Charles L.** The bibliography of philosophy; a descriptive account. Ann Arbor, Mich., Campus Publishers, 1965. 29 pp.

A brief guide to some of the most important bibliographical tools in philosophy.

See also: 8.3.17.

French

5.1.10 **Hoffmans, Jean.** La philosophie et les philosophes; ouvrages généraux. Bruxelles, Van Oest, 1920. 395 pp.

Reprinted: N. Y., Burt Franklin, 1968.
Lists dictionaries, manuals, histories, editions and translations, journals and bibliographies. Neoscholastic in emphasis. Now dated and useful only for older works.

5.1.11 **Le Senne, René.** Introduction à la philosophie. 4. éd. Paris, Presses Universitaires de France, 1958. 480 pp.

Has approximately 21 pages of bibliography and philosophically useful works.

5.1.12 **Raeymaeker, Louis de.** Introduction à la philosophie. 5. éd. Louvain, Publications Universitaires de Louvain, 1964. 320 pp.

Pp. 197–304 list many useful books and bibliographies and contain a great deal of information on philosophical centers and organizations.

Orientation is primarily scholastic and neo-thomistic.

5.1.13 Varet, Gilbert. Manuel de bibliographie philosophique. Paris, Presses Universitaires de France, 1956. 2v.

Vol. I, pp. 1–39 list basic reference works in philosophy; pp. 45–494 list books dealing with classical philosophy, historically ordered (Orient, antiquity, Christian philosophy, Descartes, Cartesianism, English classical philosophy, Rousseau, Kant and Kantianism).

Vol. II: lists works on philosophical ideologies, culture, philosophy of history, of religion, of art, logic, epistemology, philosophy of the sciences, social philosophy, philosophy of law, of education, of being and value, and ethics.

Not only a guide but a bibliography which is particularly full in its coverage of the period 1914–34, which corresponds to the hiatus between the literature covered by Ueberweg (5.3.2) and de Brie (5.3.5).

German

5.1.14 Bochenski, I. M. Bibliographische Einführungen in das Studium der Philosophie. Bern, Francke, 1948–1953.

A collection of small booklets, each dedicated to a particular philosopher or movement. Not exhaustive in any instance, but useful as an introduction and guide to the study of the authors and movements included.

No. 1: I. M. Bochenski and F. Monteleone, Allgemeine philosophische Bibliographie, 1948, 42 pp.

No. 2: R. B. Winn, Amerikanische Philosophie, 1948, 32 pp.

No. 3: E. W. Beth, Symbolische Logik und Grundlegung der exakten Wissenschaften, 1948, 28 pp.

No. 4: R. Jolivet, Kierkegaard, 1948, 33 pp.

No. 5: O. Gigon, Antike Philosophie, 1948, 52 pp.

No. 6: P. J. DeManasce, Arabische Philosophie, 1948, 49 pp.

No. 7: M. F. Sciacca, Italienische Philosophie der Gegenwart, 1948, 36 pp.

No. 8: M.-D. Philippe, Aristoteles, 1948, 48 pp.

No. 9: R. Jolivet, Französische Existenz-philosophie, 1948, 36 pp.

No. 10: M. F. Sciacca, Augustinus, 1948, 32 pp.

No. 11: K. Dürr, Der logische Positivismus, 1948, 24 pp.

No. 12: O. Gigon, Platon, 1950, 30 pp.

No. 13/14: P. Wyser, Thomas von Aquin, 1950, 78 pp.

No. 15/16: P. Wyser, Der Thomismus, 1951, 120 pp.

No. 17: F. Van Steenberghen, Philosophie des Mittelalters, 1950, 52 pp.

No. 18: O. Perler, Patristische Philosophie, 1950, 44 pp.

No. 19: G. Vajda, Jüdische Philosophie, 1950, 40 pp.

No. 20/21: C. Regamey, Buddhistische Philosophie, 1950, 86 pp.

No. 22: O. Schäfer, Johannes Duns Scotus, 1953, 34 pp.

No. 23: O. F. Bollnow, Deutsche Existenz-philosophie, 1953, 40 pp.

See also: 5.3.3.

Italian

5.1.15 Ferro, C. Guida storico-bibliografica allo studio della filosofia. Milano, "Vita e Pensiero," 1949. 196 pp.

Bibliographies of "sources" and "studies" in the history of philosophy.

5.2 GENERAL BIBLIOGRAPHIES

5.2.1 Arnim, Max. Internationale Personalbibliographie 1800–1943. 2 Aufl. Stuttgart, Hiersemann, 1944–52. 2v.

———— Bd. III, 1944–1959 und Nachträge, von Gerhard Bock und Franz Hodes. 1963. 659 pp.

Useful for bibliographies of individual philosophers, especially Germans. Includes bibliographies in books, periodicals, biographical dictionaries and other publications. Indexed. The first edition (1936) covered 1850–1935.

5.2.2 Besterman, Theodore. A world bibliography of bibliographies. 4th ed. Lausanne, Societas Bibliographica, 1965–66. 5v.

V. 5 is an index. Contains bibliographies on individuals and general topics. For general bibliographies in philosophy, see "Philosophy," vol. III, cols. 4809–4827; but this section does not list bibliographies of individuals or of special subjects, which should be searched under the appropriate separate headings. Restricted to bibliographies which are published separately.

5.2.3 **Bibliographic index;** a cumulative bibliography of bibliographies, 1937– . New York, Wilson, 1938– .

Quarterly until mid-1951, then semiannually, with annual and more inclusive cumulations.
This is the best source for keeping up with new personal and subject bibliographies, published separately, as parts of books, or in periodicals.

5.2.4 **Bohatta, Hanns,** und **Franz Hodes.** Internationale Bibliographie der Bibliographien. Ein Nachschlagewerk, unter Mitwerkung von Walther Funke. Frankfurt am Main, Klostermann, 1950. 652 pp.

Covers general, national, and subject bibliographies.

5.2.5 **Book review digest,** 1905– . New York, Wilson, 1905– .

Monthly, with annual cumulations and five-yearly cumulative subject and title indexes. Includes excerpts from 80 book-review periodicals, some of which review books in philosophy.

5.2.6 **British humanities index,** 1962– . London, Library Association, 1963– .

Quarterly, with annual cumulations.
A partial continuation of *Subject Index to Periodicals,* 1915–61. Indexes only British periodicals.

5.2.7 **Index bibliographicus;** directory of current periodical abstracts and bibliographies. Compiled by Theodore Besterman. 3d ed. Paris, UNESCO, 1952. 2v.

Lists periodicals with abstracts, reviews, and bibliographies. Vol. I: Science and technology.

Vol. II: Social sciences, education, humanistic studies.
A 4th ed. is in progress, 1959– .

5.2.8 **Index to book reviews in the humanities.** Detroit, Phillip Thomson, 1960– . Annual.

Indexes reviews which appear in about 700 journals.

5.2.9 **Index translationum.** *See* 8.2.1.

Lists works translated; arranged by country.

5.2.10 **Internationale Bibliographie der Zeitschriftenliteratur** aus allen Gebieten des Wissens (International bibliography of periodical literature covering all fields of knowledge). Osnabrück, Felix Dietrich, 1965– . Semiannual.

The most comprehensive of all indexes, covering more than 7600 periodicals. Very useful, especially to fill in gaps in coverage supplied by the philosophical bibliographies. Previously published in three sections:
Abteilung A: Bibliographie der deutschen Zeitschriftenliteratur, 1896–1964. A supplement in 20v. covers 1861–95.
Abteilung B: Bibliographie der fremdspachigen Zeitschriftenliteratur, 1911–1964.
Abteilung C: Bibliographie der Rezensionen und Referate, 1900–1942.
Reprinted: N. Y., Kraus Reprint Corp., 1960–62, 238v. (up to 1944).

5.2.11 **Nineteenth century readers' guide** to periodical literature, 1890–1899, with supplementary indexing, 1900–1922. Ed. by Helen Grant Cusing and Ada V. Morris. New York, Wilson, 1944. 2v.

An index to 51 periodicals. Only of peripheral philosophical interest.

5.2.12 **Poole's index to periodical literature,** 1802–1881. Rev. ed. Boston, Houghton Mifflin, 1891. 2v.

Supplements: Jan. 1882–Jan. 1, 1907. Boston, 1887–1908. 5v.
A subject index of 470 American and English journals.

5.2.13 **Readers' guide to periodical literature,** 1900– . New York, Wilson, 1905– .

Issued semimonthly (monthly July and August) with annual and larger cumulations. Indexes primarily popular, nontechnical periodicals. Of limited use in preparing the ordinary philosophical bibliography, but of value in locating popular articles by philosophers or on philosophers or philosophical topics.

5.2.14 Social sciences and humanities index. New York, Wilson, 1916– .

Quarterly with annual and larger cumulations. Formerly, *International Index; a Guide to Periodical Literature in the Social Sciences and Humanities.* Name changes with v. 53, no. 1, June, 1965.

Indexes scholarly journals, some of them in philosophy.

5.3 GENERAL PHILOSOPHICAL BIBLIOGRAPHIES

The Basic Bibliographies

These are the most important sources for working up a bibliography in philosophy. They are listed in the order of their coverage, and so in the order in which they would generally be used in developing a retrospective bibliography.

5.3.1 Rand, Benjamin. Bibliography of philosophy, psychology and cognate subjects. New York, Macmillan, 1905. IV. in 2.

Reprinted: N. Y., Peter Smith, 1949.
This is vol. III of Baldwin (1.2.1).
Pt. 1 deals with general works and the history of philosophy. Pt. 2 deals with systematic philosophy. It is especially good in its 16th, 17th, 18th, and 19th century references. Though not exhaustive in its coverage, which goes up to 1902, it is extremely comprehensive.
Supplements appeared in the *Psychological Index* from 1901–08.

5.3.2 Ueberweg, F. Grundriss der Geschichte der Philosophie. 11.–12. Aufl. See 3.1.16.

Covers the period of roughly up to 1920. Extremely full bibliographical information, with some emphasis on German scholarship. Some duplication with Rand.

5.3.3 Totok, Wilhelm. Handbuch der Geschichte der Philosophie: I. Altertum; Indische, Chinesische, Griechisch-Römische Philosophie. Unter Mitarbeit von Helmut Schröer. Frankfurt, V. Klostermann, 1964. 400 pp.

Very full bibliographies from 1920 on, and so vol. I completes Ueberweg for Ancient Indian, Chinese, and Greek and Roman philosophy. Pp. 1–11 are a systematic bibliographical overview of the history of philosophy. Two additional volumes covering the Middle Ages and modern times are in progress.

5.3.4 Varet, G. Manuel de bibliographie philosophique. See 5.1.13.

By intent, especially full for the period between Ueberweg (5.3.2) and De Brie (5.3.5).

5.3.5 De Brie, G. A. Bibliographia philosophica 1934–1945. Bruxellis, Editiones Spectrum, 1950–1954. 2v.

Vol. I, "Bibliographia historiae philosophiae," contains a chronological list of works on and by philosophers. Vol. II, "Bibliographia philosophiae," is divided by branches of philosophy. Though the headings are in Latin, the "Introduction" and other service material are in six languages, including English. Included are books, articles (over 400 philosophical journals searched), and reviews, published during 1934–45 in Danish, Dutch, English, French, German, Italian, Latin, Norwegian, Portuguese, Spanish, Catalan, and Swedish. Vol. II ends with an index of names appearing in the two volumes.

5.3.6 Répertoire bibliographique de la philosophie. 1949– .

From 1934–49 it appeared as a supplement to the *Revue néoscholastique de philosophie* (see 7.3.19). Since 1949 it has been issued separately, though still an annex to the *Revue philosophique de Louvain* (called the *Revue néoscholastique* until 1945). It contained the "Sommaire idéologique des ouvrages et des revues de philosophie" which appeared under varying titles 1895–1905, 1906–07, 1908–14. Not published 1915–33, 1941–45. Since 1939 the

Repertoire has also appeared with Dutch headings as "Bibliographisch Repertorium" in *Tijdschrift voor Philosophie.* This appeared during the war when the *Revue néoscholastique* was suspended.

A quarterly listing books and articles in philosophy. Divided like De Brie (5.3.5), two sections in each issue. The fourth (Nov.) issue carries a list of book reviews and an index of names.

5.3.7 **Bibliographie de la philosophie.** Institute international de philosophie. 1937–52/53. Paris, Vrin, 1937–58. 10v.

Lists books and articles. Vol. I (1) catalog of editors; (2) catalog of philosophical journals; (3) catalog of names of authors. Vol. II (1) historical (by period) and geographical (by country); (2) philosophers (on whom books and articles have been written); (3) topics (based on Lalande, 1.2.12). It provides a brief résumé in the language of the book in question where the title is not selfexplanatory. It did not appear from July 1939–December 1945. After 1953 it was continued as 5.3.8.

5.3.8 **Bibliography of philosophy.** *See* 7.2.6.

A continuation of 5.3.7. It lists only books (no articles) but gives brief summaries of many. Divided into nine subject (topical) headings. Alphabetical classification according to author under each of the subject headings. The last issue each year has an author index and an analytic subject index.

5.3.9 **Bulletin analytique:** philosophie. Paris, Centre de documentation du C.N.R.S., 1944–55. v. 1–9.

Lists journal articles only, and provides a brief noncritical résumé of each. Continued as 5.3.10.

5.3.10 **Bulletin signalétique:** sciences humaines, philosophie. Paris, Centre de documentation de C.N.R.S., v. 10– , 1956– . Quarterly.

A continuation of 5.3.9. Series 19 (1961–63); series 19–23 (1964); series 19–24 (1965–). Lists abstracts in French of philosophical articles and reviews. Coverage is worldwide and attempts to be exhaustive.

5.3.11 **The philosopher's index;** an international index to philosophical periodicals. Quarterly.

See 7.2.57. Covers the major philosophical periodicals and attempts to index and summarize all articles published in the preceding quarter.

Auxiliary Bibliographies

Each of the following is of limited scope and usefulness, but may be used to supplement the preceding list in various ways.

5.3.12 **Bibliographie critique.** Paris, G. Beauchesne, 1924– . 1922–29, annual; 1930– , biennial.

Contains reviews of the principal philosophical works of the year or biennium. A supplement to *Archives de philosophie* (7.3.2).

5.3.13 **Bibliography of current philosophical works** published in North America. St. Louis, St. Louis University, 1948– .

May 1948–May 1955, January 1959– issued as a section of *The Modern Schoolman* (7.2.50). Nov. 1955–May 1958 issued as separately paged supplement. Title varies slightly.

5.3.14 **Bibliography of philosophy,** 1933–36. New York, Journal of Philosophy, 1934–37.

An annual bibliography which appeared in the *Journal of Philosophy* (7.2.35). It included books and articles published in English, French, German, and Italian, but was selective in its coverage.

5.3.15 **Decennial index to philosophical literature,** 1939–1950. New York, Russell F. Moore, 1952. 115 pp.

Author, title, and subject list of "important books" in philosophy and cognate fields. Prepared in connection with 5.3.18.

5.3.16 **McLean, George F.** Philosophy in the 20th century; Catholic and Christian. New York, Frederick Ungar, 1967. 2v.

Vol. I, An annotated bibliography of philosophy in Catholic thought 1900–1964. Restricted to entries in English; primarily American.

Vol. II, A bibliography of Christian philosophy and contemporary ideas. International in coverage.

Both volumes interpret "Catholic and Christian" in a very broad sense, and include the writings of non-Christians if they bear on religion.

5.3.17 Index philosophique; philosophie et science. Année 1–2 (1902–03). Paris, Chevalier, 1903–05. 2v.

Indexes both articles and books for the years indicated.

5.3.18 Philosophic abstracts. New York, Philosophic Abstracts, 1939–54.

Contains English abstracts of books from many countries and lists of periodical articles. *Decennial Index to Philosophical Literature, 1939–1950*, New York, R. F. Moore, 1952, is an index of v. 1–12.

5.3.19 Philosophical books. Leicester University Press, 1960– . *See* 7.2.59.

A review of books, foreign and English. Selective in its coverage.

5.3.20 Philosophie; chronique des années de guerre, 1939–1945; d'après guerre, 1946–1948. Publié par l'Institut International de Philosophie. Editeur, Raymond Bayer. Paris, Hermann, 1950. 5v.

Covers history of philosophy, metaphysics, philosophy of value, philosophy of science, psychology, phenomenology, and existentialism.

5.3.21 Die Philosophie der Gegenwart: eine internationale Jahresübersicht. Heidelberg, Weiss, 1910–15.

Annotated lists of books and periodical articles, especially German, covering the years 1908–13. Edited by Arnold Ruge.

5.3.22 Philosophischer Literaturanzeiger. Meisenheim/Glan, Anton Hain KG, 1949– .

Published in conjunction with *Zeitschrift für philosophische Forschung* (7.3.34). Contains reviews of the most significant books of the preceding period. Appears six times a year.

5.3.23 Répertoire bibliographique de philosophie des sciences. Paris, 1950– .

A supplement of the *Bulletin de l'Académie internationale de philosophie des sciences (Actualités scientifiques et industrielles. Archives de l'Institut international des sciences théoriques).*

5.3.24 Revue internationale de philosophie. *See* 7.3.17.

Each issue dedicated to one subject, e.g., no. 6 (Aug. 1948) "Liberté"; no. 9 (July 1949) "Existentialisme."

5.3.25 Scripta recenter edita. Nijmegen, Netherlands, 1959– .

Issued 10 times a year. Lists books on philosophy and theology. Each issue contains about 400 entries, with some emphasis on theology.

5.4 PHILOSOPHICAL BIBLIOGRAPHIES: SPECIALIZED BY LANGUAGE OR AREA

For philosophical works of individual countries, see also the various national bibliographies listed in Collison (5.1.1), Walford (5.1.2), and Winchell (5.1.3).

Anglo-American

5.4.1 Kurtz, Paul, *ed.* The American philosophers. New York, Macmillan, 1965–66. 2v.

Vol. I, American thought before 1900; a sourcebook, from puritanism to Darwinism. 448 pp.

Vol. II, American philosophy in the twentieth century; a sourcebook, from pragmatism to philosophical analysis. 573 pp.

Bibliographies throughout and at the end of each volume.

5.4.2 ★ Rorty, Amelie, *ed.* Pragmatic philosophy; anthology. New York, Doubleday, 1966. 548 pp.

Bibliography: pp. 523–48.

See also: 3.6.1–3.6.14, 3.6.22, 5.1.14 (No. 2), 5.3.13, 5.3.16, 5.5.1–5.5.5, 5.5.17.

Arabic

5.4.3 **Calverley, E.** "A brief bibliography of arabic philosophy," The Moslem world, XXXII (1942), 60–68.

5.4.4 **Chauvin, V.** Bibliographie des ouvrages arabes ou relatifs aux Arabes publiées dans l'Europe chrétienne de 1810 à 1885. Liège, H. Vaillant-Carmanne, 1892–1922. 12v.

5.4.5 **Pearson, J.** Index Islamicus 1906–55. Cambridge, Heffer, 1958. 897 pp.

1st supplement 1956–60, Cambridge, Heffer, 1962, 312 pp.
2nd supplement 1961–65, Cambridge, Heffer, 1967, 342 pp.

5.4.6 **Pfannmüller, P. G.** Handbuch der Islam-Literatur. Berlin, de Gruyter, 1923. 436 pp.

5.4.7 **Sarton, Georges.** Introduction to the history of science. *See* 5.6.42.

A rich source of bibliography for Arabic, as well as Western, philosophy and science.

5.4.8 **Sauvaget, J.** Introduction to the history of the Muslim East: a bibliographical guide. Berkeley, University of California Press, 1965. 252 pp.

Based on the 2d edition of J. Sauvaget, *Introduction à l'histoire de l'orient muselman; eléments de bibliographie,* refondue et completée par Claude Cahen, Paris, Adrien-Maisonneuve, 1961, 252 pp.

See also: 5.1.13 (pp. 159–169), 5.1.14 (No. 6), 5.3.3.

Chinese

5.4.9 **Wing-tsit Chan.** An outline and annotated bibliography of Chinese philosophy. New Haven, Yale Far Eastern Publications, 1959. 127 pp.

5.4.10 ★ **Wing-tsit Chan.** Chinese philosophy, 1949–1963; an annotated biliography of mainland China publications. Honolulu, East-West Center Press, 1967. 290 pp.

See also: 3.6.15–3.6.19.

French

5.4.11 **"Bibliographie philosophique française de l'année,"** L'année philosophique, v. 1–24, 1890–1913. *See* 7.3.1.

An annual bibliography of philosophical books in French which appeared during the years of its publication.

5.4.12 **Union française des organismes de documentation** (Paris). Manuel de la recherche documentaire en France; . . . Philosophie. Pub. sous la direction de Raymond Bayer. Bayeux, Colas, 1950. 421 pp.

See also: 3.6.20–3.6.22, 5.3.20.

German

5.4.13 **Die deutschen Universitätsschriften zur Philosophie** und ihre Grenzgebieten. Erfurt, 1924–30. Annual.

Ed. Kurt Gassen.

5.4.14 **Koehler & Volckmar-Fachbibliographien:** Philosophie und Grenzgebiete 1945–1964. Stuttgart, Koehler & Volckmar, 1965. 434 pp.

Bibliography of all philosophical works in the German language, 1945 to 1964, with a list of periodicals.

5.4.15 **Literarische Berichte aus dem Gebiete der Philosophie.** Erfurt, 1–26, 1923–32. Semiannual.

Bibliography of German periodicals, together with bibliographies of individual philosophers.

5.4.16 **Philosophischer Literaturanzeiger.** *See* 5.3.22.

In 1959 it absorbed *Deutsche philosophische Bibliographie.* A section entitled "Neue Bücher" lists new books in philosophy published in German.

See also: 3.6.23, 3.6.24.

Greek

5.4.17 **Voumvlinopoulous, Georges E.** Bibliographie critique de la philosophie grecque depuis la chute de Constantinople à nos jours, 1453–1953. Athènes, Institut français d'Athènes, 1966. 236 pp.

Indian

5.4.18 **Dandekar, R. N.** Vedic bibliography; an up-to-date comprehensive and analytically arranged register of all important work done since 1930 in the field of the veda and allied antiquities. Bombay, Karnatak, "New Indiana Antiquary," 1946. 395 pp.

5.4.19 **Renou, L.** Bibliographie védique. Paris, Maisonneuve, 1931. 339 pp.

5.4.20 **Renou, L.** "Travaux récents sur la philosophie indienne," Diogène, 1954, pp. 133–41.

5.4.21 **Riepe, Dale.** "Recent Indian philosophical literature," Philosophy and phenomenological research, XV (1955), 563–570.

5.4.22 **Riepe, Dale.** "Indian philosophical literature 1955–1957," Philosophy and phenomenological research, XVIII (1957–58), 384–387.

5.4.23 ★ **Radhakrishnan, Sarvepalli,** and **C. S. Moore,** eds. A source book in Indian philosophy. Princeton, N. J., Princeton University Press, 1957. 683 pp.

Bibliography: pp. 643–669.

See also: 3.6.25, 3.6.26.

Italian

5.4.24 **Bibliografia filosofica italiana** dal 1900 al 1950. Roma, Delfino, 1950–56. 4v.

Continued by 5.4.25.

5.4.25 **Bibliografia filosofica italiana.** Milano, Marzorati, 1951– . Annual.

Continues 5.4.24 in periodical form.

See also: 3.6.29 and 5.1.14 (No. 7).

Jewish

5.4.26 **Kirjath Sepher.** 1923– .

Useful for recent bibliographies.
Index: v. 1–15, 1923–39; v. 16–25, 1940–50.

5.4.27 **Shunami, S.** Bibliography of Jewish bibliographies. Jerusalem, University Press, 1936. 399 pp.

See also: 3.6.30, 3.6.31, 5.1.13 (pp. 170–190), 5.1.14 (No. 19).

Oriental

5.4.28 **Moore, Russell Franklin.** Bibliography for Oriental philosophies. New York, Russell F. Moore, Co., 1951. 11 pp.

Reprinted from W. D. Gould, G. B. Arbaugh, R. F. Moore, *Oriental Philosophies*, 3d ed., New York, R. F. Moore Co., 1951, 220 pp.

5.4.29 **Müller, A., E. Kuhn, L. Scherman.** Orientalische Bibliographie 1887–1911. Berlin, Reuther, 1888–1922. 24v.

The best bibliography for the period covered.

5.4.30 **Senny, I.** Tranductions françaises de littératures orientales. Bruxelles, Commission Belge de bibliographie, 1958. 299 pp.

See also: 5.1.13, pp. 45–67.

Russian

5.4.31 **Bibliographie der sowjetischen Philosophie.** Dordrecht, Holland, D. Reidel Publishing Co., 1959–68. 7v.

Lists Soviet philosophical books and articles, 1947–66. Continued by bibliographies in *Studies in Soviet Thought* (7.2.84).

5.4.32 * **Edie, James M., James P. Scanlan,** & **Mary-Barbara Zeldin;** with the collaboration of George L. Kline. Russian philosophy. Chicago, Quadrangle Books, 1965. 3v.

An anthology of Russian philosophy with bibliographies throughout of primary and secondary sources.

5.4.33 **Küng, Guido.** "Bibliography of Soviet work in the field of mathematical logic and the foundations of mathematics, from 1917-1957," Notre Dame journal of formal logic, III (1962), 1-40.

See also: 3.6.32, 3.6.33.

Scandinavian

5.4.34 **"Scandinavian bibliography"**, Theoria (7.2.88).

Philosophical works published in Denmark, Finland, Norway, and Sweden are listed once a year.

Spanish and Spanish American

5.4.35 **Bibliografía Argentina de Filosofía.** La Plata, Inst. Bibliográfico, 1960– .

Irregular, but attempts to issue one volume a year.

5.4.36 **Martínez Gómez, Luis.** Bibliografía filosófica española e hispanoamericana. Barcelona, Flors, 1961. 502 pp.

Covers the period from 1940 to 1958.

See also: 3.6.34.

5.5 PHILOSOPHICAL BIBLIOGRAPHIES: SPECIALIZED BY MOVEMENTS, TRENDS, OR TRADITIONS

Analytic Philosophy

5.5.1 * **Ayer, A. J.,** ed. Logical positivism. Glencoe, Ill., The Free Press, 1959. 455 pp.

Bibliography: pp. 381-446. An excellent bibliography of the philosophical literature in the analytic tradition. The best bibliography available on this topic.

5.5.2 **Black, M.,** ed. Philosophical analysis; a collection of essays. Ithaca, Cornell University Press, 1950. 429 pp.

Bibliography: pp. 421-426.

5.5.3 **New, J.,** and **R. Rorty.** "Bibliography of writings in English on linguistic method in philosophy and related issues, 1930-1965," in Rorty, Richard, ed., Linguistic turn; recent essays in philosophical method, University of Chicago Press, 1967, pp. 361-393.

5.5.4 **Feigl, H.,** and **W. Sellars,** eds. Readings in philosophical analysis. New York, Appleton-Century-Crofts, 1949. 626 pp.

Bibliography: pp. 617-626.

5.5.5 **Williams, Bernard,** and **Alan Montefiore,** eds. British analytical philosophy. New York, Humanities Press, 1966. 346 pp.

Bibliography: pp. 335-343.

See also: 3.5.9.

Buddhism

5.5.6 **Bibliographie bouddhique.** Paris, Maison-neuve, 1928– .

An international periodical with résumés.

5.5.7 **Hanayama, S.** Bibliography on Buddhism. Tokyo, Hokuseido Press, 1961. 869 pp.

See also: 5.1.13 (pp. 45-67), and 5.1.14 (No. 20/21).

Existentialism

5.5.8 **Douglas, Kenneth.** "A critical bibliography of existentialism (The Paris School)," Yale French Studies, 1950. See 4.4.41.

5.5.9 **Valentini, Francesco.** "Esistenzialismo e marxismo; rassegna di scritti francesi," Giornale critico della filosofia italiana, XXXI (1952), 78-96.

5.5.10 **Yanitelli, Victor R.** "A bibliographical introduction to existentialism," Modern schoolman, XXVI (1949), 345–363.

See also: 5.1.14 (Nos. 9 and 23), 5.3.20, 5.3.24, 7.2.33.

Idealism

5.5.11 **Ewing, A. C.,** *ed.* The idealist tradition; from Berkeley to Blanshard. Glencoe, Ill., Free Press, 1957. 369 pp.

Bibliography: pp. 347–362.

Marxism

5.5.12 ★ **The American bibliography of Russian and East European studies.** Indiana University Press, 1958– .

An annual bibliography of works in the Slavic and Soviet Area, including Marxist philosophy; 1947–57 in one volume (1958).

5.5.13 **Kolarz, Walter.** Books on Communism; a bibliography. 2d ed. New York, Oxford University Press, 1964. 568 pp.

1st ed. 1959, by R. N. C. Hunt.

5.5.14 **Lachs, John.** Marxist philosophy; a bibliographical guide. Chapel Hill, University of North Carolina Press, 1967. 166 pp.

A partially annotated list of articles and books in English, German, and French on various aspects of Marxist philosophy. A useful guide to the literature.

See also: 4.3.82, 5.4.31, 5.4.32, 5.6.2, 7.2.84.

Phenomenology

5.5.15 **Spiegelberg, H.** The phenomenological movement; a historical introduction. *See* 3.5.8.

Bibliographies of Franz Brentano, Edmund Husserl, Max Scheler, Martin Heidegger, Nicolai Hartmann, Gabriel Marcel, J.-P. Sartre, Maurice Merleau-Ponty, as well as of general works.

See also: 5.5.17, 7.2.39.

Positivism

5.5.16 **Ducassé, Pierre.** La méthode positive et l'intuition comtienne; bibliographie. Paris, Alcan, 1939. 172 pp.

See also: 5.1.14 (No. 11), 5.5.1.

Realism

5.5.17 **Chisholm, Roderick M.,** *ed.* Realism and the background of phenomenology. Glencoe, Ill., The Free Press, 1960. 308 pp.

Bibliography: pp. 283–304.

Thomistic Philosophy

5.5.18 **Mandonnet, P.,** et **J. Destrez.** Bibliographie thomiste. La Saulchoir, Kain (Belgique), Revue des sciences philosophiques et theologiques, 1921. 116 pp.

Includes works pertaining to the study of the life, work, and thought of St. Thomas Aquinas, 1800–1920.
Continued by 5.5.19 and 5.5.20.

5.5.19 **Bourke, Vernon J.** "Thomistic bibliography, 1920–1940," The modern schoolman. Suppl. to vol. XXI. St. Louis, 1945. 312 pp.

A continuation of 5.5.18. It lists both books and articles and covers theological as well as philosophical topics.

5.5.20 **Bulletin thomiste,** 1924– . *See* 7.3.5.

Carries critical bibliographical information concerning Thomism, often with résumés or critical analyses, as a continuation of 5.5.18.

See also: 3.3.1–3.3.3, 3.3.6, 3.3.8–3.3.11, 4.2.93, 5.1.14 (No. 15/16), 5.3.16.

5.6 PHILOSOPHICAL BIBLIOGRAPHIES: SPECIALIZED BY BRANCH OF PHILOSOPHY

Aesthetics

5.6.1 **Albert, Ethel M.,** and **Clyde Kluckhorn.** A selected bibliography on values, ethics and aesthetics in the behavioral sciences and philosophy, 1920–1958. Glencoe, Ill., Free Press, 1959. 342 pp.

An annotated list of books and articles.

5.6.2 **Baxandall, Lee.** Marxism and aesthetics; a selective annotated bibliography; books and articles in the English language. New York, Humanities Press, 1968. 261 pp.

5.6.3 **Bibliographie d'esthétique** (1950). Revue esthétique, V (1952), 71–110, 177–206.

5.6.4 **Beardsley, M. C.** Aesthetics. New York, Harcourt, Brace, 1958. 614 pp.

Copious bibliographies follow each section.

5.6.5 **Chandler, Albert R.,** and **Edward H. Barnhart.** A bibliography of psychological and experimental aesthetics, 1864–1937. London, Cambridge University Press, 1938, 190 pp.

5.6.6 **Draper, J. W.** Eighteenth century English aesthetics; a bibliography. Heidelberg, Winter, 1931. 140 pp.

Supplemented by: W. D. Tempelman, "Contributions to the bibliography of eighteenth-century aesthetics," *Modern Philology,* XXX (1932–33), 309–316.

5.6.7 **Hammond, W. A.** A bibliography of aesthetics and of the philosophy of the fine arts from 1900 to 1932. Rev. ed. New York, Longmans, Green & Co., 1934. 205 pp.

Covers 1900–32 and continues Rand (5.3.1). Continued by "Selective current bibliography for aesthetics and related fields," in the June issue of *Journal of Aesthetics and Art Criticism,* from 1941.

Reprinted: N. Y., Russell & Russell, 1966.

5.6.8 **Pinilla, Norberto.** Bibliografía de estética. Santiago de Chile, M. Barros Borgoño, 1939. 64 pp.

5.6.9 * **Wollheim, Richard.** Art and its objects; an introduction to aesthetics. New York, Harper, 1968. 152 pp.

Bibliography: pp. 135–152.

See also: 2.2.1 (I, 33–35), 3.7.1–3.7.3, 5.1.13 (II, 562–608), 5.3.1 (II, 704–744).

Ethics

5.6.10 **Bastide, Georges.** Ethics and political philosophy. French bibliographical digest, No. 34. New York, Cultural Center of the French Embassy, 1961. 96 pp.

Also published as: *Morale et philosophie politique,* Paris, Assoc. pour la diffusion de la pensée française, 1961. 91 pp.

5.6.11 * **Rescher, Nicholas.** Introduction to value theory. Englewood Cliffs, N. J., Prentice-Hall, 1969. 199 pp.

"Bibliography on the Theory of Value," pp. 149–186.

5.6.12 **Sellars, W.,** and **J. Hospers.** Readings in ethical theory. New York, Appleton-Century-Crofts, 1952. 707 pp.

Bibliography: pp. 701–707.

See also: 1.3.4, 1.3.7, 2.2.1 (III, 112–117; 133–134), 3.7.4–3.7.8, 5.1.13 (II, 848–864), 5.3.1 (II, 812–891), 5.6.1, 5.6.51.

Logic

5.6.13 **Ainvelle, Varin d'.** Logic and the philosophy of science. French bibliographical digest, No. 29. New York, Cultural Center of the French Embassy, 1959. 60 pp.

5.6.14 **Cheng, Chung-ying.** "Selected bibliography with annotations and comments," in his "Inquiries into classical Chinese logic," Philosophy East and West, XV (1965), 204–215.

5.6.15 **Church, Alonzo.** "A bibliography of symbolic logic," Journal of symbolic logic, I (1936), 121–218.

Covers the years 1666–1935 Additions and corrections: *Journal of Symbolic Logic,* III (1938), 178–212.

5.6.16 **Church, Alonzo.** "Brief bibliography of formal logic," Proceedings of the American Academy of Arts and Sciences, LXXX (1952), 155–172.

5.6.17 **Risse, Wilhelm.** Bibliographia logica. Hildesheim, Olms, 1965– .

V. 1 includes separately printed works on logic from 1472–1800. 293 pp.

V. 2 will cover 1801–1964, v. 3 review articles, and v. 4 manuscripts.

See also: 3.7.9–3.7.11, 5.1.13 (II, 619–646), 5.1.14 (No. 3), 5.3.1 (II, 647–703), 7.2.38, 7.2.53.

Metaphysics

5.6.18 **De George, Richard T.,** *ed.* Classical and contemporary metaphysics; a source book. New York, Holt, Rinehart and Winston, 1962. 323 pp.

Bibliographies at the end of each Part.

5.6.19 **Drennen, D. A.,** *ed.* Modern introduction to metaphysics, readings from classical and contemporary sources. Glencoe, Ill., Free Press, 1962. 738 pp.

Bibliographies at the end of each Part.

See also: 2.2.1 (V, 299–300, 306–307), 3.7.12, 5.1.13 (II, 864–910), 5.6.51.

Philosophical Anthropology

5.6.20 **Landmann, Michael,** [u.a.]. De homine, der Mensch, im Spiegel seines Gedankens. Munich, Alber, 1962. 620 pp.

Bibliography: pp. 543–614.

See also: 5.1.13 (II, 735–777).

Philosophy of Education

5.6.21 ★ **Broudy, Harry S.** [and others]. Philosophy of education; an organization of topics and selected sources. Urbana, University of Illinois Press, 1967. 287 pp.

An annotated bibliography relating philosophy and education.

See also: Review of educational research, Washington, 1931– , 5.1.13 (II, 834–848), 7.2.83.

Philosophy of History

5.6.22 **Danto, Arthur.** Analytical philosophy of history. Cambridge, University Press, 1965. 318 pp.

Bibliographical references in "Notes," pp. 285–313.

5.6.23 ★ **Nadel, George H.,** *ed.* Studies in the philosophy of history; selected essays from History and theory [7.2.22]. New York, Harper & Row, 1965. 220 pp.

Bibliographical footnotes.

5.6.24 **Nowicki, M.** "Bibliography of works in the philosophy of history 1958–1961," History and theory, 1964. 25 pp.

Beiheft 3 to 7.2.22. A continuation of 5.6.25.

5.6.25 **Rule, John C.** "Bibliography of works in the philosophy of history 1945–1957," History and theory, 1961. 87 pp.

Beiheft 1 to 7.2.22. 87 pp.

5.6.26 **Wurgaft, Lewis D.** "Bibliography of works in the philosophy of history 1962–1965," History and theory, 1967.

Beiheft 7 to 7.2.22, pp. 1–45. A continuation of 5.6.24.

See also: 7.2.22.

Philosophy of Law

5.6.27 **Conte, Amedeo G.** "Bibliografia de logica giuridica (1936–1960)," Revista internazionale di filosofia del diritto, XXXVIII (1961), 120–144.

Addenda, XXXIX (1962), 45–46.

5.6.28 **Friedmann, Wolfgang Gaston.** Legal theory. 5th ed. New York, Columbia University Press, 1967. 607 pp.

Bibliography: pp. 581–592.

5.6.29 ★ **Friedrich, C. J.** Philosophy of law in historical perspective. 2d ed. Chicago, University of Chicago Press, 1963. 296 pp.

Bibliography: pp. 277–284.

5.6.30 **Golding, M. P.** The nature of law; readings in legal philosophy. New York, Random House, 1966. 276 pp.

Bibliography: pp. 275–278.

5.6.31 ★ **Pound, Roscoe.** An introduction to the philosophy of law. Rev. ed. New Haven, Yale University Press, 1954. 201 pp.

1st ed. 1922. 307 pp.
Bibliography: pp. 285–307.

See also: 3.7.13, 3.7.15, 3.7.19, 5.1.13 (II, 778–816).

Philosophy of Mathematics

5.6.32 **Mostowski, Andrzej.** Thirty years of foundational studies; lectures on the development of mathematical logic and the study of the foundations of mathematics in 1930–1964. (Acta philosophica Fennica, no. 17.) New York, Barnes & Noble, 1966. 180 pp.

Bibliography: pp. 157–171.

See also: 2.2.1 (V, 210–213), 5.6.13–5.6.17.

Philosophy of Mind

5.6.33 **Chappell, V. C.,** *ed.* The philosophy of mind. Englewood Cliffs, N. J., Prentice-Hall, 1962. 178 pp.

Bibliography: pp. 173–178.

5.6.34 **Minnesota studies in the philosophy of science,** vol. II: Concepts, theories, and the mind-body problem. Ed. by Herbert Feigl, Michael Scriven, and Grover Maxwell for the Minnesota Center for Philosophy of Science. Minneapolis, University of Minnesota Press, 1958. 553 pp.

Bibliographies throughout; see especially pp. 484–497.

See also: 5.6.51.

Philosophy of Religion

5.6.35 **Berkowitz, Morris I.,** and **Edmund J. Johnson.** Social scientific studies of religion; a bibliography. Pittsburgh, Pittsburgh University Press, 1967. 258 pp.

Philosophy of Science

5.6.36 **"Critical bibliography of the history of science** and its cultural influences." Isis, 1913– .

The title varies.
Isis carries a continuing bibliography in the philosophy of science. *See* 7.2.28.

5.6.37 ★ **Danto, Arthur,** and **Sidney Morgenbesser,** *eds.* Philosophy of science. New York, Meridian Books, Inc., 1960. 477 pp.

Selected bibliography: pp. 471–477.

5.6.38 **Feigl, Herbert,** and **May Brodbeck,** *eds.* Readings in the philosophy of science. New York, Appleton-Century-Crofts, 1953. 811 pp.

Bibliography: pp. 783–799.

5.6.39 **Grünbaum, Adolf.** Philosophical problems of space and time. New York, Knopf, 1963. 448 pp.

Bibliography: pp. 429–446.

5.6.40 **Logic and the philosophy of science:** with an introduction by Robert Blanché. French bibliographical digest, No. 30. New York, Cultural Center of the French Embassy, 1959. 60 pp.

Annotated.

5.6.41 **Sarton, George H.** A guide to the history of science. New York, Ronald Press Co., 1952. 316 pp.

See pp. 86–93 for Scientific methods and the philosophy of science; pp. 194–248 for journals and serials concerning the history and philosophy of science.

5.6.42 **Sarton, George H.** Introduction to the history of science. Washington, D. C., Carnegie Institute, 1927–48. 3v. in 5.

Copious bibliographies throughout. "General bibliography," v. 3, 1872–1911.

5.6.43 **Wartofsky, Marx W.** Conceptual foundations of scientific thought; an introduction to the philosophy of science. New York, Macmillan, 1968. 560 pp.

Bibliography: pp. 489–548.

See also: 5.1.13 (II, 609–732), 5.3.20, 5.6.13, 7.2.8, 7.2.28.

Political and Social Philosophy

5.6.44 ★ **Benn, S. I.,** and **R. S. Peters.** Principles of political thought. New York, Collier Books, 1964. 478 pp.

First published as *Social Principles and the Democratic State,* 1959.
Bibliography in the "Notes," pp. 441–462.

5.6.45 **Brodbeck, May.** Readings in the philosophy of the social sciences. New York, Macmillan, 1968. 789 pp.

Bibliography: pp. 737–768.

5.6.46 **Connolly, William E.** Political science and ideology. New York, Atherton, 1967. 179 pp.

Bibliography: pp. 169–174.

5.6.47 **Friedrich, Carl J.** Man and his government; an empirical theory of politics. New York, McGraw-Hill, 1963. 737 pp.

Bibliography: pp. 677–715.

5.6.48 **Krimerman, Leonard I.** The nature and scope of social science; a critical anthology. New York, Appleton-Century-Crofts, 1969. 796 pp.

Bibliography: pp. 759–775.

5.6.49 **Natanson, Maurice.** Philosophy of the social sciences; a reader. New York, Random House, 1963. 560 pp.

Bibliography: pp. 509–541.

See also: 2.2.1 (VI, 386–387; 392), 2.3.12, 2.3.13, 3.7.14, 3.7.16–3.7.18, 5.6.10.

Theory of Knowledge

5.6.50 **Canfield, John V.,** and **Franklin H. Donnell,** *eds.* Readings in the theory of knowledge. New York, Appleton-Century-Crofts, 1964. 520 pp.

Bibliographies at the end of each Part.

5.6.51 **Edwards, Paul,** and **Arthur Pap,** *eds.* A modern introduction to philosophy; readings from classical and contemporary sources. Rev. ed. New York, Free Press, 1965. 797 pp.

Excellent annotated bibliographies after each section.

5.6.52 **Nagel, Ernest,** and **Richard Brandt,** *eds.* Meaning and knowledge; systematic readings in epistemology. New York, Harcourt, Brace & World, 1965. 668 pp.

Bibliographies at the end of each chapter.

See also: 3.7.22, 5.1.13 (II, 647–662).

6. LIBRARY CATALOGS, TRADE BIBLIO-GRAPHIES, AND AMERICAN DOCTORAL DISSERTATIONS

THE CATALOGS of some of the largest libraries of the world are printed and so available in many smaller libraries. These catalogs are valuable both for completing, checking, and building bibliographies on a particular author or topic and for ascertaining where particular books may be found. The *National Union Catalog* (6.1.4) and the *Union List of Serials* (6.1.5) indicate which cooperating libraries other than the Library of Congress have the book or periodical listed. This is especially useful in requesting a book through interlibrary loan.

Many works not available in their original form are available on microfilm or microcards or in photocopied or Xeroxed form. The Library of Congress, among others, makes photocopies of materials in its collections available for research use. Copyright material, however, will not be copied without the written permission of the copyright holder. Recent articles unavailable through other sources can often be obtained through the Institut International de Philosophie.★

Trade bibliographies (6.2) are another source of bibliographical information and are especially useful in discovering recent books not yet listed in printed library catalogs and not yet indexed in the general philosophical bibliographies.

Doctral dissertations frequently contain excellent bibliographies and form a part of the philosophical literature. If they are not published, however, they are not listed in the usual bibliographical journals or trade bibliographies. Many doctoral dissertations are available on microfilm; others can only be obtained from the university at which they were written. The list in section 6.3 applies only to dissertations written in the United States or Canada. For lists of sources reporting dissertations accepted by universities in other countries see Winchell (5.1.3), pp. 163–167. For more detailed information on library collections and trade bibliographies of many countries, see Collison (5.1.1), Malclès (5.1.4), Walford (5.1.2), and Winchell (5.1.3).

★ L'Institut International de Philosophie, 173 Blvd. Saint-Germain, Paris 6e, France, has a catalog of all philosophical works since 1946. If one has difficulty obtaining an article elsewhere, he can usually obtain a microfilmed copy by writing to: Centre de Documentation et de Bibliographie Philosophiques, Faculté des Lettres, 18 rue Chifflet, Besançon, Doubs, France.

6.1 LIBRARY CATALOGS

6.1.1 **U.S. Library of Congress.** Catalog of books represented by Library of Congress printed cards, issued to July 31, 1942. Ann Arbor, Mich., Edwards Brothers, 1942–46. 167 v.

Supplement: cards issued Aug. 1, 1942–Dec. 31, 1947. Ann Arbor, Mich., Edwards, 1948. 42v.
Both reprinted: New York, Rowman & Littlefield.

6.1.2 **Library of Congress author catalog:** a cumulative list of works represented by Library of Congress printed cards, 1948–1952. Ann Arbor, Mich., Edwards, 1953. 24v.

Reprinted: New York, Rowman & Littlefield.

6.1.3 **U.S. Library of Congress catalog.** Books: subjects, 1950–1954. A cumulative list of works represented by Library of Congress printed cards. Ann Arbor, Mich., Edwards, 1955, 20v.; 1955–1959, Paterson, N. J., Pageant Books, 1960, 22v.; 1960–1964, 25v.

Supplements issued quarterly, with annual and five-yearly cumulations.

6.1.4 **National union catalog;** a cumulative author list representing Library of Congress printed cards and titles reported by other American Libraries, 1953–1957. Ann Arbor, Mich., Edwards, 1958. 28v.

1958–62. New York, Rowman & Littlefield, 1963. 54v.
1952–55 imprints: an author list representing Library of Congress printed cards and titles reported by other American libraries. Ann Arbor, Mich., Edwards, 1961. 30v.
Lists cards from over 700 cooperating libraries. Supplemented by nine monthly issues, with three quarterly and annual cumulations.

6.1.5 **Union list of serials** in libraries of the United States and Canada. 3d ed. Ed. by Edna Brown Titus. New York, Wilson, 1965. 5v.

Lists more than 156,000 titles which began publication before 1950, which are held in 956 libraries in the United States and Canada. Gives information on title, beginning date, interruptions in publication, and holdings in all reporting libraries. Continued by *New Serial Titles* (6.1.6).

6.1.6 **New serial titles,** 1950–1960; supplement to the Union list of serials. 3d ed. A union list of serials commencing publication after Dec. 31, 1949. Washington, D. C., Library of Congress, 1961. 2v.

———, 1966–67. Washington, D. C., Library of Congress, 1968.
Continued by monthly supplements, and cumulated at annual and longer intervals.

6.1.7 **New serial titles**—classed subject arrangement. Jan./May, 1955– . Washington, D. C., Library of Congress, Card Division, 1955– . Monthly.

No cumulations. Arranged by Dewey Decimal Classification.

6.1.8 **British Museum. Department of Printed Books.** General catalog of printed books. London, Trustees, 1959–66. 263v.

Primarily an author catalog, covering books cataloged through 1955. Supersedes all previous incomplete editions. Descriptions are for the most part quite full.
———. Ten-year supplement, 1956–1965. London, Trustees, 1968. 50v.

6.1.9 **British union—catalogue of periodicals;** a record of the periodicals of the world, from the seventeenth century to the present day, in British libraries. Ed. by James Douglas Stewart, Muriel E. Hammond, and Erwin Saenger. London, Butterworths Scientific Publications; New York, Academic Press, 1955–58. 4v.

——— Supplement to 1960. 1962. From 1964 there are also quarterly and annual cumulations of new periodical titles

6.1.10 **Paris. Bibliothèque Nationale.** Catalogue général des livres imprimés: Auteurs. Paris, Imprimerie Nationale, 1900– . In progress.

An author list. Each volume includes works

up to the time of publication. Vol. 189 and following do not include works published after 1959. Entries are detailed.

Quinquennial supplements: 1960–64.

6.1.11 Berlin. Preussische Staatsbibliothek. Berliner Titeldrucke. Berlin, 1892–1944.

Title varies; also called Deutscher Gesamt-katalog. Weekly with quarterly and annual cumulations.

Partially cumulated and supplemented by 6.1.12 and by two *Fünfjahrs-Katalog*, 1930–34 (1935), 1935–39 (1940).

6.1.12 Deutscher Gesamtkatalog. Hrsg. von der Preussischen Staatsbibliothek. Berlin, Preussische Druckerei- u. Verlags Aktiengesellschaft, 1931–39. v. 1–14.

V. 1–14, A-Beethordnung. No more published. An author and main entry list of books published to 1930 and held by German and Austrian libraries.

6.1.13 Centro nazionale per il catalogo unico delle biblioteche italiane e per le informazioni bibliografiche. Primo catalogo collettivo delle biblioteche italiane. Roma, 1962– .

Includes books published from 1500–1957.

6.2 TRADE BIBLIOGRAPHIES

6.2.1 U.S. Library of Congress. General Reference Bibliography Division. Current national bibliographies, comp. by Helen F. Conover. Washington, D. C., Library of Congress, 1955. 132 pp.

An annotated list of the book trade in 67 countries.

6.2.2 Cumulative book index: a world list of books in the English language. New York, H. W. Wilson, 1898– .

Issued monthly (except July and Aug.), cumulated quarterly. Permanent volumes used to cover five-year periods, now cover two-year periods. As of 1929 covers all books published in English. Author, title, and subject listings.

6.2.3 Publisher's weekly; the American book trade journal. New York, R. R. Bowker, 1872– .

A weekly list of books published. Cumulated as 6.2.4.

6.2.4 American book publishing record. New York, R. R. Bowker, 1960– .

A monthly cumulation of the *Publisher's Weekly* (6.2.3).

6.2.5 Publishers' trade list annual. New York, R. R. Bowker, 1873– .

Annual collection of catalogs of American publishers. Gives fuller information than *Books in Print* (6.2.6).

6.2.6 Books in print; an author-title-series index to the publishers' trade list annual. New York, R. R. Bowker, 1948– .

6.2.7 Subject guide to books in print; an index to the publishers' trade list annual. New York, R. R. Bowker, 1957– .

A subject guide to *Books in Print* (6.2.6).

France

6.2.8 "Biblio," catalogue des ouvrages parus en langue française dans le monde entier, Oct. 1933– . Paris, Service Bibliographique des Messageries Hachette, 1933– .

Ten issues a year with annual cumulations. The French trade list, giving full information, with author, subject, and title entries.

6.2.9 Bibliographie de la France; journal général de l'imprimerie et de la librairie. Paris, Cercle de la Librairie, 1811– .

Weekly.
The official list of acquisitions of the *dépôt légal*.

Germany

6.2.10 Deutsche Nationalbibliographie und Bibliographie des im Ausland erschienenen deutschsprachigen Schrifttums. Leipzig, Verlag für Buch- und Bibliothekswesen 1931– .

Reihe A, weekly; Reihe B, semimonthly. Cumulates into 6.2.11.

6.2.11 Jahresverzeichnis des deutschen Schrifttums, 1945/46– , bearb. und hrsg. von der Deutsch Bücherei und dem Börsenverein der Deutschen Buchhändler zu Leipzig. Leipzig, Börsenverein, 1948– .

An annual cumulation of 6.2.10.

6.2.12 Deutsches Bücherverzeichnis; Verzeichnis der in Deutschland, Osterreich, der Schweiz und im übrigen Ausland herausgegeben deutschsprachigen Verlagsschriften sowei der wichtigsten Veröffentlichungen asserhalb des Buchhandels, 1911– . Leipzig, Verlag für Buch-und Bibliothekswesen, 1915– .

Five-year cumulations of 6.2.11.

6.2.13 Deutsche Bibliographie; wöchentliches Verzeichnis. Frankfurt am Main, Buchhändler-Vereinigung GMBH, 1947– . Weekly.

Cumulated semiannually into Deutsche Bibliographie; Halbjahres-Verzeichnis. Frankfurt am Main, Buchhändler-Vereinigung GMBH, 1951– , which is in turn cumulated quinquennially into Deutsche Bibliographie, 1945/50– . Bücher und Karten. Frankfurt am Main, Buchhändler-Vereinigung GMBH, 1952– .
A competitor of the trade journals published in Leipzig (6.2.10–6.2.12), with much duplication.

Great Britain

6.2.14 British national bibliography, 1950– . London, Council of the British National Bibliography, British Museum. 1950– .

Weekly with four cumulations a year, and annual and five-year cumulations. Based on the copyright accessions of the British Museum.

6.2.15 The bookseller: The organ of the booktrade. London. Whitaker, 1858– .

Weekly since 1909, with monthly cumulations. Cumulates into *Whitaker's Cumulative Book List* (6.2.16).

6.2.16 Whitaker's cumulative book list. London, Whitaker, 1924– .

Quarterly, cumulating into yearly and five-yearly cumulations. The complete list of all books published in the United Kingdom, giving details as to author, title, subtitle, size, number of pages, price classification, and publisher. Subtitle varies.

6.3 AMERICAN DOCTORAL DISSERTATIONS

6.3.1 U. S. Library of Congress. Catalog Division. List of American doctoral dissertations printed in 1912–38. Washington, D. C., Government Printing Office, 1913–40. 26v.

6.3.2 Doctoral dissertations accepted by American universities. Published and unpublished. New York, Wilson, 1934–56. Annual. 1933/34–1954/55.

Lists dissertations accepted by U. S. and Canadian universities.
Continued by 6.3.5.

6.3.3 Microfilm abstracts; a collection of abstracts of doctoral dissertations which are available in complete form on microfilm. Ann Arbor, Mich., University Microfilms, 1935–51. v. I–II.

Lists dissertations accepted by universities in the U. S. and Canda.
Continued as 6.3.4.

6.3.4 Dissertation abstracts; abstracts of dissertations and monographs in microform. Ann Arbor, Mich., University Microfilms, 1952– . v. 12– . Monthly.

Beginning with Vol. 27, No. 1, it is divided into two sections: Humanities and Social Sciences (A) and Sciences (B). Issued with Keyword Title and Author Indexes for A and B cumulated separately each year as Part II of Issue 12, Sections A and B. Continued as 6.3.5.

6.3.5 Dissertation abstracts international. Ann Arbor, Mich., University Microfilms, 1969– . v.30– . Monthly.

The name change reflects the enlargement of University Microfilm's publication program by the addition of dissertations from European universities.

A continuation of 6.3.4.

Access to doctoral dissertations has been simplified by DATRIX (Direct Access to Reference Information: a Xerox service), which is a service of University Microfilms whereby they will search and supply appropriate references to microfilmed dissertations (from 1938 on) based on the reader's individual needs and "Key Work Lists."

See also: *The Review of Metaphysics* (7.2.76).

7. PHILOSOPHICAL SERIALS

PERIODICALS are the lifeblood of contemporary philosophy, and provide a ready outlet for the writings of philosophers. Articles are an ideal medium in which to develop or approach a single problem, present a new insight, or analyze a particular argument. Being relatively short they usually require less time to write and can be published more quickly than a book. They also offer the possibility of philosophical discussion in print. Consequently philosophical journals can be used to keep up with current philosophical developments, philosophical problems, and continuing discussions and debates.

Many philosophical journals list new books in philosophy as they appear, often giving brief summaries of them and carrying review articles of the more important and significant ones. By following the journals one can keep abreast of new books as they appear and can often decide from the summaries and reviews which of the many books that are published he should read, buy for himself, or recommend to his university or public library.

Some journals also list philosophical meetings, appointments, and other news of interest to the philosophical community. They are thus useful for keeping up with news of the profession.

The items in 7.1 are either guides or can be used to obtain information on journals in related areas or on philosophical journals not included in the following lists, which do, however, contain the most important philosophical journals in English (7.2) and in the major European languages (7.3). If foreign journals publish articles in English, this is indicated. For each journal the beginning date, information about breaks in the series, affiliation (if any), editor and/or editorial address, frequency of publication and types of contents are included. Some journals have a particular orientation and the policy or orientation of the more important journals can be found in the annotations.

Serials other than journals are listed in 7.4.

7.1 PHILOSOPHICAL PERIODICAL DIRECTORIES AND GUIDES

7.1.1 **Gerber, William.** "Philosophical Journals," the Encyclopedia of philosophy (2.2.1), vol. VI, pp. 199–216.

Contains a discussion of philosophical journals, treated chronologically.

7.1.2 **Irregular serials and annuals:** an international directory. A classified guide to current foreign and domestic serials, excepting periodicals issued more frequently than once a year. First edition, edited by Emery Koltay. New York & London, R. R. Bowker Co., 1967. 668 pp.

Covers 14,500 publications in the bibliographically confused area between books and periodicals, including "serials and continuations, such as proceedings, transactions, progresses, advances, reports, yearbooks, annual reviews, handbooks, periodical supplements, etc."

A companion volume to Ulrich (7.1.5).

The announced policy is to publish new editions biennially with annual supplements.

7.1.3 New York Public Library. A check list of cumulative indexes to individual periodicals in the New York Public Library, compiled by Daniel C. Haskell. New York, Library, 1942. 370 pp.

7.1.4 The standard periodical directory. 2d ed. New York, Oxbridge Publishing Co., 1967. 1019 pp.

Lists U. S. and Canadian periodicals.

7.1.5 Ulrich's international periodicals directory, 1967–68. 12th ed. New York, R. R. Bowker, 1968. 2v.

A classified guide to a selected list of current periodicals, American and foreign. Lists periodicals by subject. Issued triennially.

——. ⋆ *Supplement.* 1969.

7.1.6 U. S. Library of Congress. Reference Department. Philosophical periodicals; an annotated world list by David Baumgardt. Washington, D. C., Government Printing Office, 1952. 89 pp.

Contains 489 entries.

7.1.7 Varet, Gilbert and Paul Kurtz. International directory of philosophy and philosophers. New York, Humanities Press, 1965. 235 pp.

Part I, International organizations; Part II, countries and territories.

Contains detailed information by country on university departmental staffs, philosophical

institutes, organizations, journals, and publishers.

7.1.8 World list of specialized periodicals in philosophy; Liste mondiale des périodiques spécialisés en philosophie. Paris, Mouton, 1967. 124 pp.

See also: 5.2.14, 5.3.6, 5.3.11, 6.1.5–6.1.7, 6.1.9.

7.2 SELECTED PHILOSOPHICAL JOURNALS: ENGLISH LANGUAGE

7.2.1 American philosophical quarterly. Jan. 1964–to date. Quarterly (Jan., Apr., July, Oct.) Ed., Nicholas Rescher, Dept. of Philosophy, University of Pittsburgh, Pittsburgh, Pa. 15213.

Publishes only self-sufficient articles (no book reviews, critical studies, etc.), varying in length from 2000–25,000 words on any aspect of philosophy, substantive or historical. Primarily analytically inclined. Also irregularly publishes a supplementary monograph series since 1968.

7.2.2 Analysis. 1933–40 (v. 1–7); 1947–to date. Six nos. yearly (Oct., Dec., Jan., Mar., Apr., June), plus a supplement for longer papers. Ed., Peter Winch, Dept. of Philosophy, King's College, Strand, London, W. C. 2.

Suspended Nov. 1940–Sept. 1947; v. 1. No. 1 (Oct. '47) also called ns. no. 1.

Articles and discussion papers of 3000 words or less on metaphysics, logic, ethics, and aesthetic; index. Oriented towards analytic philosophy and logic.

7.2.3 Apeiron. 1969–to date. Twice yearly. Eds., P. J. Bicknell and H. D. Rankin, Monash University, Clayton, Victoria, Australia 3168, and R. W. Hall, University of Vermont, Burlington, Vt. 05401.

Deals with ancient philosophy and science.

7.2.4 Australasian journal of philosophy. 1947 (v. 25)–to date. Three nos. yearly (May, Aug., Dec.) Pub. by Australiasian Assoc. of

Philosophy. Ed., Graham Nerlich, Dept. of Philosophy, University of Sydney, Sydney, Australia.

Articles, critical notices, reviews, books received, notes and news, index. A continuation of 7.2.5.

Reprinted: (up to v. 44, no. 3), New York, Kraus Reprint Corp.

7.2.5 **Australasian journal of philosophy and psychology.** 1923–46 (v. 1–24).

Cum. index: 1–24 (1923–46).
Continued as 7.2.4.

7.2.6 **Bibliography of philosophy;** a quarterly bulletin. Published under the auspices of the International Institute of Philosophy and with the aid of UNESCO. U. S. Director: Paul Kurtz, Dept. of Philosophy, SUNY at Buffalo, 4244 Ridge Lea Rd., Amherst, N. Y. 14226.

Title also in French. Text in several languages. Provides abstracts of new philosophical books published throughout the world and comprehensive bibliographical information on reeditions. *See* 5.3.8.

7.2.7 **Blackfriars** (Oxford). 1920–to date. Monthly. Ed. by English Dominicans, Blackfriars Publications, 2 Serjeants' Inn, Fleet St., London, E. C. 4.

Articles, book reviews, index. A learned Catholic journal of theology, philosophy, sociology, art, literature and contemporary affairs

Supplement: *Life of the spirit*, 1–3 (no. 1–28), Feb. 1944–June 1948; continued as separate publication under the same name.

7.2.8 **The British journal for the philosophy of science.** May 1950–to date. Quarterly (May, Aug., Nov., Feb.). Organ of the British Society for the Philosophy of Science. Eds., Mary B. Hesse, D. H. Mellor, Whipple Museum, Free School Lane, Cambridge, England.

Articles (not exceeding 5000 words), discussions, reviews, recent publication, lists of articles in the philosophy of science, and abstracts of articles published in *Dialectica*, *Methods*, and *Philosophy of Science*.

Reprinted: v. 1–12 (1950/51–1961/62), New York, Kraus Reprint Corp.

7.2.9 **The British journal of aesthetics;** a journal for the understanding of the principles of criticism and appreciation. 1960–to date. Quarterly (Jan., Apr., July, Oct.). Official organ of the British Society of Aesthetics. Ed. Harold Osborne, 90A St. John's Wood High St., London. N. W. 8.

Articles, book reviews, books received, correspondence.

7.2.10 **Cross currents.** 1950–to date. Quarterly (Winter, Spring, Summer, Fall). Ed., Joseph E. Cunneen, 103 Van Houten Fields, West Nyack, N. Y. 10994.

Original articles, translations from European journals, notes, reviews, plus an Annual Review of Philosophy by James Collins. Concerned with exploring "the implications of Christianity for our times."

7.2.11 **Darshana international;** an international quarterly of philosophy, psychology, psychical research, religion, mysticism, and sociology. 1961–to date. Ed., J. P. Atreya, Darshana International, Moradabad, India.

Title varies (v. 1–2, 1961–62, *Darshana*). Articles, book reviews, index.

7.2.12 **Dialectica;** international review of philosophy of knowledge. 1947–to date. Quarterly. Ed., P. Bernays (and others), 12 Chemin du Muveran, 1012 Lausanne, Switzerland.

Text and subtitle in English, French, and German.

Articles (with some emphasis on philosophy of science), books received, book reviews, abstracts from *Philosophy of Science* and *The British Journal for the Philosophy of Science*, index. Cumulative index (subject, 1966; authors, 1967).

Partially reprinted: Johnson Reprint Corp.

7.2.13 **Dialogue;** Canadian philosophical review/revue canadienne de philosophie. 1962–to date. Quarterly (June, Sept., Dec., Mar.). Organ of the Canadian Philosophical

Association. Eds., H. M. Estall, Dept. of Philosophy, Queens University, Kingston, Ontario, and V. Cauchy, Faculté de Philosophie, Université de Montréal, Montréal, Canada.

Text in English and French. No specific orientation. Articles, notes, discussions, critical notices, many book reviews, books received, announcements, index.

7.2.14 **Diogenes;** an international review of philosophy and humanistic studies. 1953–to date. Quarterly (Dec., Mar., June, Sept.). Publication of the International Council for Philosophy and Humanistic Studies. Ed., Roger Caillois, Place de Fontenoy, Paris 7, France.

English, French, Spanish, Arabian parallel editions. Articles, notes and discussion. Often has an issue devoted to a single general topic, e.g., No. 39, "Esthetic Problems: Past and Present." Articles of a technically philosophical nature are not usually carried.

7.2.15 **Erkenntnis.** *See* Journal of unified science (7.2.42).

7.2.16 **Ethics;** an international journal of social, political and legal philosophy. 1937/38 (v. 48)– to date. Quarterly (Oct., Jan., Apr., July). Eds., Charles W. Wegener and Warner A. Wick, The University of Chicago Press, 5750 Ellis Avenue, Chicago, Ill., 60637.

Articles, discussions, book reviews, shorter notices, books received index. "Devoted to study of the ideas and principles which form the basis for individual and social action. It publishes articles in ethical theory, social science, and jurisprudence contributing to an understanding of the basic structure of civilization and society. It is not the organ of any group and is not committed to any policy or program." A continuation of 7.2.26. Cum. index: 1890–1965.
Reprinted: v. 1–25 (1891–1915), Johnson Reprint Corp.

7.2.17 **Foundations of language;** international journal of language and philosophy. 1965–to date. Quarterly (Feb., Aug., May, Nov.). Ed., Morris Halle (and others), M. I. T., Cambridge, Mass. 02139.

Articles, short notices, reviews, and publications received for review. Deals with language and the foundations of its study, including the impact of language on various disciplines.

7.2.18 **Franciscan studies.** 1924–to date. Annual. Ed. by the Franciscan Education Conference, St. Bonaventure University, St. Bonaventure, N. Y. 14778.

V. 22, 1941– also as ns. v. 1– . Formerly quarterly; annual as of 1963. Articles on topics related to Franciscan philosophy or theology, published in English, Latin, French, German, or Italian.

7.2.19 **The Harvard theological review.** 1908–to date. Quarterly (Jan., Apr., July, Oct.). Issued by the Faculty of Divinity in Harvard University. Ed., Krister Stendahl, The Divinity School, Harvard University, Cambridge, Mass. 02138.

Articles, notes and observations, books received. Includes theology, ethics, the history and philosophy of religion, and cognate subjects.

7.2.20 **The Heythrop journal;** a review of philosophy and theology. 1960–to date. Quarterly. Ed., Rev. B. R. Brinkman, Heythrop College, Oxon, England.

Articles, bibliographies, book reviews, index.

7.2.21 **Hibbert journal.** 1902–1968 (v. 1–66, no. 262/3). Quarterly (Winter, Spring, Autumn Summer).

A review of religion, theology, and philosophy, containing articles, book reviews, index.
Cum. index: v. 1–10 (1902–11).

7.2.22 **History and theory:** studies in the philosophy of history. 1960–to date. Three nos. yearly, and 1 Beiheft. Ed., George H. Nadel, Wesleyan Station, Middletown, Conn. 06457.

Monographs, reviews, essays, exchanges, comments, and bibliographies. Devoted to theory of history, historiography, method of history, and the relation of historical theory and method of the social sciences.

Index to v. 1–5 (1960–66) contains an annotated list of articles, a list of review articles, and titles of the Beihefte.

7.2.23 The humanist. 1941–to date. Six nos. yearly (Jan., Mar., May, July, Sept., Nov.). Published by the American Humanist Association and the American Ethical Union. Ed., Paul Kurtz, 4244 Ridge Lea Rd., Amherst, N. Y. 14226.

Editorials, articles, film, drama, book reviews, news, index. Attempts to bridge theoretical philosophical discussion and practical applications of humanism.

7.2.24 Inquiry; an interdisciplinary journal of philosophy and the social sciences. 1958–to date. Quarterly (Spring, Summer, Autumn, Winter). Ed., Arne Naess, Institute of Philosophy, P. O. Box 307, Blidern, Oslo 3, Norway.

Articles, reviews, discussion, books received, abstracts of articles from *Philosophy of Science.* Orientation is somewhat analytic, but not entirely so. Some issues devoted to special topics.

7.2.25 The international archives of the history of ideas. 1963–to date. Irregular. Ed., P. Didon and R. Popkin, Nijhoff, The Hague, Netherlands.

Articles in English and French. Devoted to the history of ideas, especially of the 16th, 17th, and 18th centuries.

7.2.26 International journal of ethics. 1890/91–1936/37 (v. 1–47).

Continued as 7.2.16. Index, v. 1–41 (Oct. 1890–July 1931).
Reprinted: v. 1–25 (1891–1915), Johnson Reprint Corp.

7.2.27 International philosophical quarterly. 1961–to date. Quarterly (Mar., June, May, Sept., Dec.). Ed., W. Norris Clarke, Fordham University, Bronx, N. Y. 10458. (In collaboration with Joseph F. Donceel, Heverlée-Louvain, Belgium.)

Articles, critical discussion, feature review, briefer book notices, contemporary currents, books received, index. "IPQ has been founded to provide an international forum in English for the interchange of basic philosophical ideas between the Americas and Europe and between East and West. Its primary orientation is to encourage vital contemporary expression—creative, critical and historical—in the intercultural tradition of theistic, spiritualist, and personalist humanism, but without further restriction of school within these broad perspectives."

7.2.28 Isis; an international quarterly review devoted to the history of science and its cultural influences. 1913–to date. Quarterly (Mar., June, Sept., Dec.) with a special Critical bibliography, issued annually in Aug. by Univ. of California Press. Official journal of the History of Science Society. Ed., Robert P. Multauf, Smithsonian Institution, Washington, D. C. 20560.

Subtitle varies. Suspended July 1914–Aug. 1919. Articles, notes and correspondence, news.
Cum. Index: v. 1–3 in v. 3; v. 1–20 (1913–33) in v. 21.

7.2.29 The Islamic review. 1913–to date. Monthly [irregular] Ed., The Shah Jehan Mosque, Woking, Surrey.

Title varies: Feb. 1913–Jan. 1914 as *Muslim India and Islamic world*; Feb. 1914–20 as *Islamic Review and Muslim India.*
Articles, book reviews, index. A cultural journal dealing with the world of Islam.

7.2.30 The Jewish quarterly review. 1888–to date. Quarterly (July, Oct., Jan., Apr.). Eds., A. I. Katsh and S. Zeitlin, Dropsie College for Hebrew and Cognate Learning, Broad and York Streets, Philadelphia, Pa.

V. 1–20 (1888–1908); ns. v. 1 July 1910–to date.
Cum. Index: v. 1–20 (1910–1930).

7.2.31 Journal for the scientific study of religion. 1961–to date. Semiannual (Fall and Spring). Official journal of the Society for the Scientific Study of Religion. Ed. James E. Dittes, 409 Prospect St., New Haven, Conn. 06510.

Articles, reviews, notes, index.

7.2.32 **Journal of aesthetics and art criticism.** 1941–to date. Quarterly (Fall, Winter, Spring, Summer). Published by the American Society for Aesthetics. Ed., Herbert M. Schueller, Dept. of English, Wayne State University, Detroit, Mich. 48202.

Studies of visual arts, literature, music, theatre arts from a philosophic or other theoretical point of view; book reviews, index.
Cum. index: v. 1–20 (1941–1963), N. Y., AMS Reprint Co.

7.2.33 **Journal of existentialism;** the international quarterly of existential thought. 1960–67.

Title varies: v. 1–4, *Journal of Existential Psychiatry*. Associated with the Association for Phenomenology and Existential Philosophy. Articles on philosphy, psychology, psychiatry, social sciences, and literature; bibliography, book reviews, index.
Reprinted: v. 1–3 (1960–63), Johnson Reprint Corp.

7.2.34 **Journal of philosophical studies.** 1926–1930. (v. 1–5).

Continued as 7.2.66.

7.2.35 **Journal of philosophy.** 1921 (v. 18)–to date. 24 nos. yearly. Eds., J. Randall (honorary), S. Morgenbesser, A. Danto, C. Parsons, J. Walsh, 720 Philosophy Hall, Columbia University, New York, N. Y. 10027.

Articles, reviews, new books, notes, and news of the profession; index; carries major papers of the American Philosophical Association Eastern Division Meetings prior to the meetings. A continuation of 7.2.36.
50–yr. Index: 1904–1953; 10-yr. supplement, 1954–1963.

7.2.36 **Journal of philosophy, psychology and scientific methods.** 1904–1920 (v. 1–17).

Continued as 7.2.35.

7.2.37 **The journal of religion.** 1921–to date. Quarterly (Jan., Apr., July, Oct.). A publication of the Divinity School of the University of Chicago. Eds., J. C. Rylaarsdam and N. A. Scott, Jr., University of Chicago, 1025 E. 58th St., Chicago, Ill. 60637.

Formed by the union of the *American Journal of Theology* and *Biblical World*.
Articles, reviews, book notes, index.

7.2.38 **The journal of symbolic logic.** 1936–to date. Quarterly (Mar., June, Sept., Dec.). Official organ of the Association for Symbolic Logic. Eds., Burton Dreben, Dept. of Philosophy, Emerson Hall, Harvard University, Cambridge, Mass. 02138, and others.

Articles (sometimes in French and German), reviews, bibliographies, news of the Association, abstracts of papers delivered at meetings of the Association, offices and members of the Association, official notices of the Division of Logic, Methodology and Philosophy of Science of the International Union of the History and Philosophy of Science, index. Technical papers in logic, the history of logic and the philosophy of logic.
V. 26 is an index for v. 1–25.

7.2.39 **The journal of the British Society for Phenomenology.** 1969–to date. Three nos. yearly. Ed., D. W. Mays, Dept. of Philosophy, University of Manchester, Manchester 13, England.

Articles on phenomenology and related topics in the humanities, discussion notes, book reviews, bibliography, reports of the Society, correspondence.

7.2.40 **Journal of the history of ideas;** a quarterly devoted to cultural and intellectual history. 1940–to date. Quarterly (Jan./Mar., Apr./June, July/Sept., Oct./Dec.). Ed., Philip Wiener, Temple University, Philadelphia, Pa. 19122.

Articles, discussion, notes, reviews, index. Fosters studies which emphasize the interrelations of several fields of historical study.
Cum. index: v. 1–25.
Partially reprinted: Johnson Reprint Corp.

7.2.41 **Journal of the history of philosophy.** 1963–to date. Quarterly (Jan., Apr., July, Oct.). Ed., Richard Popkin, University of California, San Diego, La Jola, California.

Articles on the history of Western philosophy broadly conceived, in English, French, and German, notes and discussions, book reviews, book notes, books received.

7.2.42 The journal of unified science (Erkenntnis). 1930–40 (v. 1–8, no. 5/6). Eds., Rudolf Carnap and Hans Reichenbach.

Superseded Annalen der Philosophie und philosophischen Kritik. v. 1–7 (1930–39) as Erkenntnis.
Articles and reviews in English and German. Carried discussions of the Vienna Circle.

7.2.43 The journal of value inquiry. 1967–to date. Quarterly (somewhat irregular). Ed., James Wilbur and others, Dept. of Philosophy, SUNY, Geneseo, N. Y. 14454.

Articles on any aspect of value theory without restriction of method, scope, or orientation, discussion, book reviews, books received. One issue per year contains the proceedings of the Conference on Value Inquiry.

7.2.44 Main currents in modern thought; journal of the foundation of integrative education. 1940–to date. Five nos. yearly (Sept., Nov., Jan., Mar., May). Ed., F. L. Kunz, 12 Church St., New Rochelle, N. Y. 10805.

Suspended Apr.–Dec. 1943.
Articles, news and views, reviews. Promotes the integration of all knowledge.

7.2.45 Man and world; an international philosophical review. 1968–to date. Quarterly (Feb., May, Aug., Nov.,). Ed., Calvin O. Schrag and others, P. O. Box 173, State College, Pa. 16801.

Articles in English, French, German, and Spanish (with short summaries in English of articles not written in English), reviews, critical discussions, chronicles. Aims at increasing contact among countries of North, Central, South America, and Europe by discussing philosophical issues of mutual interest; not explicitly related to any one trend or school.

7.2.46 Mediaeval studies. 1939–to date. Annual. Ed., J. P. Mooro, 59 Queen's Part, Toronto 5, Canada.

7.2.47 Metaphilosophy. 1969–to date. Quarterly (Jan., Apr., July, Oct.). Ed., T. W. Bynum and W. L. Reese, Dept. of Philosophy, SUNY, 1400 Washington Ave., Albany, N. Y. 12203.

Articles and reviews of books *about* philosophy or some particular school, method, or field of philosophy.

7.2.48 Methodos; language and cybernetics; linguaggio e cibernetica. 1949–to date. Quarterly. Pub. under the auspices of the Center of Cybernetics and Linguistic Activities of the University of Milan and of CNR. Ed., Marsilio Editori, via S. Eufemia, 5, Padova.

Subtitle varies: Quarterly review of methodology and symbolic logic until 1954.
Articles (in original language often followed by complete English translation [after 1954 there are more articles in English but articles in other languages are not always translated into English]), book reviews, books received, news, notes, index. Publishes unconventional essays on language, cybernetics, and applications to the design of intelligent machines of the results obtained by the Italian Operational School.

7.2.49 Mind; a quarterly review of psychology and philosophy. 1876–1891 (v. 1–16); 1892 (ns. v. 1)–to date. Quarterly (Jan., Apr., July, Oct.). Publication of the Mind Association. Ed., Gilbert Ryle, Magdalen College, Oxford University, Oxford.

Articles, critical notices, book reviews, new books, notes (primarily British) list of officers and members of Mind Association. Analytic in orientation. 1896–1900 contain papers of the Aristotelian Society.
Cum. index: v. 1–16 (1876–91) in v. 16; ns. v. 1–12)1892–1903); ns. v. 13–32 (1904–23); ns. v. 33–42 (1924–33).
Partially reprinted: Kraus Reprint Corp.

7.2.50 The modern schoolman; a quarterly journal of philosophy. 1925–to date. Quarterly (Nov., Jan., Mar., May). Ed., George P. Klubertanz, St. Louis University, 3700 West Pine Blvd., St. Louis, Mo. 63108.

Articles, notes and discussions, book reviews, book notes, books received, index. "Dedicated to furthering the work begun by the great Schoolmen of the Middle Ages."

See also: 5.5.19.

7.2.51 The monist; an international quarterly journal of general philosophical inquiry. 1890–1936 (v. 1–46); 1962 (v. 47)–to date. Quarterly (Jan., Apr., July, Oct.). Ed., Eugene Freeman, Dept. of Philosophy, San José State College, San José, Calif. 95114.

Subtitle varies.

Articles, books received, authors' abstracts of recent books, index. Each issue devoted to a particular topic, announced in advance (e.g., Winter 1963, "Metaphysics Today"; Summer, 1963, "Ethics and Anthropology").

Reprinted: v. 1–46, Kraus Reprint Corp.

7.2.52 The new scholasticism; a quarterly of philosophy. 1927–to date. Quarterly (Jan., Apr., July, Oct.). Journal of the American Catholic Philosophical Association. Ed., John A. Oesterle, University of Notre Dame, Notre Dame, Ind. 46556.

Articles, discussion, book reviews, chronicle, index. The Secretary's notes are extremely full as of Oct. 1963, and include news of the Association, other meetings, special studies, collections, lecture programs, news of other societies, periodicals and series, research instruments, classical works, translations, and appointments.

Cum. index, v. 1–40 (1927–1966).

Reprinted: v. 1–10 (1927–1936), Johnson Reprint Corp.

7.2.53 Notre Dame journal of formal logic. 1960–to date. Quarterly (Jan., Apr., July, Oct.). Ed., Boleslaw Sobocinski, Box 28, Notre Dame, Ind. 46556.

Articles on symbolic logic, foundations of mathematics, history of logic, metalogic, semantics, and the fields immediately related to logic.

10-yr. index in last issue of v. 10.

7.2.54 Nous. 1967–to date. Quarterly (Feb., May, Sept., Nov.). Ed., Hector-Neri Castañeda, Dept. of Philosophy, Indiana University, Bloomington, Ind. 47401.

Articles, critical studies, symposia, publications received, index. Emphasis on articles which apply the techniques of formal logic to philosophical questions.

7.2.55 Pacific philosophy forum. *See* Philosophy forum (7.2.70).

7.2.56 Personalist; an international review of philosophy. 1920–to date. Quarterly (Jan., Apr., July, Oct.). Ed., John Hospers, for the School of Philosophy, University of Southern California, 3518 University Avenue, Los Angeles, California. 90007. Articles, reviews, verse.

Subtitle varies.

Articles, book reviews, notices, index. Previously included articles on religion and literature; now devoted exclusively to philosophy.

7.2.57 The philosopher's index; an international index to philosophical periodicals. 1967–to date. Quarterly (Jan., Apr., July, Oct.). Ed., Richard H. Lineback, Bowling Green University, Bowling Green, Ohio. 43402.

A keyword subject and author index to more than 90 major American and British philosophical periodicals, selected foreign journals, and related interdisciplinary publications. Cumulations in hardback every two years. From v. 3 includes abstracts written by authors of articles indexed.

7.2.58 Philosophia mathematica. 1964–to date. Semiannually (June, Dec.). Official journal of the Association for Philosophy of Mathematics. Ed., J. Fang, Memphis State University, Memphis, Tenn. 38111.

Devoted to the philosophy of mathematics. Articles, discussion, reviews, recent publications.

7.2.59 Philosophical books. 1960–to date. Three nos. yearly (Jan., May, Oct.). Ed., J. Kemp, The University, Leicester, England.

Frequency varies.

Reviews of philosophical books, primarily from an analytic point of view.

7.2.60 The philosophical forum. 1943–to date. Quarterly (Fall, Winter, Spring, Summer).

Eds., Joseph Agassi and Walter Emge, Dept. of Philosophy, Boston University, 232 Bay State Road, Boston, Mass. 02215.

Annual until Sept. 1968.
Articles, replies, critical studies, translations. "Open to contributions of all types and schools."

7.2.61 **Philosophical journal;** transactions of the Royal Philosophical Society of Glasgow. 1964–to date. Semiannually (Jan., July). Ed., Carl Barbier, Dept. of French, The University, Edinburgh 8, Scotland.

Articles, book reviews, index. "Publishes not only papers given before the Society but also outside contributions on topics within the general aims of the Society."

7.2.62 **The philosophical quarterly.** 1950–to date. Quarterly (Jan., Apr., July, Oct.). Publication of the Scots Philosophical Club of the University of St. Andrews. Ed., G. P. Henderson, Dept. of Philosophy, The University, Dundee, Scotland.

Articles, discussions, critical studies, book reviews, books received. Primarily analytic in orientation, it publishes works from philosophers in any part of the world and gives "special attention to surveys of philosophical literature and to book reviews."

7.2.63 **Philosophical review.** 1892–to date. Quarterly (Jan., Apr., July, Oct.). Ed. by Faculty of the Sage School of Philosophy, 218 Goldwin Smith Hall, Cornell University, Ithaca, New York. 14850.

Articles, discussions, many book reviews, books received, notes, index. Orientation is analytic; "widely regarded as the best philosophical periodical in the English-speaking world at the present time," Anthony Quinton, 9.2.9, p. 107.
Cum. index: v. 1–3 (1892–1926).
Reprinted: v. 1–70 (1892–1961), AMS Reprint Co.

7.2.64 **Philosophical studies** (Maynooth). 1951–to date. Annual. Ed., James D. Bastable, St. Patrick's College, Maynooth, Ireland.

Articles, critical notices, and a large number of book reviews. Aims at the development and diffusion of Christian philosophy by way of exact analysis and specialized study with emphasis on contemporary problems and movements.

7.2.65 **Philosophical studies** (Minneapolis). 1950–to date. Six nos. yearly (Jan., Feb., Apr., June, Oct., Dec.). Eds., Wilfrid Sellars (Univ. of Pittsburgh) and Herbert Feigl (Univ. of Minnesota).

Articles (of less than 3000 words), books received, index. Analytic in orientation.
Partially reprinted: Johnson Reprint Corp.

7.2.66 **Philosophy.** 1931 (v. 6)–to date. Quarterly (Jan., Apr., July, Oct.). The journal of the Royal Institute of Philosophy. Ed., H. B. Acton, 14 Gordon Square, London W. C. 1, England.

Articles, discussions, book reviews, books received, Institute news and notes, index.
A continuation of 7.2.34.
Reprinted: v. 1–11 (1926–1945), Johnson Reprint Corp.

7.2.67 **Philosophy and phenomenological research.** 1940–to date. Quarterly (Sept., Dec., Mar., June). Organ of the International Phenomenological Society. Ed., Marvin Farber, SUNY, Buffalo, N. Y. 14214.

Articles, discussions, reviews, notes and news, recent publications, index. In addition to papers on phenomenology it publishes articles in most of the branches of philosophy.
Partially reprinted: Kraus Reprint Corp.

7.2.68 **Philosophy and rhetoric.** 1968–to date. Quarterly (Winter, Spring, Summer, Fall). Ed., Henry W. Johnstone, Jr., Pennsylvania State University, University Park, Pa. 16802.

Concerned primarily with rhetoric as a philosophical concept, the role of rhetoric, and the relation of rhetoric and other human activities.

7.2.69 **Philosophy east and west;** a quarterly journal of oriental and comparative thought.

1951–to date. Quarterly (Jan., Apr., July, Oct.). Ed., Eliot Deutsch, 1993 East-West Road, The University of Hawaii, Honolulu, Hawaii. 96822.

Articles on Oriental and comparative philosophy and culture, book reviews, current periodicals (i.e., a listing of articles in Oriental and comparative philosophy appearing in other journals), news and notes pertaining to Oriental and comparative philosophy.

Reprinted: v. 1–14 (1951–1964), Johnson Reprint Corp.

7.2.70 The philosophy forum. 1962–to date. Quarterly (Sept., Dec., Feb., May). Ed., Rubin Gotesky, Northern Illinois University, De Kalb, Ill. 60115.

Called *The Pacific Philosophy Forum,* v. 1–6 (1962–68). Each volume has a common theme (e.g., v. 2, 1963/64, "The Democratic Idea"). Each number contains a longer essay developing a philosophical thesis on that theme, two shorter articles developing a counter-thesis, and an article examining the thesis and counter-theses. Beginning with vol. IX each issue also includes uncommissioned articles dealing with topics associated with the sub-theme of a given issue, and reviews of recent works.

7.2.71 Philosophy of science. 1934–to date. Quarterly (Mar., June, Sept., Dec.). Official journal of the Philosophy of Science Association. Ed., Richard S. Rudner, Dept. of Philosophy, Washington University, St. Louis, Mo. 63130.

Cosponsored by the Institute for the Unity of Science and by Section L of the American Association for the Advancement of Science.

Articles on the philosophy of science, book reviews, membership list of the Association, abstracts of articles from *Inquiry, Dialectica,* and *The British Journal for the Philosophy of Science,* index.

Reprinted: v. 1–25 (1934–58), Johnson Reprint Corp.

7.2.72 Philosophy today. 1957–to date. Quarterly (Spring, Summer, Fall, Winter). Published by the Society of the Precious Blood, St. Joseph's College, Collegeville, Ind. Ed.,

Robert F. Lechner, Carthegena Station, Celina, Ohio. 45822.

Articles, index. Frequently contains reprints or translations of articles which have appeared elsewhere.

7.2.73 Phronesis; a journal for ancient philosophy. 1955–to date. Semiannually. Ed. David Furley, Princeton University, Princeton, N. J. 08540 (and others).

Text in English, French, German, Latin. Articles only, index.

7.2.74 Praxis; international edition. 1965–to date. Quarterly (Jan., Apr., July, Oct.). Eds., Gajo Petrović and Rudi Supek, Filosofski Fakultet, Zagreb, Dure Salaja b.b., Yugoslavia.

Text in English, French, German. Articles, "Portraits and situations," "Thought and reality," discussion, reviews, notes, philosophical life. Marxist in orientation. Issues frequently focus on some theme or problem.

7.2.75 Ratio. 1957–to date. Semiannually (June, Dec.). Official organ of the Society for the Furtherance of Critical Philosophy. Ed., Stephen Körner, Dept. of Philosophy, University of Bristol, Bristol 8, England.

Published in an English and a German edition.

Articles, book reviews, books received, announcements, index. Deals with all branches of philosophy; is opposed to irrationalism and scepticism.

7.2.76 Review of metaphysics. 1947–to date. Quarterly (Sept., Dec., Mar., June). Ed., Richard Bernstein, 214 Lyman-Beecher Hall, Haverford College, Haverford, Pa. 19041.

Articles in all branches of philosophy, critical studies, problems and perplexities, exploration, discussion, summaries and comments of books received, announcements, abstracts of articles from other leading philosophical journals, annual list of doctoral dissertations (since 1958; listing is incomplete), emeriti professors, visiting philosophers from abroad, index. No special orientation. Annually publishes the presidential address of the Metaphysical Society of America.

Cum. index: v. 1–20 (1947–67). Reprinted: v. 1–20, A. M. S. Reprint Co.

7.2.77 **Science and society;** an independent journal of Marxism. Quarterly (Winter, Spring, Summer, Fall). Ed. Board: Edwin B. Burgum, and others, 30 E. 20th St., New York, N. Y. 10003.

Articles, communications, book reviews, index. Marxist in orientation; sometimes carries articles in philosophy.

7.2.78 **Scientia;** international review of scientific synthesis. Bimonthly. Ed., N. Bonetti, via Donizetti 55, 20122 Milano, Italy.

Articles in English, Italian, French, Spanish, German (supplement with a French translation of non-French articles), book reviews, analysis, chronicle. Multidisciplinary, with emphasis on the convergence of the various branches of knowledge.

7.2.79 **Social theory and practice;** an international and interdisciplinary journal of social philosophy. 1970–to date. Quarterly. Ed., K. T. Fann (and others), Dept. of Philosophy, The Florida State University, Tallahassee, Fla. 82306.

Part of each issue is devoted to a specific theme. Concerned with the relevance of philosophical criticism to the solution of pressing social problems.

7.2.80 **The southern journal of philosophy.** 1963–to date. Quarterly (Spring, Summer, Autumn, Winter). Ed., W. B. Barton, Jr., Dept. of Philosophy, Memphis State University, Memphis, Tenn. 38111.

Articles, book reviews, news, index. "The journal does not confine itself to any particular set of issues or problems, nor to any particular orientation, regional or other."

7.2.81 **Soviet studies in philosophy;** selected articles from Soviet journals in English translation. 1962–to date. Quarterly (Summer, Fall, Winter, Spring). Ed., John Sommerville, California Western University, San Diego, Calif. 92106.

Publishes translations of Russian articles in philosophy.

7.2.82 **Speculum;** a journal of mediaeval studies. 1926–to date. Quarterly (Jan., Apr., July, Oct.). Published by the Mediaeval Academy of America. Cambridge, Mass. Ed., Van Courtlandt Elliott, 1430 Mass. Ave., Cambridge, Mass. 02138.

Articles, book reviews, bibliography, index. An important journal in its field.

7.2.83 **Studies in philosophy and education.** 1960–to date. Quarterly (Winter, Spring, Summer, Autumn). Ed., Francis T. Villemain, Southern Illinois University, Edwardsville, Ill. 62025.

Essays, articles, reviews and rejoinders, book reviews, bibliographies. Once a year an issue is devoted to the literature in and related to the philosophy of education.

7.2.84 **Studies in Soviet thought.** 1961–to date. Quarterly (Mar., June, Sept., Dec.). Eds., J. M. Bochenski (Fribourg, Switzerland) and T. J. Blakeley, Dept. of Philosophy, Boston College, Chestnut Hill, Mass. 02167.

V. 1 published in one bound issue.
Text in English, French, German.
Articles, notes and comments, bibliography, chronology, book reviews, report from the Institute of East European Studies, Fribourg, Switzerland, index. Concerned with all aspects of Soviet and East European philosophy from both a descriptive and a critical point of view.

7.2.85 **Synthese;** an international journal for epistemology, methodology and philosophy of science. 1936–1963 (v. 1–15); 1966 (v. 16)–to date. Quarterly (Mar., June, Sept., Dec.). Ed., Jaakko Hintikka, University of Helsinki and Dept. of Philosophy, Stanford University, Stanford, Calif. 94305.

Suspended 1940–Apr. 1946; 1964–65. Subtitle varies. Text in English, French, and German.
Articles, reviews, abstracts, books received, index. Also publishes selected papers read at the Boston Colloquium for the Philosophy of Science, and minutes and announcements of the

Division of Logic, Methodology and Philosophy of Science, International Union of History and Philosophy of Science. Most issues are partially devoted to symposia on a prescribed theme.

Cum. index: v. 1–17 (1936–67).

7.2.86 **Systematics;** the journal of the Institute for the Comparative Study of History. Philosophy and the Sciences. 1963–to date, Quarterly (Mar., June, Sept., Dec.). Eds., John G. Bennett and Karl S. Schaffer, 23 Brunswick Road, Kingston-upon-Thames, Surrey, England.

Articles, reviews, review discussions. Interdisciplinary, with emphasis on "the field of structural thinking and organization."

7.2.87 **Theological studies.** 1940–to date. Quarterly (Mar., June, Sept., Dec.). Publication of the Theological Faculties of the Society of Jesus in the U. S. Edited by the Theological Faculty, Woodstock, Md. 21163.

Articles, notes, book reviews, books received, index.

7.2.88 **Theoria;** a Swedish journal of philosophy. 1935–to date. Three nos. yearly. Ed., Mats Furberg (and others), The Philosophical Institute, Kungshuset, Lundagard, Lund, Sweden.

Subtitle varies. Text primarily in English, also in French and German.
Articles, discussions, annual bibliography of Scandinavian literature and of articles in philosophy and related fields, index. Emphasis on analytic philosophy and articles employing symbolic logic.

7.2.89 **The thomist;** a speculative quarterly of theology and philosophy. 1939–to date. Quarterly (Jan., Apr., July, Oct.). Edited by the Dominican Fathers of the Province of St. Joseph. Ed., Nicholas Halligan, 487 Michigan Ave., N. E., Washington, D. C. 20017.

Articles, book reviews, books received, index.
Cum. index: v. 1–15 (1939–52).
Reprinted: v. 1–25 (1939–67), Kraus Reprint Corp.

7.2.90 **Thought;** a review of culture and ideas. 1926–to date. Quarterly (Spring, Summer, Autumn, Winter). Published by Fordham University. Ed., Joseph E. O'Neill, S. J., Fordham University, Bronx, N. Y. 10458.

Subtitle varies.
Articles and book reviews, some of them in or on philosophy, index.

7.2.91 **Traditio;** studies in ancient and medieval history, thought, and religion. 1943–to date. Annual. Ed., S. Kuttner, Fordham University Press, Bronx, N. Y. 10458.

Articles, miscellany, bibliography, Institute of Medieval Canon Law Bulletin. Carries some articles on philosophy.

7.2.92 **Transactions of the Charles S. Peirce Society;** a journal in American philosophy. 1965–to date. Three nos. yearly (Winter, Spring, Fall). Ed., Edward C. Moore, Dept. of Philosophy, SUNY, Binghamton, N. Y. 13901.

Articles on American philosophy and source materials on American pragmatism and Peirce in particular, proceedings and members of the Society, books received, book reviews, news and notes.

7.2.93 **Vivarium;** a journal for mediaeval philosophy and the intellectual life of the Middle Ages. 1963–to date. Semiannually (May, Nov.). Ed., L. M. De Rijk, Sophiaweg 73, Nijmegan, The Netherlands.

Articles in English, French, German; reviews, books received, index.
Concerned with medieval philosophy in relation to the field of liberal arts.

7.2.94 **Zygon;** journal of religion and science. 1966–to date. Quarterly (Mar., June, Sept., Dec.). Published by the Institute on Religion in an Age of Science *and* Meadville Theological School of Lombard College. Ed., Ralph W. Burhoe, 5700 Woodlawn Ave., Chicago, Ill. 60637.

Editorial, articles, book reviews, a survey of periodicals, announcements. Seeks to bridge the gap between science and religion.

See also: 5.3.8, 7.3.3, 7.3.19, 7.3.28, 7.3.32, 7.3.35, 7.3.41, 7.3.42 7.3.48.

7.3 SELECTED PHILOSOPHICAL JOURNALS: OTHER LANGUAGES

French

7.3.1 L'année philosophique. 1890–1913 (v. 1–24). Paris. Annual. Superseded *Critique philosophique*. Paris, no. 1–26, 1872–85; ns. v. 1–10, 1885–89.

Articles, bibliography of French philosophy for the year.

7.3.2 Archives de philsophie; recherches et documentation. 1923–to date. Quarterly. Ed., M. Régnier, 117 rue de Rennes, 75 Paris (6ᵉ).

Suspended between v. 18, no. 2 (1952) and v. 19, no. 1 (1955). v. 18– , called "nouvelle série."
Articles, book reviews, bibliographies, index. Each issue devoted to a particular topic.
Cum. index: v. 1–12 (1923–34).

7.3.3 Archives internationales d'histoire des sciences. 1947–to date. Quarterly. Published by Académie internationale d'histoire des sciences. Ed., Pierre Costabel, 115 Blvd. St. Germain, Paris 6, France.

Text in French and English.
Articles, reviews, bibliographies, news.

7.3.4 Bulletin de la société française de philosophie. 1901–to date. Quarterly. Organ of the Société. Ed., Librairie Colin, 103 Blvd. Saint-Michel, Paris 5, France.

Suspended 1915–16, 1918–20. Numbering irregular. V. 20–24 omitted in numbering; v. 26, no. 5 (Dec. 1936) never published.
Texts and communications of the society, followed by the complete discussion.

7.3.5 Bulletin thomiste. 1924–to date. Quarterly. Organ of the Société Thomiste. Ed., Università S. Tommaso, Largo Angelicum 1, I–00184 Roma, Italy.

V. 1–7 (1924–30) in *Revue thomiste;* v. 8 (1931) published separately. V. 12 (years 1940–42, 1963–65), the last of the old series contains book reviews and a Thomistic bibliography up through 1965 (p. 209–435). See 5.5.20.
Cum. index: 1924–33.

7.3.6 Etudes franciscaines. 1899–1936; ns. 1950–to date. Semiannual. Ed., Bibliothèque Franciscaine Provinciale, Couvent des Capucins, 26 rue Boissonade, Paris 14, France.

Subtitle varies. Articles and bibliographies connected with the Franciscans.
Cum. index: v. 1–20 (1899–1928).

7.3.7 Les études philosophiques. 1926–1945 (v. 1–20); 1946 (ns. v. 1)–to date. Quarterly. Ed., G. Bastide, 173 Blvd. Saint Germain, 75–Paris 6, France.

Articles, critical studies, book reviews (which encompass about half of each issue), philosophical life (international), news (international), doctoral defenses, index. Each issue is devoted to a particular theme.

7.3.8 Laval théologique et philosophique. 1945–to date. Semiannual. Ed., Emmanuel Trépanier, Université Laval, Québec 10, P. Q., Canada.

1928–45, published irregularly as *Bulletin Laval des sciences philosophiques et théologiques*. Articles, theses extracts, bibliography.

7.3.9 Recherches de philosophie. 1955–to date. Annual. Publication of the Association des professeurs de philosophie de facultés catholiques de France. Ed., R. P. Stanislas Breton, 1 rue du sud, Clamart, S. & O; and Jean Chatillon, 61 rue Madame, Paris 6, France.

Articles, confrontations, notes, chronicle. Each volume dedicated to a particular theme; some issues of book length.
A continuation of *Revue de philosophie* (7.3.12).

7.3.10 Revue d'esthétique. 1948–to date. 4 nos. yearly (irregular). Organ of the Société française d'esthétique. Eds., E. Souriau and M. Dufrenne, 16 rue Chaptal, Paris 9, France.

Articles, chronicle, book reviews, news of the society, index.

7.3.11 Revue de métaphysique et de morale. 1893–1941 (v. 1–48); 1944 (v. 49)–to date. Quarterly. Ed., Jean Wahl, Lib. Armand Colin,

103 Blvd. Saint-Michel, 75-Paris 5e, France.

Suspended Jan.-Dec. 1915; 1942–1944; 1944 replaced by *Etudes de métaphysique et de morale*, later considered v. 49 of the *Revue*.

Articles, critical studies, book reviews, critical notes, index. Publishes articles on topics other than metaphysics and ethics. The major French philosophical journal.

Cum. index: v. 1–30 (1893–1923).

Reprinted: v. 1–17 (1893–1909), Johnson Reprint Corp.

7.3.12 Revue de philosophie. 1900–1939 (v. 1–39).

Suspended 1915–18. 1931–39 also called ns. v. 1–8. Some irregularity in numbering.

Cum. index: v. 1–23 (1900–13).

1902–03 published *Index philosophique*, v. 1–2. Continued as 7.3.9.

7.3.13 Revue de théologie et de philosophie. 1868–1911 (v. 1–44); 1913–50 (ns. v. 1–38); 1951 (s3, v. 1)–to date. Quarterly. Ed., Henri Meylan, 7 Chevnin des Cèdres, 1000 Lausanne, Switzerland.

V. 1–5 (1868–72), as *Théologie et philosophie*. Six nos. yearly, 1868–1920; quarterly from 1921.

Articles, discussion, reviews.

Reprinted: v. 1–44 (1868–1911), Johnson Reprint Corp.

7.3.14 Revue des études augustiniennes. 1955–to date. Quarterly. Ed., 8 rue Francois ler, Paris 8, France.

Continues *Année théologique augustinienne*, v. 1–14 (1940–54).

Publishes articles related to the work and thought of St. Augustine; reviews of related books, index.

7.3.15 Revue des études juives; historia judaica. 1880–to date. Quarterly. Publication of Ecole Pratique des Hautes-Etudes (6e section) *and* Société des Etudes Juives. Ed., Georges Vajda, 20 rue de La Baume, 75–Paris 8e, France.

N . 101, 1937 also as ns. v. 1.

Articles, notes, reviews.

Cum. index: v. 1–50 (1880–1905); v. 51–100 bis.

7.3.16 Revue des sciences philosophiques et théologiques. 1907–1941 (v. 1–30); 1947 (v. 31)–to date. Quarterly. Published by the Professeurs aux Facultés de Philosophie et de Théologie, O. P., Le Saulchoir, Ed., B. Quelquejeu, Le Saulchoir, Etoilles, 91 Soisy-sur-Seine, France.

Suspended 1941–46.

Articles, notes, bulletins, reviews (sometimes two-thirds of an issue), contents of articles from many journals (with one-sentence summaries of some), bibliographies, index.

7.3.17 Revue internationale de philosophie. 1938–to date. Quarterly. Ed., P. Devaux (and others), 99 avenue de l'Université, Bruxelles 5, Belgium.

Suspended after v. 2, no. 5, Oct. 1939; resumed with special no. v. 2, no. 6, pub. Aug. 1948, which completes v. 2.

Articles (in French, English, German, Italian, Spanish), notes and discussions, book reviews, books received, contents of a number of journals, philosophical life, index. Each number dedicated to a study of a philosopher, movement, or a problem of philosophy, often with an extensive bibliography on the topic. See 5.3.24.

Reprinted: Johnson Reprint Corp.

7.3.18 Revue philosophique de la France et de l'étranger. 1876–to date. Quarterly. Ed., Pierre-Maxime Schuhl, 12, rue Jean-de-Beauvais, Paris 5e, France.

Articles, critical reviews, notes, information, news correspondence, index.

Cum. index: 1876–1920 in 5v.

7.3.19 Revue philosophique de Louvain. 1894–to date. Quarterly. Published by the Société Philosophique de Louvain. Ed., Albert Dondeyne, Place Cardinal Mercier 2, Louvain 2, Belgium.

1894–1909 as *Revue néo-scholastique*; 1910–45 as *Revue néo-scholastique de philosophie*. v. 1–25 also called no. 1–100; 26–43 also called s2, no. 1–67/68; v. 44– , also called s3. Suspended Aug. 1914–Nov. 1919 (v. 21, no. 84 called Nov. 1914–1919): May 1940-Aug. 1945 (v. 43, no. 3 dated Aug. 1940–Aug. 1945).

Articles (some in English, some in French with English summary), book reviews, index. Supplement: *Repertoire bibliographique de la philosophie* (5.3.6).

Cum. index: v. 1–20 (1894–1913).

7.3.20 Revue Teilhard de Chardin. 1960–to date. Quarterly. Organ of the Société Teilhard de Chardin. Ed., 99 rue Souveraine, Bruxelles 5, Belgium.

No. 1/2–12, June 1960–Sept. 1962; v. 4, No. 14, Mar. 1963– .

7.3.21 Revue thomiste. 1893–to date. Quarterly. Ed., M. V. Jean Leroy, Desclée de Brouwer, 23 Quai au Bois, Bruges, Belgium.

Suspended Oct./Dec. 1939–Jan./Mar. 1946.

Articles, reviews of books, reviews of reviews, summaries of articles, index.

7.3.22 Les temps modernes. 1945–to date. Monthly. Ed., Jean-Paul Sartre, Editions Julliard, 30 rue de l'Université, Paris 7e, France.

Supersedes *Nouvelle revue française*.

Articles, debates, chronicles. An outlet for articles by Sartre and members of the Paris existentialist school, and their debates with others.

See also: 5.3.6–5.3.10, 5.3.12, 5.3.23, 5.4.11, 7.3.26, 7.3.28, 7.3.35, 7.3.41, 7.3.43, 7.3.48.

German

7.3.23 Archiv für Geschichte der Philosophie. 1888–1932; 1959–to date. Three nos. yearly. Ed., Dr. Hans Wagner, Philosophisches Seminar A der Universität, Bonn, Germany.

Suspended 1933–59.

V. 37–39, 1925–30 as *Archiv für Geschichte der Philosophie und Soziologie*; v. 8–39 (1895–1930) as v. 1–32; v. 8–33 (1895–1924) as *Archiv für Philosophie*, Abteilung 1.

Articles (in English, French, German, Italian), critical reviews.

7.3.24 Archiv für Philosophie. 1947–to date. Quarterly. Ed., Jürgen v. Kempski, 3491 Hembsen über Bad, Driburg/Wesf., Germany.

Articles, book reviews, index.

7.3.25 Deutsche Zeitschrift für Philosophie. 1953–to date. Monthly. Ed., Rolf Kirchhoff, 104 Berlin, Marienstrasse 19/20, Germany.

Frequency varies.

Table of contents also in Russian, English, French, Spanish.

Articles, remarks and discussion, book reviews, notes index.

Marxist in orientation; emphasis on Eastern European philosophy and dialectical materialism.

7.3.26 Freiburger Zeitschrift für Philosophie und Theologie. 1954–to date. Quarterly. Ed., Dr. Paul Wyser, O. P., Place G. Python 1, Fribourg, Switzerland.

Superseded *Divus Thomas*, 1887–1953; also numbered *Jahrbuch für Philosophie und speculative Theologie*, ser. 4.

Text in French and German. Articles, book reviews, bibliography, index.

7.3.27 Hegel-Studien. 1955–to date. Irregular. Ed., F. Nicolin and O. Pöggeler, H. Bouvier Verlag, Bonn, Germany.

Published in connection with the Hegel-Kommission der Deutschen Forschungsgemeinschaft.

Articles on Hegel, Hegel texts, reviews of Hegel literature.

7.3.28 Kant-Studien; philosophische Zeitschrift der Kant-Gesellschaft. 1897–to date. Quarterly. Ed., Gottfried Martin, 5301 Röttgen/bei Bonn, Am alten Forsthaus, Germany.

Suspended 1937–41, 1945–52.

Articles (in German, English, French, Italian), discussions, book reviews, bibliography, information, index. Not exclusively on Kant.

Reprinted: Würzburg, Arnulf Leibing OHG.

7.3.29 Philosophia naturalis; Archiv für Naturphilosophie und die philosophischen Grenzgebiete der exakten Wissenschaftsgeschichte. 1950–to date. Quarterly. Ed. Joseph Meurers, Wien, Direktor der Universitätssternwarte.

Articles, book reviews, index. Emphasis on analytic philosophy, logic and philosophy of science.

7.3.30 Philosophische Rundschau. 1957–to date. Quarterly. Eds., G. Gadamer (Heidelberg) and Helmut Kuhn, U. of Munich, Germany.

Articles, book reviews, bibliography, index.

7.3.31 Philosophisches Jahrbuch im Auftrag der Görres-Gesellschaft. 1888–to date. Two nos. yearly. Ed., Max Müller, Philosophisches Seminar I der Universität München, 8 München 22, Geschwister-School-Platz, Germany.

Frequency varies.
Articles, reviews, reports.

7.3.32 Studium Generale; Zeitschrift für interdisziplinäre Studien; Journal for interdisciplinary studies. 1947–to date. Monthly. Ed., G. H. Müller, 6900 Heidelberg 1, Postfach 1780, Germany.

Subtitle and frequency vary.
Articles (in German and English), short summaries of journal articles (but no book reviews). Emphasis on philosophy of science and analytic philosophy.

7.3.33 Theologie und Philosophie. 1966–to date. Quarterly. Ed. Alois Grillmeier, Offenbacher Landstrasse 224, Frankfurt am Main, Germany.

Supersedes *Scholastik*, 1926–1965. Published by the Jesuit Faculty of Theology and Philosophy of St. Georgen in Frankfurt.

7.3.34 Die Zeitschrift für philosophische Forschung. 1946–to date. Quarterly. Ed. G. Schischkoff, 809 Wasserburg/Inn, bei München, Mozartstrasse 15, Germany.

Articles, discussion, book reviews, contents of other journals, reports and information. See also 5.3.22.
Cum. index every 10 years.

See also: 5.3.21, 5.3.22, 5.4.13–5.4.16, 7.2.42, 7.3.17, 7.3.35, 7.3.38, 7.3.41, 7.3.48.

Italian

7.3.35 Archivio di filosofia. 1931–to date. Quarterly. Organ of the Istituto di Studi Filosofici dell'Universita di Roma. Ed., Enrico Castelli, Edizioni CEDAM, Padua, Italy.

Suspended 1943–45.
Articles (in Italian, English, French, German), bibliography, information on activities of the Institute.

7.3.36 Aut aut; rivista di filosofia e di cultura, 1951–to date. Bi-monthly. Ed., Enzo Paci, c/o A. Lampugnani Nigiri, Via S. Gregorio 10, Milano, Italy.

Articles, book reviews in the Kierkegaardian tradition of *Either/Or*, emphasizing freedom: to free examination, to follow alternatives of the irrational, and to uncover new problems.

7.3.37 Ethica; rassegna di filosofia morale. 1961–to date. Three nos. yearly. Ed., M. Gianfranco Morra, Via Zanchini 24, Forli, Italy.

Articles, book reviews, notes.

7.3.38 Filosofia. 1950–to date. Quarterly. Ed., Augusto Guzzo, Via Po 18, Turino, Italy.

Four nos. in Italian, one international number in English, French, German, or Spanish.
Articles on all branches of philosophy, book reviews, index.
Cum. index every 10 years.

7.3.39 Giornale critico della filosofia italiana. 1920–32 (v. 1–13); 1933 (s2 v. 1)–to date. Quarterly. Ed., Ugo Spirito, Piazza Grazioli 5, Roma, Italy.

Suspended 1946–1953. s2 v. 1 (1933) also v. 14. Text in Italian, English, French. Founded by G. Gentile.
Articles, discussion, book reviews, notes, bibliography, index.

7.3.40 Giornale di metafisica. 1946–to date. Bimonthly. Ed., Michele Sciacca, Società Editrice Internationale, 176 Corso Regina, Margherita, Turino, Italy.

Studies, notes, book reviews, chronicle, index.

7.3.41 Gregorianum; periodicum trimestre a Pontifica Universitate Gregoriana edita. 1920–to date. Quarterly. Ed., Peter Henrici, I–00187 Roma, Piazza della Pilotta, 4, Italy.

Subtitle varies.

Articles (in English, French, German, Italian, Latin, Spanish), notes, reviews, bibliography. Thomistic in orientation.

7.3.42 Rassegna bibliografica di storia della filosofia—ricavata dalle riviste; Bibliographic review of the history of philosophy—extracted from magazines. 1968–to date. Annual. Published by L'Instituto di Filosofia dell'Università de Parma. Ed., D. Pesce, Liviana Editrice, 35100 Padova, Via S. Biagio, 18, Italy.

Aims to provide researchers with information on what has been published every year in the major journals concerning the history of philosophy by way of articles, notes, and reviews.
Vol. I (1968) covered 1966; vol. II (1969) covered 1967; etc.

7.3.43 Rivista critica di storia della filosofia. 1946–to date. Quarterly. Organ of the Ist. di Storia della Filosofia dell'Universita di Milano. Ed., Mario Dal Pra (and others).

Text in Italian, French, Greek, Latin. Articles on historical studies broadly conceived, documents, notes, discussion, book reviews, information, index. Some numbers dedicated to an author or subject, with exhaustive bibliographies.

7.3.44 Rivista di filosofia. 1909–to date. Quarterly. Ed., Norberto Bobbio, Casa Editrice Taylor, Torino, Corso Stati Uniti, 53, Italy.

Suspended 1922. Supersedes *Rivista filosofica*, 1899–1908.
Articles on all aspects of philosophy, discussion, book reviews, chronicle, index.

7.3.45 Rivista di filosofia neoscholastica. 1909–to date. Bimonthly. Published by Universita Cattolica del Sacro Cuore, Faculta di Filosofia, Largo A. Gemelli 1, 20133 Milano, Italy.

Articles, notes and discussions, announcements, bibliographies, book reviews, index.

7.3.46 Rivista di studi Crociani. 1964–to date. Quarterly. Ed., Alfredo Parente, Società Napoletana di Storia Patria, Piazza Municipio, Maschio Angioino, 80133 Napoli, Italy.

Dedicated to the study and continuation of Croce's thought.

7.3.47 Sapienza; rivista internationale di filosofia e teologia. Edited by the Dominicans of Italy. 1948–to date. Quarterly. Ed., Benedetto d'Amore, Via Luigi Palmieri 19, 80133 Napoli, Italy.

Subtitle varies.
Articles, discussions, critical notes, book reviews, books received.

7.3.48 Sophia; rassegna critica di filosofia e storia della filosofia. 1933–to date. Quarterly. Ed., Carmelo Ottaviano, Via Mesopotamia 21, Roma, Italy.

Subtitle varies.
Articles (in English, French, German, Italian), book reviews, index. Emphasis on the history of philosophy, with an annual bibliography of new works.

See also: 5.4.25, 7.2.48, 7.2.78, 7.3.17, 7.3.28.

Russian

7.3.49 Nauchnye doklady vysshei shkoly; filosofskie nauki. 1958–to date. Bimonthly. Ed., M. T. Iovchuk, Moskva, K-19, prospekt Marksa 18, Korpus 5, U. S. S. R.

Articles, book reviews, discussions and debates, new books in philosophy. Table of contents also in English, French, German. Exclusively Marxist-Leninist in orientation.

7.3.50 Voprosy filosofii. 1947–to date. Monthly. Published by Akademiia Nauk SSSR. Institut Filosofii. Ed., I. T. Frolov, Moskva, G–19, Volkhonka 14, Komm. 103, U. S. S. R.

Summaries in English of the major articles. Table of contents also in English, French, German, Spanish.
Articles, consultation, notes, discussion, book reviews, bibliography, index. Exclusively Marxist-Leninist. The major Soviet philosophical journal.

Spanish

7.3.51 Augustinus. 1956–to date. Quarterly. Published by Padres Agustinos Recoletos,

Cea Bermudez 59, Madrid–3, Spain. Eds., Victorino Capanaga y Adolfo Muñoz Alonso.

Articles, book reviews, news, index. Dedicated to all aspects of the writings of St. Augustine; devotes much space to bibliography.

7.3.52 **Crítica;** revista hispanoamericana de filosofia. 1967–to date. Three nos. yearly. Ed., A. Rossi (and others), Apartado 27–414, México, D. F.

Articles (in Spanish and English with summaries in the other language), discussions, bibliographical notes. Represents the various philosophical tendencies in Latin America, with some emphasis on analytic philosophy.

7.3.53 **Estudios filosóficos.** 1951–to date. Three nos. yearly. Published by the Dominicans, Estudio General de Filosofía, La Caldas de Besaya (Santander), Spain. Ed., P. Téofilo Urdánoz, O. P.

Articles, notes, commentaries, chronicles, bibliography, book reviews. Thomistic in orientation.

7.3.54 **Pensiamento;** revista de investigacíon e información filosófica. 1945–to date. Quarterly. Published by the Facultades de Filosofia de la Compañía de Jesús en Espagña. Ed., Juan Roig Gironella, Pablo Aranda 3, Madrid–6, Spain.

Articles, notes, commentaries, reviews of books, extracts of articles, chronicle, annual bibliography of Spanish and hispanoamerican philosophy.

7.3.55 **Revista de filosofía.** 1942–to date. Quarterly. Pub. by Instituto "Luis Vives" de Filosofía. Ed., Manuel Mindan, Serrano 127, Madrid–6, Spain.

Articles, notes, texts, book reviews, chronicle, and acts of the Soc. Esp. de Fil., bibliography, notices. Primarily scholastic in orientation.

7.3.56 **Sapientia.** 1946–to date. Quarterly. Published by the Fac. de Fil., Univ. Católica "Santa María de los Buenos Aires." La Plata, Argentina. Eds., O. N. Derisi and J. E. Bolzán.

Articles, notes, bibliography. Thomistic in orientatio

Cum. index: 1946–1955.

See also: 5.4.35, 7.3.17, 7.3.38, 7.3.41.

7.4 OTHER PHILOSOPHICAL SERIALS

7.4.1 **American Catholic philosophical association.** Proceedings. 1926–to date. Annual.

1944 not published.
Contains all papers presented at annual meetings; Association reports; list of members. Each annual meeting is devoted to a particular problem.
Issued by the Office of the National Secretary of the Association, The Catholic University of America, Washington, D. C. 20017.
Cum. index: v. 1–39 (1926–65).
Partially reprinted: Johnson Reprint Corp.

7.4.2 **American philosophical association.** Proceedings and addresses. 1926–to date. Annual.

Presidential addresses, proceedings, officers, Association reports, list of members.
Proceedings 1902–26 were printed in the *Philosophical Review* (7.2.63). Now published by the Association, 117 Lehigh Road, College Park, Md., 20740.
Cum. index: v. 1–39 (1926–1965).

7.4.3 **American philosophical society.** Proceedings. 1838–to date. Early proceedings . . . from the manuscript of its meetings from 1744 to 1838 in v. 22, pt 3.

Cum. index: v. 1–100 (1838–1957). 3v.
———. Transactions. 1769–1809 (v. 1–6); 1818 (ns. v. 1)–to date.
Though not concerned only with philosophy, papers and monographs on philosophy are included.
Published by the Society, 104 S. Fifth St., Philadelphia, Pa. 19106.

7.4.4 **Aristotelian society** for the systematic study of philosophy. Proceedings. 1887–96 (v. 1–3); 1900 (ns. v. 1)–to date. Annual.

1897–1900 published in *Mind* (7.2.49), v. 5–9 (1896–1900).

Contains papers read before the Society. Supplementary volumes of symposia, 1918–to date.

Reprinted: Johnson Reprint Corp.

7.4.5 **Boston college studies in philosophy.** The Hague, Martinus Nijhoff, 1966–to date. Annual.

Each volume contains a group of essays, usually on a common theme.

7.4.6 **California university publications in philosophy.** Berkeley, University of California Press, 1904–to date. Frequency varies.

Contains monographs and, since 1923, lectures delivered before the Philosophical Union. Reprinted: v. 1–25, 1904–1950. Johnson Reprint Corp.

7.4.7 **Catholic university of America.** Philosophical studies. Catholic University of America Press. Irregular.

V. 1–33 issued without series title and numbering. Contains dissertations in philosophy accepted at Catholic University.

7.4.8 **Catholic university of America.** Studies in philosophy and the history of philosophy. Washington, D. C., Catholic University of America Press, 1961–to date. Irregular.

Each volume is a collection of essays, sometimes on a specific topic.

7.4.9 ★ **Danish year-book of philosophy.** Organ of the Danish Society for Philosophy and Psychology. 1964–to date. Annual. Eds., Mogens Blegvad [et al], Munksgaard, 47 Prags Boulevard, Copenhagen, Denmark.

English, occasionally French or German, papers of varying length on philosophical topics, preferably written by Danish philosophers.

7.4.10 ★ **Duquesne studies.** Philosophical series. Published by Duquesne University. 1952–to date. Irregular.

Contains primarily monographs, with some

tendency towards phenomenology. Though irregular, volumes have appeared on the average of one a year.

7.4.11 **Iowa publications in philsosophy.** The Hague, Martinus Nijhoff, 1963–to date. Irregular.

Sponsored by the Department of Philosophy, Iowa University. "A series of analytical studies—essay collections, monographs, books —in ontology, the history of philosophy, the philosophy of science, and other branches of philosophy."

7.4.12 **Mediaeval philosophical texts in translation.** Published by Marquette University. 1942–to date. Irregular.

Monograph-length translations.

7.4.13 **Nomos.** Yearbook of the American society for for politcal and legal philosophy. 1958–to date. Annual.

Each volume contains papers on a particular theme or topic (e.g., v. 1, Authority). Publisher varies. Recent volumes have been published by The Atherton Press (New York).

7.4.14 **Philosophy of education society.** Proceedings of the annual meeting. 1958 (v. 14)–to date. Annual.

V. 1–13 not published.

7.4.15 **Studia philosophica;** Jahrbuch der schweizerischen philosophischen Gesellschaft; annuaire de la société suisse de philosophie. Basel, Verlag für Recht und Gesellschaft, 1941– to date. Annual.

Also supplements, 1943–to date. Contains articles, book reviews, critical studies.

Supplementary vol. II: *Bibliographie der philosophischen, psychologischen und pädagogischen Literatur in der deutschsprachigen Schweiz 1900– 1940.* Continued in v. 5 for 1941–44, and in later volumes.

7.4.16 **Tulane studies in philosophy.** The Hague, Martinus Nijhoff, 1952–to date. Annual.

Each volume dedicated to a particular theme or topic.

Lecture Series

7.4.17 Aquinas lecture. 1937–to date. Annual.

Sponsored by Marquette University and the Aristotelian Society of Milwaukee, Wis. Published by Marquette University Press.

Lecturers have included M. Adler, J. Maritain, E. Gilson, J. Collins, and P. Weiss.

7.4.18 Paul Carus lectures. 1925–to date.

Sponsored by the American Philosophical Association (the lecturer is selected biannually by a special committee) and the Edward C. Hegeler Foundation. The lectures are delivered alternately at one of the divisional meetings of the A. P. A. (e.g., R. Chisholm presented the 16th annual lectures at the 1967 meetings of the Pacific Division; C. Hempel presented the 17th annual lectures at the 1970 meetings of the Western Division). Published by Open Court Publishing Co.

Lecturers have included J. Dewey, G. H. Mead, C. I. Lewis, C. J. Ducasse, G. Boas, B. Blanshard, E. Nagel, and R. McKeon.

7.4.19 Deems lectures. 1895–to date. Irregular.

Sponsored by New York University; endowed by the American Institute of Christian Philosophy. Publisher varies, though recent lectures have been published by the New York University Press.

Lecturers have included F. S. C. Northrop and J. M. Bochenski.

7.4.20 Dewey lectures. 1968–to date.

Sponsored by Columbia University. The lectures are given once every two years.

The first lecturer was W. V. O. Quine.

7.4.21 Howison lecture. 1927–to date. Irregular.

Sponsored by California University, Berkeley, Published in 7.4.6.

Lecturers have included C. I. Lewis, W. H. Sheldon, G. Boas, and B. Blanshard.

7.4.22 Lindley lecture. 1961–to date. Annual.

Sponsored by the Department of Philosophy, The University of Kansas. Lectures on the theme "Values of Living," broadly conceived. Published by the Department.

Lecturers have included R. B. Brandt, R. M. Chisholm, S. Hampshire, W. K. Frankena, and W. Sellars.

7.4.23 Terry lectures. 1925–to date. Irregular.

Sponsored by Yale University. Lectures on Religion in the Light of Science and Philosophy. Published by Yale University Press.

Lecturers have included W. P. Montague, C. G. Jung, J. Dewey, W. E. Hocking, J. Maritain, C. Hartshorne, P. Tillich, and E. E. Harris.

7.4.24 William James lectures on philsophy. 1929–to date. Irregular.

Sponsored by Harvard University to honor the memory of William James.

Lecturers have included John Dewey (*Art as Experience*), A. O. Lovejoy (*The Great Chain of Being*), E. Gilson (*The Unity of Philosophical Experience*), and J. L. Austin (*How to Do Things with Words*).

Publisher varies.

7.4.25 Woodbridge lectures. 1943–to date. Irregular.

Sponsored by Columbia University and published by Columbia University Press.

Lecturers have included W. Sheldon, S. P. Lamprecht, C. I. Lewis, and I. Berlin.

8. PHILOSOPHICAL RESEARCH, REPORTS, AND PUBLISHING

SCHOLARLY WORK on a particular author demands that the student or scholar ascertain as closely as possible what the philosopher in question really wrote. It is necessary both to identify a text as being from the author concerned and as being his latest thought on the matter (or as being from a certain period in his development). This always remains a difficulty, though it becomes less acute as one approaches nearer to the present time. The establishing of a text is not itself a philosophical task, but may well be a necessary prelude to carrying out the philosophical task.

Analytical (or critical) *bibliography* consists in the examination of books with respect to their physical characteristics and details of their manufacture. It is divided into *descriptive bibliography*, which is concerned with establishing the physical form of a book for purposes of identification, and *textual bibliography* or *criticism*, which is concerned with coming as close as possible to the original or lost manuscript. Works dealing with analytical bibliography are listed in 8.1.

Research in philosophy often involves working with languages other than one's own, to consult, verify, read, or translate texts, articles, or material written in a foreign tongue. Translations are useful for some purposes, and guides to what has been translated or to what is in the process of translation are available. The translator will require dictionaries of the language in which he is working. But both the expert and the novice can use bilingual dictionaries with profit. A recommended list, together with translation guides, can be found in 8.2.

The results of research are frequently submitted by students in the form of term papers, theses, and dissertations, and by scholars in book or article form. It is primarily by publication that knowledge is disseminated widely among specialists in any field, and that discoveries or insights can be shared with others, criticized, corrected, and used in turn to advance knowledge further. Form and style guides are listed in 8.3; books concerning the various facets of publishing (copyrights, indexing, proofreading, etc.) are listed in 8.4.

8.1 ANALYTICAL BIBLIOGRAPHY AND TEXTUAL ANALYSIS

Descriptive Bibliography

8.1.1 **Aldis, H. G.** The printed book. 3d ed. New York, Bowker, 1951. 141 pp.

A history of book printing and construction.

8.1.2 **The bookman's glossary.** 4th ed. New York, R. R. Bowker Co., 1961. 212 pp.

Includes information on the production of books, classical names of towns and cities; foreign book trade names; private book clubs; proofreaders' marks; and a selected reading list.

8.1.3 **Bowers, Fredson.** Principles of bibliographical description. Princeton, Princeton University Press, 1949. 505 pp.

A basic guide to descriptive bibliography.

8.1.4 **Cowley, John D.** Bibliographical description and cataloguing. London, Grafton, 1939. 256 pp.

A textbook of bibliographical description including information on handling "awkward material."

8.1.5 **Dictionary of printing terms.** 5th ed. Salt Lake City, Porte Publishing Co., 1950. 173 pp.

8.1.6 **Esdaile, Arundell.** A student's manual of bibliography. 4th ed. rev. by Roy Stokes. London, Allen & Unwin and the Lib. Assoc., 1967. 336 pp.

1st ed. 1931.
A basic guide to bibliographies and book descriptions, with discussions of the history and makeup of the book.

8.1.7 **Freer, Percy.** Bibliography and modern book production; notes and sources for student librarians, printers, booksellers, stationers, book-collectors. Johannesburg, Witwatersrand University Press, 1954. 345 pp.

8.1.8 **Hostettler, Rudolf.** Printer's terms. St. Gallen, Hostettler, 1949. 204 pp.

Lists English, German, French, and Italian terms.

Textual Bibliography

8.1.9 **Bowers, Fredson.** Bibliography and textual criticism (The Lyell Lectures, Oxford, Trinity Term 1959). Oxford, Clarendon Press, 1964. 207 pp.

A discussion of evidence in textual criticism.

8.1.10 **Bowers, Fredson Thayer.** "Textual criticism," Encyclopaedia Britannica (1965), v. 22, 14–19.

A succinct introduction.

8.1.11 **Capelli, Adriano.** Lexicon abbreviaturarum; dizionario di abbreviature latine ed italiano, usate nelle carte e codici specialmente del Medio-Evo riprodotte con oltre 14000 segni incisi, con l'aggiunta di uno studio sulla brachigrafia medioevale, un prontuario di sigle epigrafiche, l'antica numerazione romana ed arabica ed i segni indicanti monete, pesi, misure, etc. 4. ed. Milano, Hoepli, 1949. 431 pp.

Bibliography: pp. 517–531.

8.1.12 **Chassant, Alphonse A. L.** Dictionnaire des abréviations latines at françaises usitées dans les inscriptions lapidaires et métalliques, les manuscrits et les chartes du Moyen Age. 5. éd. Paris, J. Martin, 1884. 172 pp.

Gives manuscript abbreviations and their equivalents.

8.1.13 **Clark, A. C.** The descent of manuscripts. Oxford, Clarendon Press, 1918. 464 pp.

8.1.14 **Dearing, Vinton A.** A manual of textual analysis. Berkeley, University of California Press, 1959. 108 pp.

A handbook of techniques of textual criticism.

8.1.15 **Goldschmidt, E. P.** Medieval texts and their first appearance in print. London, printed for the Bibliographical Society at the Oxford University Press, 1943. 143 pp.

8.1.16 Greg, W. W. The calculus of variants; an essay on textual criticism. Oxford, Clarendon Press, 1927. 63 pp.

A basic guide to the technique of comparing manuscripts which "aims at nothing but defining and making precise for formal use the logical rules which textual critics have always applied" (p. vi).

8.1.17 Kenyon, F. G. Books and readers in ancient Greece and Rome. Oxford, Clarendon Press, 1931. 136 pp.

Treats the use of books in ancient Greece, papyrus roll books, reading in Rome, vellum, and the codex.

8.1.18 Maas, Paul. Textual criticism. Trans. from German by Barbara Flower. Oxford, Clarendon Press, 1958. 59 pp.

A basic guide.

8.1.19 Madan, Falconer. Books in manuscript; a short introduction to their study and use. With a chapter on records. 2d ed. London, Kegan Paul, 1920. 208 pp.

1st ed. 1893.
"A plain account of the study and use of manuscripts" (p. v). Includes a list of books useful for the study of manuscripts.

8.1.20 McKerrow, Ronald B. An introduction to bibliography for literary students. Oxford, Clarendon Press, 1927. 359 pp.

2d impression with corrections, 1928; reprinted frequently.
A standard work on the making of early printed books.

8.1.21 National union catalog of manuscript collections. 1959–1961. Ann Arbor, Mich., J. W. Edwards, 1962. 1061 pp.

———. 1962–1966. Hamden, Conn., The Shoe String Press, 1964–67.
5v., including indexes.
A continuing series.
"Based on reports from American repositories of manuscripts."

8.1.22 Scriptorium; revue internationale des études relatives aux manuscrits. 1946/47–to date. Semiannual.

Text in English, French, German, Spanish. Carries bibliographies of manuscript studies.

8.1.23 Thompson, *Sir* **Edward Maunde.** An introduction to Greek and Latin palaeography. Oxford, Clarendon Press, 1912. 600 pp.

Reprinted: New York, Burt Franklin.
Still a standard guide.

8.1.24 Van Hoesen, H. B., and **F. K. Walter.** Bibliography; practical, enumerative, historical; an introductory manual. New York, Scribner's, 1928. 519 pp.

Contains chapters on subject bibliography, general reference, special bibliography, national bibliography, bibliography of bibliography, history of writing and printing, bookselling and publishing.
Bibliography: pp. 425–502.

8.1.25 Williamson, Derek. Bibliography; historical analytical and descriptive. London, Clive Bingley, 1967. 129 pp.

"An examination guidebook," which reviews some of the literature on bibliography.

8.2 TRANSLATION GUIDES AND BIBLINGUAL DICTIONARIES

Translation Guides

8.2.1 ★ Index translationum. Répertoire international des traductions. International bibliography of translations. Ns. v. 1, 1948– . Paris, UNESCO, 1949– . Annual.

1st series, no. 1–31, Paris, International Institute of Intellectual Cooperation, 1932–40.
Covers 75 countries and lists works which have been translated during the preceding period. *See* 5.2.9.

8.2.2 Delos; a journal on and of translation. 1968–to date.

Publishes translations, reports, articles, and information on translations. It is the journal of the National Translation Center, 2621 Speedway, Austin, Texas, 78705, which aims "to support the quality, availability, and financial reward of literary translation into English of texts having cultural and artistic significance." The "clearing house" section lists translations known to be in progress and titles for which publishers are seeking translators."

The Center also awards fellows and grants.

8.2.3 **Nida, Eugene A.** Toward a science of translating. Leiden, E. J. Brill, 1964. 331 pp.

Bibliography: pp. 265–320.

A discussion of meaning, communication, correspondences, and translation problems and procedures, with special reference to Bible translation.

8.2.4 **Scholarly translation program.** ACLS, 345 East 46th St., New York, N. Y. 10017.

8.2.5 **Translation Center,** Humanities Division, Southern Illinois University, Edwardsville, Ill. 62025.

Advises translators whether or not the work they intend to translate is already in progress elsewhere.

See also: 4.2.4.

Bilingual Dictionaries

For a detailed account of foreign language dictionaries see Winchell (5.1.3), pp. 102–132.

8.2.6 **Collison, Robert Lewis.** Dictionaries of foreign languages; a bibliographical guide to the general and technical dictionaries of the chief foreign languages, with historical and explanatory notes and references. New York, Hafner, 1955. 210 pp.

Lists general, special, and bilingual dictionaries of the languages of Europe, Asia, and Africa.

8.2.7 **U. S. Library of Congress. General reference and bibliography division.** Foreign language–English dictionaries. Washington, D. C., 1955. 2v.

Vol. I lists subject dictionaries; vol. II, general language dictionaries.

8.2.8 **Walford, Albert John.** A guide to foreign language grammars and dictionaries. 2d ed., revised and enlarged. London, The Library Association, 1967. 240 pp.

Annotated list of grammars, dictionaries, and audio-visual aids for the major foreign languages of Western Europe, plus Russian and Chinese.

French

8.2.9 **Concise Oxford French dictionary.** Oxford, Clarendon Press. 2v.

French-English, compiled by A. Chevalley and M. Chevalley, 1934, 895 pp.; English-French, compiled by G. Goodridge, 1940, 295 pp. Frequently reprinted; also available in one joint volume.

8.2.10 **Mansion, J. E.** Harrap's standard French and English dictionary. London, Harrap, 1962. 2v.

V. 1, French-English, 912 pp.; v. 2, English-French, 488 pp.

1st ed. 1934–1939; American edition: Heath's Standard French and English Dictionary, 2d ed., Boston, Heath, 1939, 2v.

Generally considered the best French-English, English-French dictionary.

German

8.2.11 **English-German and German-English dictionary.** K. Wildhagen and W. Héraucourt. 12th ed., rev. and enl. Wiesbaden, Brandstetter; London, Allen & Unwin, 1936–65. 2v.

Helpful for translation; gives examples.

8.2.12 **Langenscheidt's new Muret-Sanders encyclopedic dictionary** of the English and German languages. Completely rev. 1962. Ed. by Otto Springer. London, Methuen; New York, Barnes & Noble, 1962– .

Pt. I (English-German), 2v., 1962–64.

1st ed. 1908. Long considered an excellent bilingual dictionary.

Greek

8.2.13 Greek-English lexicon. H. G. Liddell and R. Scott. 9th ed. rev. Oxford, Clarendon Press, 1925–40. 2111 pp.

1st ed. 1843.
The standard Greek-English lexicon.

See also: 1.4.2.

Italian

8.2.14 Hoare, A. A short Italian dictionary. Cambridge, University Press, 1926. 2v.

Abridged from the A. Hoare, *Italian dictionary*, 2d ed., Cambridge, University Press, 1925, 906 pp., which is out of print.

8.2.15 Reynolds, B. The Cambridge Italian dictionary. Cambridge, University Press, 1962– .

V. 1, Italian-English, 900 pp. Based in part on A. Hoare, *Italian Dictionary* (see 8.2.14).

Latin

8.2.16 Harpers' Latin dictionary. A new Latin dictionary founded on the translation of Freund's Latin-German lexicon. Ed. by E. A. Andrews, rev., enl., and in great part rewritten by Charlton T. Lewis and Charles Short. New York, American Book Co., 1907. 2019 pp.

Reprinted: Oxford, Clarendon Press, 1955.

Russian

8.2.17 Müller, V. K. English-Russian dictionary. 6th ed. New York, Dutton, 1959. 699 pp.

8.2.18 Smirnitskii, A. I. Russian-English dictionary. 3d ed. rev. and enl. under the editorship of O. S. Akhmanova. New York, Dutton, 1959. 951 pp.

Spanish

8.2.19 Appleton's revised English-Spanish and Spanish-English dictionary. Arturo Cuyas. 4th ed. rev. and enl. by Lewis E. Brett and Helen S. Eaton. New York, Appleton, 1961. 2v.

8.2.20 Raventós, Margaret H. A modern Spanish dictionary. London, English Universities Press, 1953. 1,230 pp.

American Edition: *McKay's Modern Spanish-English, English-Spanish Dictionary.* New York, McKay, 1954.

8.2.21 Velázquez de la Cadena, Mariano, [and others]. New revised Velázquez Spanish and English dictionary. Newly revised by Ida Navarro Hinojosa. Chicago and New York, Follett, 1959.
Pt. 1 Spanish-English, 698 pp.; pt. 2, English-Spanish, 778 pp.

8.3 THE PHILOSOPHIC REPORT: FORM AND STYLE

8.3.1 Albaugh, Ralph M. Thesis writing; a guide to scholarly style. Patterson, N. J., Littlefield, Adams & Co., 1960. 149 pp.

A short practical guide to the mechanical aspects of preparing a thesis in final form.

8.3.2 Bernstein, Theodore M. The careful writer; a modern guide to English usage. New York, Atheneum, 1965. 487 pp.

Idioms, corrections, errors; alphabetical arrangement.

8.3.3 ★ Blanshard, Brand. On philosophical style. Bloomington, Indiana University Press, 1954. 69 pp.

An urbane essay on clear writing as a vehicle of clear thought.

8.3.4 ★ Campbell, William Giles. Form and style in thesis writing. Boston, Houghton Mifflin, 1954. 114 pp.

8.3.5 Chicago University Press. A manual of style for authors, editors, and copywriters. 12th ed. Chicago, The University of Chicago Press, 1969. 546 pp.

A basic manual used and recommended by many publishers. Contains information on manuscript preparation, copyright, obtaining permissions, matters of style, specimens of type, and production and printing.

8.3.6 **Copperud, Roy H.** Words on paper; a manual of prose style for professional writers, reporters, authors, editors, publishers, and teachers. New York, Hawthorn Books, 1960. 286 pp.

8.3.7 ★ **Coyle, William.** Research papers. 2d ed. New York, Odyssey, 1965. 124 pp.

8.3.8 **Evans, Begen,** and **Cornelia Evans.** A dictionary of contemporary American usage. New York, Random House, 1957. 567 pp.

8.3.9 **Fowler, Henry Watson.** A dictionary of modern English usage. 2d ed., rev. by Sir Ernest Gowers. Oxford, Clarendon Press, 1965. 725 pp.

1st ed. 1926.

8.3.10 ★ **Guitton, Jean.** A student's guide to *intellectual* work. Trans. by Adrienne Foulke. Notre Dame, Indiana, The University of Notre Dame Press, 1964. 155 pp.

A presentation of the author's view on *how* to study, think, and write.

8.3.11 **Gourmont, Robert de.** La dissertation philosophique; conseils pour préparer et rédiger la dissertation philosophique et méthode pour faire des progrès en cet exercice. 3. éd. Paris, O. R. A. C., 1966. 78 pp.

8.3.12 ★ **Hook, Lucyle,** and **Mary Virginia Gaver.** The research paper. 2d ed. New York, Prentice-Hall, 1952. 85 pp.

8.3.13 ★ **Hurt, Peyton.** Bibliography and footnotes; a style manual for students and writers. 3d ed., revised and enlarged by Mary L. Hurt Richmond. Berkeley and Los Angeles, University of California Press, 1968. 163 pp.

8.3.14 **Jordan, Lewis,** *ed.* The New York Times style book. New York, McGraw-Hill, 1962. 124 pp.

A guide for manuscript preparation.

8.3.15 **Kinney, Mary R.** Bibliographical style manuals; a guide to their use in documentation and research. Chicago, Association of College and Reference Libraries, 1953. 21 pp.

8.3.16 **Koefod, Paul E.** The writing requirements for graduate degrees. Englewood Cliffs, N. J., Prentice-Hall, 1964. 268 pp.

A discussion of thesis and dissertation writing and of graduate schools in general; an appendix reprints some pertinent articles by others, and lists model prospectuses of theses and dissertations.

8.3.17 **Koren, Henry J.** Research in philosophy; a bibliographical introduction to philosophy and a few suggestions for dissertations. Pittsburgh, Duquesne University Press, 1966. 203 pp.

Chapter 6: A few suggestions about dissertations.

8.3.18 ★ **The MLA style sheet.** By William Riley Parker. Revised ed. 1968. 32 pp.

Obtainable from The Materials Center, Modern Language Association, 62 Fifth Ave., New York, N. Y. 10011.

A style sheet recommended by many philosophical journals. Contains information on preparing the manuscript, documentation, abbreviations, submitting the manuscript, proofreading, preparation of Masters' and Doctors' theses, and guideline for abstracting scholarly articles.

8.3.19 **Nicholson, Margaret.** A dictionary of American-English usage based on Fowler's modern English usage. New York, Oxford University Press, 1957. 671 pp.

8.3.20 ★ **Pugh, Griffith Thompson.** Guide to research writing. Boston, Houghton Mifflin, 1955. 64 pp.

8.3.21 **Richards, Paul I.,** and **Irving T. Richards.** Proper words in proper places; writing to inform. Boston, The Christopher Publishing House, 1964. 206 pp.

The strategy and mechanics of writing and proofreading.

8.3.22 ★ **Strunk, William, Jr.,** and **Elwyn Brooks White.** The elements of style. Rev. ed. New York, Macmillan, 1959. 71 pp.

A small, concise guide. One of the best.

8.3.23 ★ **Seeber, Edward D.** A style manual for authors Bloomington, Indiana University Press, 1965. 96 pp.

Endeavors to clarify the author-printer relationship and publishers' requirements. Its procedures correspond to those of the *MLA Style Sheet* (8.3.18).

8.3.24 ★ **Turabian, Kate L.** A manual for writers of term papers, theses, and dissertations. Rev. ed. Chicago, University of Chicago Press, 1955. 82 pp.

A widely used guide for undergraduate and graduate students.

8.3.25 **U. S. Government Printing Office.** Style manual. Rev. ed. Washington, D. C., Government Printing Office, 1959. 496 pp.

Gives the practices of the Government Printing Office on preparing copy and rules of style.

8.3.26 **U. S. Library of Congress. General reference and bibliography division.** Bibliographical procedures and style; a manual for bibliographers in the Library of Congress. By Blanche P. McCrum and Helen D. Jones. Washington, D. C., Government Printing Office, 1954; reprinted 1966 with list of abbreviations. 133 pp.

A guide to the forms of entry used by the Library of Congress.

8.3.27 **Van Steenberghen, Fernand.** Directives pour la confection d'un monographie scientifique avec applications concrètes aux recherches sur la philosophie médiévale. 2. éd. Louvain, Editions de l'Institut Supérieur de Philosophie, 1949. 86 pp.

See also: 1.1.4.

8.4 SCHOLARLY PUBLISHING

8.4.1 **American book trade directory;** lists of publishers, booksellers, periodicals, trade organizations, wholesalers, etc. New York, Bowker, 1915– .

Title varies. Published about every three years. 17th ed., 1965–66.

Information about the American book market and markets abroad.

8.4.2 **Association of American University Presses.** Directory. New York, American University Press Service. 1947–to date.

Frequency varies; now issued every two years.

Available from the AAUP.

Lists addresses, officers, organizations, and publication interest of each university press.

8.4.3 **Association of American University Presses.** Scholarly books in America. 1959–to date. Quarterly. Published by the University of Chicago with the cooperation of the Association of American University Presses.

A quarterly bibliography sent free to scholars and libraries to keep them informed about scholarly publishing in North America. Contains brief articles and notes about university press publishing, and an annotated listing of publications issued by AAUP members.

8.4.4 ★ **Cargill, O.** [et al]. The publication of academic writing. New York, Modern Language Association, 1966. 24 pp.

"How to prepare a book for publication, how to choose a publisher, how to negotiate with him."

8.4.5 **Cassell's directory of publishing** in Great Britain, the Commonwealth and Ireland. 2d ed., 1962–63. London, Cassell. 443 pp.

1st ed. 1960–61.

8.4.6 **Collison, Robert.** Indexing books; a manual of basic principles. New York, John de Graff, 1962. 96 pp.

A succinct and useful guide.

8.4.7 **Gill, Robert S.** The author-publisher-printer complex. 3d ed. Baltimore, Williams & Wilkins, 1960. 138 pp.

A brief guide to terms, copy, proof, etc., including royalties.

8.4.8 **Hawes, Gene R.** To advance knowledge; a handbook on American university press publishing. New York, American University Press Service, 1967. 148 pp.

A discussion of scholarly publishing, with a chapter on "what the scholar and publisher expect of each other."

8.4.9 **Lasky, Joseph.** Proofreading and copy-preparation; a textbook for the grafic arts industry. New York, Mentor Books, 1954. 656 pp.

1st ed. 1941.
A useful guide.

8.4.10 ★ **Literary market place;** the business directory of American book publishing. New York, Bowker, 1940–   . Annual.

Lists personnel and addresses of book publishers, advertising agencies, authors' agents, associations, book manufacturers, and other aspects of commercial publishers.

8.4.11 **Nicholson, Margaret.** A manual of copyright practice for writers, publishers, and agents. 2d ed. New York, Oxford University Press, 1956. 273 pp.

A useful guide. The appendix reprints the text of the U. S. Copyright Law and of the Universal Copyright Convention.

8.4.12 ★ **On the publication of research;** essays by R. B. McKerrow and Henry M. Silver. New York, Modern Language Association, 1964. 20 pp.

"Trenchant advice on how to turn research into readable articles."

8.4.13 ★ **Pilpe, Harriet F.,** and **Morton D. Goldberg.** A copyright guide. 2d ed. New York, Bowker, 1963. 40 pp.

A brief guide in question and answer form.

8.4.14 **Scholarly publishing;** a journal for authors and publishers. 1969–to date. Quarterly. Ed., Eleanor Harman, University of Toronto Press, Toronto 181, Canada.

Articles, book reviews, correspondence, editorial positions available, index.

An international quarterly which aims to encourage scholarly publication by providing a forum for discussion and a source of current information and advice on developing manuscripts, editorial techniques, book production, sales and promotion, and related areas.

8.4.15 **Skillen, Marjorie E.,** and **Robert M. Gay.** Words into type; a guide in the preparation of manuscripts, for writers, editors, proofreaders and printers. 2d ed. New York, Appleton-Century-Crofts, 1964. 596 pp.

Sections on manuscript preparation, copy and proof, typography and illustration, printing style, grammar, and use of words.

8.4.16 **Smith, Datus C., Jr.** A guide to book publishing. New York, Bowker, 1966. 244 pp.

Explains the general principles of book publishing. Chapters include "The book-publishing process" and "Kinds of book-publishing."

Bibliography: pp. 229–233.

8.4.17 ★ **Spiker, Sina.** Indexing your book; a practical guide for authors. 2d ed. Madison, University of Wisconsin Press, 1963. 40 pp.

8.4.18 **Turner, Mary C.** The bookman's glossary. 4th ed. New York, Bowker, 1961. 212 pp.

8.4.19 **United Nations Educational, Scientific and Cultural Organization.** Copyright laws and treaties of the world. Washington, D. C., UNESCO and the Bureau of National Affairs, 1956–   . Loose-leaf.

Yearly supplements.

8.4.20 **Welter, Rush.** Problems of scholarly publication in the humanities and social sciences; a report prepared for the Committee on Scholarly Publication of the American

Council of Learned Societies. New York, American Council of Learned Societies, 1959. 81 pp.

An informative report on both book and scholarly journal publication.

8.4.21 **Unwin, Stanley.** The truth about publishing. 6th ed. London, George Allen & Unwin Ltd., 1950. 352 pp.

1st ed. 1926.
An informal discussion of book publishing written for authors by a distinguished publisher.

8.4.22 ★ **Wiles, Roy M.** Scholarly reporting in the humanities. 3d ed. Toronto, University of Toronto Press, 1961. 53 pp.

A guide to format and style.

8.4.23 **Wittenberg, Philip.** The protection of literary property. Boston, Writer Inc., 1968. 267 pp.

8.4.24 **Writer's market.** Cincinnati, Writer's Digest. 1931– . Annual.

25th ed. 1969. Frequency varied in the early years of its publication.
Contains lists of commercial book and journal publishers, but some of its notes on publishing apply equally well to scholarly publishing.

9. BIOGRAPHIES

WHILE THE BIOGRAPHIES of the more important figures in the history of philosophy are usually available in the major encyclopedias or histories of philosophy, it is often difficult to find biographical information in these sources for relatively minor figures or for contemporary or near-contemporary philosophers. General and philosophical biographies help supply this information. National biographies are useful in searching for biographical information on particular philosophers from the country covered by such biographies. Philosophical directories supply the smallest amount of information, but are the most inclusive of the biographical sources.

9.1 BIOGRAPHIES: GENERAL

Indexes

9.1.1 **Biography index;** a cumulative index to biographical material in books and magazines. New York, Wilson, 1947–to date.

Quarterly with annual and three-year cumulations. Wider in coverage than "Who's Who" books.

9.1.2 **Dictionary of international biography.** Dartmouth Chronicle Group Ltd., 1963– . Annual.

Indicates all other reference works which also contain sketches of biographies.

9.1.3 **Hyamson, Albert M. A.** A dictionary of universal biography of all ages and of all peoples. New York, Dutton, 1951, 679 pp.

1st ed. 1916.
An index to persons listed in 24 other biographical dictionaries. International in scope.

9.1.4 **Riches, Phyllis.** Analytical bibliography of universal collected biography, comprising books published in the English tongue in Great Britain and Ireland, America and the

British Dominions. London, Library Association, 1934. 709 pp.

An index to biographies written in English.

International

9.1.5 **Biographie universelle (Michaud)** ancienne et moderne. Nouv. éd., publiée sous la direction de M. Michaud. Paris, Mme. C. Desplaces, 1843–65. 45v.

1st ed. 1811–57. 84v.
Still useful.

9.1.6 **Chamber's biographical dictionary.** New ed., ed. by J. O. Thorne. New York, St. Martin's, 1962. 1432 pp.

"The great of all nations and all times." Includes an index of pseudonyms.

9.1.7 **Contemporary authors;** a biobibliographical guide to current authors and their works. Detroit, Gale Research Co., 1962–to date. Semiannual.

Frequency varies. An international biographical source on authors in a variety of fields, including philosophy. Supplies basic personal and career data plus bibliographies and work in progress.

9.1.8 **Current biography;** who's news and why. New York, Wilson, 1940–to date.

Published monthly, except August, and cumulated annually.

9.1.9 **Hoefer, Ferdinand.** Nouvelle biographie générale depuis les temps les plus reculés jusqu'à nos jours. Paris, Firmin-Didot, 1853–1866. 46v.

A rival of Michaud (9.1.5).
Reprinted: Copenhague, Rosenkilde & Bagger, 1963– .

9.1.10 **International who's who.** 1935–to date. London, Europa Publications Ltd., and Allen & Unwin. Annual.

Short biographies of prominent persons.

9.1.11 **Webster's biographical dictionary,** a dictionary of names of noteworthy persons, with pronunciations and concise biographies. Springfield, Merriam, 1962. 1697 pp.

1st ed. 1943.
Brief biographies of upwards of 40,000 persons.

9.1.12 **World of learning.** London, Europa Publications Ltd., 1947–to date. Annual.

Lists learned societies, research institutes, libraries, and all institutions of higher learning, their administrators and senior staff. Often useful for finding addresses of professors in foreign institutions.

National

For full details on national biographies see Winchell (5.1.3), pp. 171–190.

United States

9.1.13 **Dictionary of American biography.** New York, Scribner, 1928–37. 20v. and Index.

Does not include living persons.
Two supplements, 1944–58, include persons who died between original publication date and 1940.
Includes bibliographies.

9.1.14 **National cyclopedia of American biography.** New York, White, 1892– .

44 permanent volumes, plus current volumes of living persons.
The most comprehensive American biographical work.

9.1.15 **White's Conspectus of American biography;** a tabulated record of American history and biography. 2d ed. New York, White, 1937. 455 pp.

1st ed. 1906.
Major arrangement is chronological.

9.1.16 **Who was who in America.** Chicago, Marquis, 1942– .

Historical volume, 1607–1896; v. 1, 1897–1942; v. 2, 1943–1950; v. 3, 1951–1960.

9.1.17 **Who's who in America.** Chicago, Marquis 1899– . Biennial.

Includes, by virtue of their position, all professors at major American universities.

Canada

9.1.18 **Canadian who's who.** Toronto, Trans-Canada Press, 1910– .

9.1.19 **Dictionary of Canadian biography/** Dictionnaire biographique du Canada. Toronto University of Toronto Press, 1966– .

In progress. Includes bibliographies.
V. 1, 1000 to 1700.

France

9.1.20 **Dictionnaire biographique français contemporain.** 2. éd. Paris, Edit. Pharos, 1954. 708 pp.

Supplements 1–2, 1955–56.

9.1.21 **Dictionnaire de biographie française.** Paris, Letouzey, 1933– .

In progress.

9.1.22 **Who's who in France;** dictionnaire biographique. Paris, Lafitte, 1953– . Biennial.

Germany

9.1.23 Allgemeine deutsche Biographie.
Hrsg. durch die Historische Commission bei
der Königl. Akademie der Wissenschaften.
Leipzig, Duncker, 1875–1912. 56v.

The basic German biographical dictionary.
Includes bibliographies.

Reprinted: Berlin, Duncker & Humblot,
1967.

9.1.24 Neue deutsche Biographie; ein
Biographisches Lexikon. Berlin, Duncker und
Humblot, 1953– .

In progress.
20v. projected.
Supplements 9.1.23.

9.1.25 Wer ist Wer. Berlin, Arani, 1905– .

Title and frequency vary.

Great Britain

9.1.26 Dictionary of national biography.
London, Smith, Edler, 1885–1901. 63v.

Index and epitome, 1903–13. 2v. Reissue,
22v., 1908–09; reprinted, 1938. 2d–6th supplements, Oxford University Press, 1912–59. 5v.
The basic English biographical work, with
bibliographies.

9.1.27 Who was who; a companion to
Who's who. London, Black, 1929–61. 5v.

Lists deceased persons from the 1897–1960
volumes of Who's Who.

9.1.28 Who's who. London, Black, 1849– .
Annual.

Assumed its present form and coverage in
1897.

Italy

9.1.29 Chi è? Dizionario degli italiani d'oggi.
7. ed. Roma, Scarano, 1961. 714 pp.

9.1.30 Dizionario biografico degli italiani.
Roma, Istit. della Enciclopedia Italiana, 1960– .

In progress.
Does not include living persons.

**9.1.31 Enciclopedia biographica e biblio-
graphica "italiana."** Milano, Tosi, 1936–44.
Series 4–50.

Never completed.
Divided according to professions; for
philosophers see especially series XXXVIII:
Pedagogisti ed Educatori.

9.1.32 Who's who in Italy. Milano, Inter-
continental Book and Pub. S.r.l., 1958.

Published in English.

9.2 BIOGRAPHIES: PHILOSOPHICAL

9.2.1 Directory of American philosophers.
Ed., Archie Bahm. Albuquerque, 1915 Las
Lomas Rd. N. E., 1970–71. 5th ed.

Revised every two years.
Directory of U. S. and Canadian colleges
and universities and their philosophy department staffs. Includes also an index of philosophers, giving their addresses, and information
on philosophical societies, periodicals, fellowships, and employment opportunities.

9.2.2 Directory of American scholars; a
biographical dictionary. 5th ed. Ed. by the
Jacques Cattel Press, Inc. New York, Bowker,
1969. 4v.

Vol. IV, *Philosophy, Religion and Law,*
includes some 6300 biographies. It lists name,
personal data, education, positions, society
memberships, research, publications, and address. Extremely useful for finding information
on a large number of contemporary American
philosophers.

9.2.3 Kiernan, Thomas P. Who's who in the
history of philosophy. New York, Philosophical Library, 1965. 185 pp.

"The ultimate design of this book is to
acquaint rather than instruct the reader"
(p. v).

9.2.4 Lewes, George Henry. A biographical
history of philosophy. London, Routledge &
Sons, Ltd., 1900. 656 pp.

1st ed. 1845–51.

9.2.5 **Runes, D. D.** Who's who in philosophy. New York, Philosophical Library, 1942. 243 pp.

Includes only Anglo-American philosophers.

9.2.6 **Thomas, Henry.** Biographical encyclopedia of philosophy. Garden City, New York, Doubleday, 1965. 273 pp.

Short biographical sketches; no bibliographies.

9.2.7 **Thomas, Henry,** and **Dana Lee Thomas.** Living biographies of great philosophers. Garden City, New York, Garden City Books, 1959. 335 pp.

9.2.8 **Urmson, J. O.,** *ed.* The concise encyclopedia of western philosophy and philosophers. *See* 1.2.6.

Bibliography: pp. 421–431.

9.2.9 **Varet, G.,** and **P. Kurtz.** International directory of philosophy and philosophers. *See* 7.1.7.

Lists philosophy staffs at colleges, universities, etc., in more than 80 countries and territories.

French

9.2.10 **Dictionnaire des philosophes.** Paris, Editions Seghers, 1962. 376 pp.

9.2.11 **Palharies, Fortune.** Vies et doctrines des grands philosophes à travers les âges. Paris, Lamore, 1928–29. 3v.

See also: 1.2.11.

German

9.2.12 **Decurtins, Carl.** Kleines Philosophenlexikon, von den Vorsokratikern bis zur Gegenwart. Affoltern, Aehren Verlag, 1952. 312 pp.

9.2.13 **Ziegenfuss, Werner.** Philosophen-Lexikon; Handwörterbuch der Philosophie nach Personen. Unter Mitwerk von Gertrud Jung, verf. u. hersg. von Werner Ziegenfuss. Berlin, Walter de Gruyter, 1949–50. 2v.

Biographies and short bibliographies of works of and about philosophers. Includes some contemporary philosophers. The best known of the philosophical biographies.
Replaces earlier biographies by Eisler and Hauer.

See also: 1.2.15, 1.2.20.

Spanish

9.2.14 **Menchaca, José A.** Diccionario bio-bibliográfico de filosofos. Bilbao, El Mensajero del Corazon de Jesus, 1965– .

In progress.
For each author: biographical note, bibliographies in which he is listed, list of author's writings and their translations, and list of studies on the author.

10. PHILOSOPHICAL PROFESSIONAL LIFE

PHILOSOPHICAL meetings serve a variety of purposes. They give philosophers a chance to meet one another so they can discuss, exchange ideas, compare views, and engage in dialogue both formally and informally. Some meetings bring together philosophers of similar interests; some, philosophers of diverse interests. Some meetings are centered on a particular topic for intensive discussion of it; others offer discussions of a variety of topics. Many offer philosophers the opportunity to overcome both geographic and intellectual provincialism; they give young philosophers a chance to hear known and established philosophers, as well as allowing the young themselves to be heard. They sometimes provide the possibility for those seeking teaching positions to meet those who have such positions available.

Philosophical meetings take place on many levels: local, regional, national, and international. Usually they are sponsored by philosophical societies or groups at the appropriate levels. Some societies have as their sole function the calling of meetings, while others also publish a journal, represent the interests of philosophers on the regional or national scene, sponsor research by awarding or administering grants, and so on. International, American, and British associations and meetings are listed in 10.1.

The funding of scholarly research in philosophy comes largely from colleges and universities in the form of research grants and paid sabbatical leaves. Other sources of support include private foundations and government grants. Guides to research opportunities and a selected list of foundations can be found in 10.2.

10.1 PHILOSOPHICAL ORGANIZATIONS AND MEETINGS

International Associations and Congresses
For a more complete list of international philosophical societies see Varet and Kurtz (7.1.7) and World of learning (9.1.12).

10.1.1 **International congress calendar;** 1960/61– . Brussels, Union of International Associations, 1961– . Annual.

Lists forthcoming international congresses projected for as far ahead as five years.

10.1.2 **World list of future international meetings.** June 1959– , prep. by the International Organizations Section. Washington, D. C., Reference Dept. Library of Congress, 1959– . Monthly and quarterly.

Lists forthcoming international congresses projected for three years; the quarterly issues are kept current by the monthly issues.

10.1.3 **The Division of Logic, Methodology and Philosophy of Science,** of the International Union of the History and Philosophy of Science (IUHPS). Founded 1956.

Sec.: Alan Ross Anderson, Department of

Philosophy, University of Pittsburgh, Pittsburgh, Pa.

Among its purposes, it organizes periodic international congresses for logic, methodology, and the Philosophy of science. The first general congress was held in Stanford in 1960. Other congresses have been held in Amsterdam, Oxford, Warsaw, and Helsinki, and some have been devoted to special topics.

10.1.4 Inter-American Congress of Philosophy.

Meets once every three years. The Ist Congress met in Port-au-Prince, 1944; the IInd in New York, 1947; the IIIrd in Mexico City, 1950; the IVth in Santiago de Chile, 1956; the Vth in Washington, 1957; the VIth in Buenos Aires, 1959; the VIIth in Quebec, 1967; the VIIIth in Brazil, 1970.

10.1.5 International Association of Law and Social Philosophy. Founded 1909.

Gen.-sec.: Paul Trappe, Bruckfeldstr. 14, Bern, Switzerland.

Sponsors international congresses every four years. An American section (AMINTAPHIL), founded in 1963, meets every three years. Dir.: T. A. Cowan, Rutgers Law School, 53 Washington St., Newark, N. J.

10.1.6 International Center for the Study of Arabian Philosophy.

Secretariat: c/o Institut Dominicain d'études orientales, 1 rue Masna al-Tarabich, Abassiah-Le Caire.

10.1.7 International Executive Committee for International Congresses of Aesthetics.

President: Etienne Souriau, 3 rue Michelet, Paris-VIe, France. Sponsors Congresses every four years. The VIth Congress was held in Uppsala, 1968.

10.1.8 International Federation of Societies of Philosophy (IFSP). Founded 1948.

Since its founding it has assumed the organization of the five-yearly International Congress of Philosophy. The first International Congress of Philosophy was held in 1900 in Paris; the second at Geneva in 1904;

the IIIrd at Heidelberg in 1908; the IVth at Bologne in 1911; the Vth at Naples in 1924; the VIth at Cambridge, Mass., in 1926; the VIIth at Oxford in 1930; the VIIIth at Prague in 1934; the IXth at Paris in 1937; the Xth at Amsterdam in 1948; the XIth at Brussels in 1953; the XIIth at Venice in 1958; the XIIIth at Mexico City in 1963; the XIVth at Vienna in 1968.

10.1.9 International Institute of Philosophy (IIP). Founded 1937.

Sec.: 173 Boulevard Saint-Germain, Paris VIe, France.

Composed of 100 elected members, representing 30 countries.

It helps organize International meetings and publishes the *Bibliography of Philosophy* (7.2.6) and *Chroniques de Philosophie* (1937– ; every 10 years).

10.1.10 International Phenomenological Society. Founded 1939. Address: c/o Marvin Farber, State University of New York at Buffalo, Buffalo, New York.

Its aim is to further the understanding, development and application of phenomenological inquiries as inaugurated by E. Husserl.

Publishes *Philosophy and Phenomenological Research* (7.2.67).

10.1.11 International Society for the History of Ideas. Founded 1959.

Sec.: 137 Findley Center, The City College, N. Y., N. Y. 10031.

Publishes the *Journal of the History of Ideas* (7.2.40) and sponsors an international conference every three years.

10.1.12 International Society for the Study of Medieval Philosophy (ISSMP). Founded 1958.

Sec.: 2, Place Cardinal Mercier, Louvain, Belgium.

Membership is by nomination by a member. Publishes Bulletin de philosophie medievale, which covers works in progress, national chronicles, and general information for those interested in medieval philosophy. Sponsors International Congresses of Medieval Philosophy: Ist Congress, Louvain, 1958; IId Congress, Cologne, 1961; IIIrd Congress, Bolzano, Italy, 1964; IVth Congress, Montreal, 1967; Vth Congress, Spain, 1972.

10.1.13 International Society of Logic and the Philosophy of Science.

Address: c/o F. Gonseth, Goldauerstrasse 60, Zürich, Switzerland.

10.1.14 World Union of Catholic Societies of Philosophy. Founded, 1968.

Sec.-General: P. Maxmilian Roesle, Aignerstr. 25, Salzburg-Aigen.

U.S. Associations and Meetings

For a list of regional and local associations and meetings see Directory of American philosophers (9.2.1).

10.1.15 American Association for the Advancement of Science. Section L: The History and Philosophy of Science.

Holds annual meetings in December in alternate years with the Eastern Division of the APA and with the History of Science Society.

10.1.16 The American Catholic Philosophical Association (ACPA). Founded 1926.

Sec.: Catholic University of America, Washington, D.C. 20017. The second largest U. S. philosophical association. Publishes the *Proceedings of the American Catholic Philosophical Association* (7.4.1), *The New Scholasticism* (7.2.52), and a *Directory of Members*.
Holds an annual meeting devoted to a single topic during the week after Easter. Also sponsors a Speakers' Bureau and a Personnel Placement Service.

10.1.17 American Philosophical Association (APA). Founded 1901.

United with the Western Philosophical Association and Philosophical Society of the Pacific Coast in 1926. National office: Alan Pasch, Exec. Sec., 117 Lehigh Road, U. of Maryland, College Park, Md. 20740.

The largest national association. Membership is open to those holding advanced degrees in philosophy, those engaged in careers of teaching philosophy, etc. Nomination for membership must be made by two members of the Association. Associate membership is available to students working towards their Ph. D.
The national organization consists of a board of officers and a number of committees. *Proceedings and Addresses of the American Philosophical Association* (7.4.2) are published annually. They contain the three Presidential Addresses and the programs for the annual meetings of the Association's three divisions: The Eastern Division, the Western Division, and the Pacific Division. They also contain committee and other reports and list of members. The association's standing committees are: The Committee on Lectures, Publications, and Research; The Committee on International Cooperation; The Committee on Placement; and The Committee on the Status and Future of the Profession.
Persons seeking a teaching position in philosophy may register with the Association's National Registry of Philosophers, Professional Career and Information Center, IIII 20th St., N. W., Washington, D. C. 20036.

10.1.18 The American Society for Aesthetics. Founded 1942.

Address: Cleveland Museum of Art, Cleveland 6, Ohio.
Publishes the *Journal of Aesthetics and Art Criticism* (7.2.32). Annual meetings in October.

10.1.19 American Society for Political and Legal Philosophy. Founded 1955.

Address: c/o John Ladd, Dept. of Philosophy, Brown University, Providence, R. I. 02912. A candidate must be nominated by two members and elected to membership by the Membership Committee.
Publishes *Nomos* (7.4.13). Its annual meetings follow (in rotation) the meetings of the American Philosophical Association, The American Political Science Association, and the Association of American Law Schools.

10.1.20 **Association for Realistic Philosophy.** Founded 1948.

Holds an annual meeting each fall and also meets in conjunction with the annual meetings of the Eastern Division of the APA.

10.1.21 **Association for Symbolic Logic.** Founded 1936.

Business office: P. O. Box 6248, Providence, R. I. 02904.
Membership is open to all persons interested in the work of the Association.
Publishes *The Journal of Symbolic Logic* (7.2.38).
Holds annual meetings, normally in conjunction with alternate annual meetings of the Eastern Division of the APA and of the American Mathematical Society.

10.1.22 **Charles S. Peirce Society.** Founded 1946.

Publishes Transactions of the Charles S. Peirce Society (7.2.92).
Holds an annual meeting with the Eastern Division of the APA.

10.1.23 **Division of Philosophical Psychology of the American Psychological Association.** Founded 1963.

Holds annual meetings together with the Association in September.

10.1.24 **Duns Scotus Philosophical Association.** Founded 1937.

Address: Our Lady of Angels Seminary, 3644 Rocky River Drive, Cleveland, Ohio.
Holds an annual convention in April and other meetings twice a year.

10.1.25 **Hegel Society of America.** Founded 1968.

Treas.: c/o Department of Philosophy, Northern Illinois University, De Kalb, Ill. 60115.
Holds an annual meeting. Publishes a newsletter entitled *The Owl of Minerva*, ed. by Frederick G. Weiss, The Florida State University, Tallahassee, Fla. 32306.

10.1.26 **The Metaphysical Society of America.** Founded 1950.

Sec.: Marc Griesbach, Marquette University, Milwaukee, Wis. 53233.
Membership is open to those of demonstrated philosophical competence who are nominated by two members of the Society.
Holds an annual meeting during the third weekend in March.

10.1.27 **Personalist Discussion Group.** Founded 1938.

Address: Philosophy Department, Boston University, Boston, Mass. 02215.
Holds an annual meeting in conjunction with the Eastern Division of the APA.

10.1.28 **Philosophy of Education Society.** Founded 1941.

Address: c/o D. B. Gowin, Sec.-Treas., 108 Stone Hall, Cornell University, Ithaca, N. Y. 14850.
Publishes the *Proceedings of the Philosophy of Education Society* (7.4.14).
Holds an annual meeting during the week prior to Easter.

10.1.29 **Philosophy of Science Association.** Founded 1934.

Address: c/o Gerald Massey, Sec.-Treas., Michigan State University, East Lansing, Mich. 48823.
Publishes *Philosophy of Science* (7.2.71).
Holds an annual meeting together with the American Assoc. for the Advancement of Science.

10.1.30 **Society for American Philosophy.** Founded 1962.

Address: c/o Dale Riepe, SUNY at Buffalo, Amherst, N. Y. 14226.
Its annual meeting alternates between the Western and the Eastern Division meetings of the APA.

10.1.31 **Society for Ancient Greek Philosophy.** Founded 1953.

Address: Yarrow West, Bryn Mawr, Pa. 19010.

Meets with the Eastern Division of APA and with the American Philological Association.

10.1.32 Society for Phenomenology and Existential Philosophy. Founded 1962.

Co-sec.: David Carr and Edward Casey, Dept. of Philosophy, Yale University, New Haven, Conn. 06520.
Holds an annual meeting in October.

10.1.33 Society for Philosophy and Public Policy. Founded 1969.

Sec.: Prof. John M. Dolan, The Rockefeller University, New York, N. Y. 10021.
Membership is open to all teachers and graduate students of philosophy, and to others with the approval of the executive committee.
Annual national meeting with the Western Division of the APA; also regional and local meetings. The aim of the Society is to encourage and, if possible, extend concern with public issues among professional philosophers.

10.1.34 Society for the Philosophy of Creativity. Founded 1957.

Associated with The Foundation for Creative Philosophy, 1301 West Freeman St., Carbondale, Ill. 62901.
Meets with both the Western Division and the Eastern Division of the APA. The first National Conference for Philosophy of Creativity was held in 1969.
Publishes *Philosophy of Creativity Monograph Series*, v. 1– , 1969– .

10.1.35 Society for the Philosophical Study of Dialectical Materialism. Founded 1962.

Sec.-Treas.: Prof. Donald Hodges, Florida State University, Tallahassee, Fla. 32306.
Membership is open to members of the APA.
Meets concurrently with the Eastern and the Western Division meetings of the APA.

10.1.36 Society for the Scientific Study of Religion. Founded 1949.

Address: 1200 17th St., N. W., Washington, D. C. 20036.

Publishes the *Journal for the Scientific Study of Religion* (7.2.31).
Holds an annual meeting in October.

10.1.37 Society for the Study of Process Philosophies. Founded 1965.

Holds an annual meeting with the Eastern Division of the APA.

See also: 10.1.5.

British Associations and Meetings

For a more complete list see Varet and Kurtz (7.1.7).

10.1.38 Aristotelian Society. Founded 1860.

Hon. Sec. and Ed.: A. A. Kassman, 31 West Heath Drive, London, N. W. 11.
Publishes *Proceedings* and supplementary volumes (7.4.4).
Holds fortnightly meetings and annual joint sessions with The Mind Association.

10.1.39 The British Society for Phenomenology. Founded 1967.

Publishes *The Journal of the British Society for Phenomenology* (7.2.39).
Holds annual meetings at British universities.

10.1.40 British Society for the Philosophy of Science. Founded 1948.

Address: c/o B. C. Brookes, University College, Gower St., London, W. C. 1.
Publishes *The British Journal for the Philosophy of Science* (7.2.8).
Holds three meetings in each university term on Mondays at University College, London, and an annual general conference.

10.1.41 British Society of Aesthetics. Founded 1960.

Address: c/o Hon. Sec., Dept. of Philosophy, Bedford College, Regent's Park, London, N. W. 1.
Publishes *The British Journal of Aesthetics* (7.2.9).
Holds monthly lecture meetings and an annual conference.

10.1.42 Mind Association. Founded 1871.

Holds joint annual sessions with the Aristotelian Society.

Publishes *Mind* (7.2.49).

One can become a member by subscribing to *Mind*.

10.1.43 Philosophy of Education Society of Great Britain.

Secretary: Paul H. Hirst, Dept. of Philosophy of Education, Univ. of London Institute of Education, Malet Street, London, W. C. 1, England.

10.1.44 Royal Institute of Philosophy.

Secretary: 14 Gordon Sq., London W. C. 1, England.

Publishes *Philosophy* (7.2.66).

10.1.45 Society of Philosophical Letter Writers. Founded 1967.

Address: E. H. Stubbes, University of Aston in Birmingham, Gosta Green, Birmingham 4, England.

The aim of the society is to facilitate correspondence among philosophical writers of similar interests.

Membership is open to anyone, without charge.

10.2 POSTDOCTORAL RESEARCH

10.2.1 American Council on Education. Fellowships in the Arts and Sciences. Washington, American Council on Education, 1957–   . Annual.

Includes information on predoctoral and postdoctoral fellowships.

10.2.2 American foundations and their fields. 1931–   . Irregular.

Published by American Foundations Information Service, 860 Broadway, N. Y. Supplemented until Sept. 1960 by *American Foundation News.*

The 7th ed., 1955, carried information on 4289 Foundations.

Largely superseded by 10.2.9.

10.2.3 Annual register of grant support. Los Angeles, Academic Media, Inc., 1969–   .

The most comprehensive and up-to-date source of information on postgraduate awards in the English-speaking world.

Supersedes *Grant Data Quarterly* (1967–68, v. 1–2).

10.2.4 Council for Philosophical Studies.

Exec. Sec.: Prof. Jerome Shaffer, Dept. of Philosophy, University of Connecticut, Storrs, Conn. 06268.

Established "to contribute to the advancement of teaching and scholarship in the field of philosophy," the Council sponsors both individual conferences concerned with scholarly problems and summer institutes for teachers of philosophy.

10.2.5 David F. Swenson-Kierkegaard Memorial Fund.

Fellowship for study of writings of Kierkegaard. Write: Secretary of the Swenson-Kierkegaard Memorial Committee, Prof. Paul L. Homes, Yale University, 409 Prospect Street, New Haven, Conn.

10.2.6 Educational and Cultural Exchange Opportunities.

Published annually by the Dept. of State, Bureau of Educational and Cultural Affairs, Washington, D.C.

10.2.7 Feingold, S. Norman. Scholarships, fellowships and loans. Cambridge, Mass., Bellman, 1949–62. 4v.

10.2.8 Fellowships and Loans of the Organization of American States for Study Abroad.

Published by the Organization of American States, 17th & Constitution, N. W., Washington, D. C.

10.2.9 The foundation directory. New York, Russell Sage Foundations, 1960–   .

3d ed., 1967.

Contains information on 6803 foundations.

Supplemented by *Foundation News,* issued

by the Foundation Library center, 428 E. Preston St., Baltimore, Md.

10.2.10 * **Handbook on international study.** New York, Institute of International Education, 1955– . Triennial.

Since 1961 it appears in 2v. Includes exchanges, fellowships, and government regulations.

10.2.11 **Interuniversity Committee on Travel Grants.** Indiana University, Bloomington, Indiana.

Handles exchanges for study and research in the U. S. S. R. Bulgaria, Czechoslovakia, and Hungary.

10.2.12 **National register of scholarships and fellowships.** Ed., Juvenal L. Angel. 4th ed. New York, World Trade Academy Press, 1963–64. 2v.

Includes undergraduate, predoctoral, and postdoctoral opportunities.

10.2.13 **Publications of the Modern Language Association (PMLA).** 1952–to date.

Annually (in Sept.) publishes a list of fellowships and research programs, many of which apply to all areas of the humanities.

10.2.14 **A selected list of major fellowship opportunities** and aids to advanced education for United States citizens. Annual.

Published by The Fellowship Office, National Academy of Sciences—National Research Council, Washingtohn, D. C.

10.2.15 * **Study abroad;** international directory of fellowships, scholarships, and awards compiled by UNESCO. Paris, New York, 1948– . Annual.

INDEX

This index includes author and subject entries and most, but not all, title entries. In general titles of journal articles have been omitted, as well as titles of collected works of an individual philosopher, which may be found under the author entry.

A. Camus and the literature of revolt, J. Cruick-shank, 53

Abbagnano, N. Dizionario di filosofia, 6; Storia della filosofia, 17

Abelard, P.: Works, 33–34

Achievement of Jacques and Raissa Maritain, D. A. and I. Gallagher, 55

Aesthetics
  bibliography, 68–69
  congresses, 112
  dictionaries, 7
  histories, 24
  journals, 80, 83, 90
  societies, 113, 115

Aesthetics, M. C. Beardsley, 69

Aesthetics from ancient Greece to the present, M. C. Beardsley, 24

Ainvelle, V. d'. Logic and the philosophy of science, 69

Akademiia nauk SSSR. Istoria filosofii, 18

Albaugh, R. M. Thesis writing, 102

Albert, E. M. and C. Kluckhorn. Selected bibliography on values, ethics and aesthetics, 68

Albert Camus, B. T. Fitch, 53

Albert the Great: bibliography and works, 34

Aldis, H. G. Printed book, 99

Allgemeine deutsche Biographie, 109

American Association for the Advancement of Science, 113

American bibliography of Russian and East European studies, 68

American book publishing record, 75

American book trade directory, 104

American Catholic Philosophical Association (ACPA), 113

American Catholic philosophical association. Proceedings, 95

American Council on Education. Fellowships in the

Arts and Sciences, 116

American foundations and their fields, 116

American philosophic addresses 1700–1900, 21

American Philosophical Association (APA), 113

American philosophical association. Proceedings and addresses, 95

American philosophical quaterly, 79

American philosophical society. Proceedings, 95

American philosophy
  bibliography, 64–65
  histories, 21–22
  society, 114

American Society for Aesthetics, 113

American Society for Political and Legal Philosophy, 113

Analysis, 79

Analytic philosophy
  bibliography, 67
  history, 21

Analytical bibliography of universal collected biography, P. Riches, 107

Analytical philosophy of history, A. Danto, 70

Anawati, G. C. Essai de bibliographie avicennienne, 35

Ancient Christian writers, 33

Ancient philosophy
  bibliographies, 28
  dictionaries, 8
  society, 114
  sources, 29–32

Ancilla to the Pre-Socratic philosophers, K. Freeman, 29

Andresen, C. Bibliographia Augustiniana, 34

Année philosophique, 90

Annotated bibliography of the writings of William James, R. B. Perry, 45

Annotated catalogue of the papers of C. S. Peirce, R. S. Robin, 50

Bibliografia di Giordano Bruno, V. Salvestrini and
L. Firpo, 37
Bibliografia filosofica española e hispanoamericana,
L. Martínez Gómez, 67
Bibliografia filosofica italiana, 66
Bibliografia suareciana, P. Múgica, 39
Bibliografia vichiana, 52
Bibliographia Augustina, E. Nebreda, 34
Bibliographia Augustiniana, C. Andresen, 34
Bibliographia Cartesiana, G. Sebba, 42
Bibliographia de . . . J. Duns Scoti, O. Schäfer, 37
Bibliographia Franciscana, 36
Bibliographia logica, W. Risse, 70
Bibliographia patristica, 32
Bibliographia philosophica, G. A. De Brie, 62
Bibliographic index, 61
Bibliographical description and cataloguing, J. D.
Cowley, 99
Bibliographical introduction to the study of John
Locke, H. O. Christophersen, 47
Bibliographical procedures and style, U.S. Library
of Congress, 104
Bibliographical style manuals, M. R. Kinney, 103
Bibliographie bouddhique, 67
Bibliographie critique, 63
Bibliographie d'Aristote, M. Schwab, 29
Bibliographie d'esthétique, 69
Bibliographie de l'antiquité classique, S. Lambrino,
28
Bibliographie de la France, 75
Bibliographie de la philosophie, 63
Bibliographie de la philosophie greque, G. E.
Voumvlenopoulous, 66
Bibliographie der sowjetischen Philosophie, 66
Bibliographie des ouvrages Arabes, 65
Bibliographie des oeuvres de K. Marx, M. Rubel, 48
Bibliographie des oeuvres de Leibniz, E. Ravier, 46
Bibliographie des principaux travaux européens sur
Avicenne, S. Naficy, 35
Bibliographie générale des oeuvres de B. Pascal,
A. Marie, 49
Bibliographie générale des oeuvres de J.-J. Rousseau,
J. Senelier, 50
"Bibliographie philosophique française de l'année,"
65
Bibliographie thomiste, P. Mandonnet and J.
Destrez, 68
Bibliographie védique, L. Renou, 66
Bibliographies, subject and national, R. S. Collison,
58
Bibliographische Einführungen in das Studium der
Philosophie, I. M. Bochenski, 60

Bibliography
analytical, 98–100
descriptive, 98, 99
general, 60–62
general guides, 58–59
general philosophical, 62–64
indexes, 107
philosophical guides, 59–60
textual, 98, 99–100
trade, 75–76
Bibliography, H. B. Van Hoesen and F. K. Walter,
100
Bibliography, D. Williamson, 100
Bibliography and footnotes, P. Hurt, 103
Bibliography and modern book production, P.
Freer, 99
Bibliography and textual criticism, F. Bowers, 99
Bibliography for Oriental philosophies, R. F.
Moore, 66
Bibliography of aesthetics and of the philosophy of
the fine arts, W. A. Hammond, 69
Bibliography of current philosophical works, 63
Bibliography of David Hume, T. E. Jessop, 44
Bibliography of English translations from medieval
sources, C. P. Farrar and A. P. Evans, 32
Bibliography of George Berkeley, T. E. Jessop, 41
Bibliography of Jewish bibliographies, S. Shunami,
66
Bibliography of Lucretius, C. A. Gordon, 30
Bibliography of M. Buber's works, M. Catanne, 53
Bibliography of philosophy, 80
Bibliography of philosophy (1933–1936), 63
Bibliography of philosophy, C. L. Higgins, 59
Bibliography of philosophy, psychology and
cognate subjects, B. Rand, 62
Bibliography of psychological and experimental
aesthetics, A. R. Chandler and E. H. Barnhart, 69
Bibliography of the published writings of J. S. Mill,
N. MacMinn [et al.], 49
Bibliography of writings by and on Kant, 45
Bibliography on Buddhism, S. Hanayama, 67
Bibliography on the survival of the classics, 28
Bibliotheca Erasmiana, R. van der Haeghen, 37
Bibliotheca scriptorum classicorum, W. V. Engel-
mann, 28
Bibliotheca scriptorum classicorum et graecorum et
latinorum, R. Klussmann, 28
Bio-bibliographie de Cajetan, M.-J. Congar, 37
Biographical encyclopedia of philosophy, H.
Thomas, 110
Biographical history of philosophy, G. H. Lewes,
109

Keystones and theories of philosophy, W. D. Bruckmann, 4

Kierkegaard, S. A.: bibliography and works, 46

Kiernan, T. P. Aristotle dictionary, 29; Who's who in the history of philosophy, 109

Kindi, Y. ibn I. al-: bibliography, 38

Kinney, M. R. Bibliographical style manuals, 103

Kirjath Sepher, 66

Kirk, G. S. and J. E. Raven, Presocratic philosophers, 29

Klaus, G. and M. Buhr. Philosophisches Wörterbuch, 6

Kleines Philosophen-lexikon, C. Decurtins, 110

Klibansky, R. Contemporary philosophy, 21; Philosophy in mid-century, 21

Klussmann, R. Bibliotheca scriptorum classicorum et graecorum et latinorum, 28

Kneale, W. and M. Development of logic, 25

Koefod, P. E. Writing requirements for graduate degrees, 103

Koehler & Volckmar-Fachbibliographien, 65

Kolarz, W. Books on communism, 68

Kolb, W. L. and J. Gould. Dictionary of the social sciences, 10

Koren, H. J. Research in philosophy, 103

Kranz, W. Griechische Philosophie, 19

Kränzlin, G. Max Schelers phänomelogische Systematik, 57

Kratkii filosofskii slovar', M. M. Rozental' and P. F. Iudin, 7

Kratkii slovar' po estetike, M. F. Ovsiannikov and V. A. Razumni, 7

Kratkii slovar' po etike, 8

Kratkii slovar' po filosofii, I. V. Blauberg [et al.], 7

Krimerman, L. I. Nature and scope of social science, 72

Kristeller, P. O. Catalogus translationum et commentariorum, 32; Iter Italicum, 32; Latin manuscript books before 1600, 33; Studies in Renaissance thought and letters, 19

Kroner, R. Von Kant bis Hegel, 21

Kurtz, P. American philosophers, 64

Lachs, J. Marxist philosophy, 48, 68

Lalande, A. Vocabulaire technique et critique de la philosophie, 5

Lamanna, E. [et al.]. Dizionario di termini filosofici, 6

Lambrino, S. Bibliographie de l'antiquité classique, 28

La Mettrie, J. O. de: works, 46

Langenscheidt's new Muret-Sanders encyclopedic dictionary of the English and German languages, 101

Lasky, J. Proofreading and copy-preparation, 105

Latin–English dictionary of St. Thomas Aquinas, R. J. Defarrari, 40

Latin manuscript books before 1600, P. O. Kristeller, 33

Laval théologique et philosophique, 90

Law, philosophy of
bibliographies, 70–71
society, 113

Lecture series, 97

Legal philosophy from Plato to Hegel, H. Cairns, 25

Legal theory, W. G. Friedmann, 70

Leibniz, G. W.: bibliography and works, 46–47

Leibniz-Bibliographie, 46

Lenfant, D. Concordantiae Augustinianae, 34

Le Senne, R. Introduction à la philosophie, 59

Lessing, G. E.: works, 47

Lévy-Bruhl, L. History of modern philosophy in France, 20

Lewes, G. H. Biographical history of philosophy, 109

Lewis, C. I.: bibliography, 55

Lexicon abbreviaturarum, A. Capelli, 99

Lexicon . . . a B. Joanne Duns Scoto, M. Fernandez Garcia, 37

Lexicon of St. Thomas Aquinas, R. J. Defarrari [et al.], 40

Lexicon peripateticum philosophico-theologicum, N. Signoriello, 8

Lexicon philosophicum, R. Goclenius, 8

Lexikon Bonaventurianum, A. M. a Vicetia and J. a Rubino, 36

Lexikon der Weltliteratur im 20. Jahrundert, 9

Lexikon für Theologie und Kirche, 10

Lexikon platonicum, F. Ast, 31

Lexique de la langue philosophique d'Ibn Sina, A. M. Goichon, 35

Lexique philosophique de G. Ockham, L. Baudry, 41

Library of Congress author catalog, 74

Liddell, H. G. and R. Scott. Greek–English lexicon, 102

Lindley lecture, 97

List of American doctoral dissertations, U. S. Library of Congress, 76

Listes anciennes des ouvrages d'Aristote, P. Moraux, 29

Literarische Berichte aus dem Gebiete der Philosophie, 65